Advance P

Jay Michaelson is a jewel. In *Enlightenment by Trial and Error*, he invites us to walk with him, shoulder to shoulder, with his rigorous mind and wide-ranging experiences. Through sharing his heartbreaks and confusion, and his ability to have humor in the midst of it all, this book is an act of generosity inviting us into the unfolding of love.
—**Sensei Koshin Paley Ellison**, author of *Wholehearted: Slow Down, Help Out, Wake Up*

Today, spirituality is usually packaged into a few talking points. *Enlightenment by Trial and Error* is a departure from that shallow model. Ultimately, what Michaelson counsels—from experience rather than dogma—is compassion, self-awareness, mindfulness, and love. It's hard to see what could be more needed in these changing times.
—**Rabbi Jill Hammer**, author of *The Jewish Book of Days*

In this record of a personal struggle to find his place in religion, spirituality and culture, Jay has laid down a trail for those who'd follow. *Enlightenment by Trial and Error* is an embodied and authentic resource for anyone trying to make thoughtful choices about who tey are in the world.
—**Dr. Dan Friedman**, co-founder, *Zeek: A Jewish Journal of Thought & Culture*

From closeted recoiling to ecstatic uncoiling, from faithful unraveling to loving unknowing, *Enlightenment by Trial and Error* is a textured self-portrait of the quest for Self. The early essays, born from frisky honeymoons with contemplative Judaism, shimmer with genuine revelations. The later essays beam with such fearless wisdom that they must conclude "I have absolutely no idea." With humor and heresy, depth and insight, Jay's book should be relished by all seekers.
—**Professor Sam Berrin Shonkoff**, Graduate Theological Union

Like a time-lapse film following a rose from seed to blossom, Jay Michaelson's new book offers a rare peek into the elusive art of human flourishing. Beyond the beaten binary boundaries of Jewish and Pagan, soul and body,

Queer and religious, Michaelson weaves a web of possibilities for an honest, helpful, present, life.
—**Rabbi Amichai Lau-Lavie**, founder, LabShul

For over two decades, Jay Michaelson has boldly sought to remake the Jewish heritage into a tradition that can inspire a new generation. He has served us by being resolutely honest about his own journey.
—**Rabbi Jacob Staub**, Professor of Jewish Philosophy and Spirituality, Reconstructionist Rabbinical College

In these essays, Jay Michaelson serves as an expert guide to paths of awakening he explored over many years while he merged his professions and passions (scholar, journalist, teacher; mysticism, meditation, modernity). With curiosity, vulnerability and skill, he leads us through myriad milieus offering poetic inquiries and poignant insights along the way.
—**Sebene Selassie**, contributor, *Still, in the City: Creating Peace of Mind in the Midst of Urban Chaos*

To dance the love supreme deep in the desert of Burning Man, to sit with the stilling voice of silence at a Buddhist retreat—seekers from many tribes and tribulations will appreciate this decade in Michaelson's spiritual diary, at once curious and critical, naïve and neurotic. Jay Michaelson wakes up his readers to the daily truth hidden in plain sight, where all along there was an esoteric love song singing itself.
—**Rabbi Dr. Aubrey L. Glazer** author of *God Knows, Everything is Broken: The Great (Gnostic) Americana Songbook of Bob Dylan*

Jay Michaelson offers us an honest, intimate account of the contemplative path in all of its wonder, messiness, joy and confusion. In his characteristically clear, witty, and thought-provoking style, Jay weaves a tapestry of wisdom from many traditions, with powerful instructions and practical stories to guide the way. Deeply personal, sometimes humorous, and brutally honest, these self-reflective essays can inspire seekers of all ages.
—**Oren Jay Sofer**, author of *Say What You Mean: A Mindful Approach to Nonviolent Communication*

Enlightenment by Trial and Error

Also by Jay Michaelson

Is: Heretical Poems and Blessings (as Yaakov Moshe)

The Gate of Tears: Sadness and the Spiritual Path

Evolving Dharma: Meditation, Buddhism, and the Next Generation of Enlightenment

Redefining Religious Liberty: The Covert Campaign Against Civil Rights

God vs. Gay? The Religious Case for Equality

Everything is God: The Radical Path of Nondual Judaism

Another Word for Sky: Poems

God in Your Body: Kabbalah, Mindfulness, and Embodied Spiritual Practice

Enlightenment
by Trial and Error

Ten Years on the Slippery Slopes of
Jewish Spirituality,
Postmodern Buddhism, and
Other Mystical Heresies

Jay Michaelson

Ben Yehuda Press
Teaneck, New Jersey

Published by Ben Yehuda Press
122 Ayers Court #1B
Teaneck, NJ 07666

http://www.BenYehudaPress.com

To subscribe to our monthly book club and support independent Jewish publishing, visit
https://www.patreon.com/BenYehudaPress

ISBN13 978-1-934730-80-5

19 20 21/ 10 9 8 7 6 5 4 3 2 1   20191104

Contents

Part Three Unknowing

Introduction

Here's why I wrote this book. There are plenty of "spiritual" books out there, but most are written by people who have searched and found answers, and who are now reporting those answers to you. But when I was starting out "on the path," I would have loved a book by someone still searching and figuring stuff out; still highly skeptical of the things people call 'spiritual' but equally skeptical of the skeptics; and still questioning everything along the way.

So now I've written that book.

For ten years, 2002 to 2012, I wrote about these questions, mostly in an online magazine I co-founded called *Zeek: A Jewish Journal of Thought and Culture*. I'm enormously proud of those essays, actually. In fact, having now written seven books on spirituality and religion, I've often felt that my best work on the subject was in these *Zeek* essays—and, in particular, the ones written before I came to any conclusions about anything. They represent a mind (or heart or body or maybe even soul) in midflight, figuring it out as it goes along, failing sometimes, revising, revisiting, learning, unfolding.

Here, I've taken those essays (plus a few written for the *Forward* newspaper), sifted through them, reordered them into a kind of thematic/narrative arc, and put together this book. In a way, they represent a kind of memoir, or at least a postmodern heretical hedonistic travelogue. But the autobiography is, at most, a partial one. Obviously, mystical exploration was not the only thing happening in my life during that decade. In addition to co-editing *Zeek*, I worked as a professional LGBT activist and founded two queer Jewish organizations. I also was making myself semi-notorious—in a small circle, to be sure —for writing about emerging forms of Jewish identification, not to mention Israel/Palestine and other issues Jews love to argue about. These essays represent less than half of my contributions to *Zeek* in the period; all of us on the masthead were equally obsessed with politics, literary culture, and with new forms of Jewish expression that were, for a while, exciting and rebellious and fresh.

But the thread of contemplative practice ties this book together. It's a story of how I lost my religion and gained something far better, how I achieved my wildest dreams and still doubted that they'd come true, and how I eventually came to understand a few things about "God," life, and love. These subjects are not for everyone, I know. But for some people, the path of awakening is one of the most essential things in our lives. If you are one of those people, this book is for you.

* * *

For whatever psychological, karmic, or genetic reasons, I've been interested in spiritual experience—and mystical experience in particular—since childhood. As a teenager, I would walk in the woods alone, moved in some vague way by the solitude and rhythms of the natural world, years before Wordsworth articulated it for me. I read books that were more typical of a 1970s seeker than a 1980s adolescent: *The Tao of Physics*, *Zen and the Art of Motorcycle Maintenance*, everything by Hermann Hesse.

But I didn't stop there. Throughout my twenties, I deepened my spiritual explorations with the academic and non-academic study of Kabbalah (eventually getting a Ph.D. in Jewish Thought, and teaching Kabbalah myself for a while, both in and outside of the academy), as well as psychedelics, meditation, halachic Jewish practice, and more books. I was continually drawn to questions of 'ultimate' experience, truth, and God. (Even at the time, it was clear that this was just a preference; some people are into golf, I'm into mysticism.) Yet most of that investigation was mediated by books; whether there really was anything beneath the symbols remained, like Kafka's law, inaccessible. I was too busy studying the actual law, and creating something that looked like a normal life.

In 2001, my life changed when I was in a serious car accident; I was riding in a taxi that got hit by a truck. I suffered a serious concussion that temporarily made it impossible to work and permanently damaged my short-term memory (even today, I'm not just "bad with names"—I forget conversations, events, and people). Within a year, everything changed. I had co-founded a software company in 2000, but I left six months after the accident, both unable to work and uninterested in doing so. My girlfriend, fortunately, left me, realizing that my 'bisexuality' was not as real as I thought it was, and so I finally came out to myself and everyone around me.

More broadly, I started living the life I had always wanted to live, but due, I think, to the closet, I didn't think I could actually have. I went to Burning Man for the first time, and glimpsed possibilities of radical self-expression and freedom that I had not imagined before. I started a garage rock band called The Swains (we weren't that good, but we did play CBGB's, which I consider a life achievement) and started writing 'for real' rather than just in my spare time.

Perhaps most importantly, I stopped reading about spiritual practice and started doing it. In 2002, I went on my first multi-day meditation retreat, a weeklong, silent Jewish-Buddhist retreat led by Rabbi David Cooper, his wife Shoshana Cooper, together with Rabbi Jeff Roth, Eliezer Sobel and Rabbi Naomi Mara Hyman. Rather naïvely, I went on that first retreat expecting to have the mystical experiences that I'd read about in books, only to find that, in fact, meditation had something to do with seeing clearly—meaning, not the pleroma of God and angels, but my own neuroses, fears, and internalized crap. Oh, and then seeing God later.

My life changed that week in June 2002, and I spent most of the next decade figuring out how. I went on many more retreats (two weeks, six weeks, three months), and experienced many more peak experiences, plus lots of doubt, lots of silence of course, still more reading. In a sense, this book is a record of that decade of my trying to figure out the meaning of life, or my life anyway, centered around spirituality and mystical experience.

It's been an unexpected delight to revisit these essays, and the selves I inhabited fifteen years ago. I love the curiosity and the tenderness of these pieces, and precisely because they are all works in progress, I hope they can speak to you, if you're on a spiritual path yourself. Today, I'm in a different place: not lonely anymore, married with a young daughter, decently established in my two professional lives (one as a legal-political journalist, the other as a meditation teacher), and, while of course I'm continuing to grow and question, I feel relatively settled on how I relate to these still-fundamental questions of love, God, and the contemplative path.

Even within the arc represented in this book, a lot of the angst in the first few essays got resolved by the time of the last few. I got off the fence: I left the corporate world, moved to a more interesting part of New York, had the sensual and spiritual experiences I wondered if I'd ever have.

Did I get enlightened? It depends what that word means. According to my experiences, my teachers, and my several years of academic study of the subject, I did have many of the peak experiences that, in some traditions, accompany awakening. Having spent many months in intensive dharma practice, I've progressed somewhat along the way (again, according to the various maps that exist). Probably most importantly, my friends tell me that I became a kinder, wiser, and more settled human being during the decade reflected in this book. I experienced deep love and profound loss. In any case, it was all worth it.

* * *

The paths described in this book are drawn primarily from Jewish, Western Buddhist, and Western philosophical traditions. (I've tried in past books to describe how these paths intersect and interweave.) So while this book is primarily about the spiritual search in general, it is shaped by my Jewish background, my Western education, and my practice of the Buddhadharma—as well as my sex, gender, class, age, race, and many other factors, of course.

Jewish mystical traditions have always represented a tiny fringe within the wider Jewish community. At its best, mainstream Judaism is more interested in justice than spirituality. (At its least, it's about tribe.) To the extent the Jewish *summum bonum* is to be measured by demographics, texts, and history, it has more to do with how we treat one another than with how we merge into the vast oceanic oneness. It's the pursuit of justice, not mysticism.

Moreover, Jewish mysticism is remarkably rooted in communal life, especially by comparison to monastic traditions such as one finds in Christianity, Buddhism, and other religious contexts. (I talk about this at some length in the late essay, "What's Different About Jewish Enlightenment?") The ideal of the "old man [sic] sitting atop the mountain" rarely is found in Jewish sources. You don't get enlightened and stay there; you have moments of oneness and moments of multiplicity, times of expansion and times of contraction. All of these are sacred; after all, you can't raise kids, keep Shabbos, and give money to the needy if you're in a permanent state of unitive bliss. In fact, nonduality—discussed in part three here, and in my book *Everything is God* —encompasses both union and division, both the oneness of mystical experience and the multiplicity of mundane experience. Thus, in the Jewish frame, the mystical path is one of *ratzo v'shov*, running and returning, like the angels in Ezekiel's vision. Profound experiences of the Divine; ethical obligations to one another. Realization and responsibility.

Arguably, the same is true in Western Buddhism (in my book *Evolving Dharma*, I try to describe that phenomenon in depth and explore how it evolved from, and differs from, the Buddhist religious forms practiced in Asia and Asian diasporas). In this context, the Buddhadharma is primarily about suffering and the end of suffering. It provides a set of tools for realizing happiness by changing the way the mind (and even the brain) works.

Yet even as I teach a secular form of meditation today (at Ten Percent Happier, a leading meditation company), my own contemplative practice remains informed by mysticism. The mind rests in a happiness that does not depend on conditions. All things are seen as dependently originating dharmas, not self. It seems optional whether to associate that happiness and that Being with some phenomenon called "God." Optional, and confusing. But the reality is that, idiosyncratically, I came into meditation, and the contemplative path in general, through an unusual door. I didn't come looking for relief from stress or healing from pain—at least, not consciously. I came looking for truth; for experiences of ultimate reality that I'd read about in books but had never had myself; for, I admit, enlightenment.

Part one of the book ("Uncoiling") tracks my slow unfolding into the spiritual path, exploring what it means, traveling between experience and doubt. As I've said already, I'm no longer the person who wrote the essays in part one—but I think that's part of their value. They explore questions that were absolutely fundamental to what I thought was the thing most worth doing in my life: waking up.

Part two ("Unraveling") is largely about how those explorations unraveled some of my previous commitments and questioned my relationship to religion in general. Here, everything falls apart, at first without my noticing, then with my ambivalence, and finally with my enthusiasm.

Part three ("Unknowing") represents the theological and personal maturation of some of the processes from parts one and two, with some tentative conclusions about the spiritual path and where it might lead. In a sense, this part is most in need of a sequel, since in the last ten years I've tended to articulate the happiness that does not depend on conditions less in nondualistic ontological terms and more in agnostic psychological ones. As the final essay in this volume (before the epilogue) says, I have no idea if everything is one. But in spacious moments, I feel a profound rest, and a love that is curiously awake.

Throughout the ten years reflected in these pages, I was interested in a kind of pragmatism of the head, heart, and spirit. What worked, and what didn't? What's true, and what isn't? I wanted to apply the same rigor I used in my political and cultural writing to questions of meaning and mysticism. I wanted a contemplative practice that felt as authentic and serious as my legal practice, and as honest as I could make it. I hope that what I learned resonates with my fellow seekers, wherever and whoever you are.

I've tried to maintain a light editorial hand in putting this book together, leaving intact the curiosity and directness of the essays, even where I disagree with them now. Where I've cut, it's mostly to avoid repetition, as well as to take out some passages that I truly don't want to see in print. Finally, the large majority of what I wrote from 2002-2011 landed on the cutting room floor, either because it wasn't about the topics of this book or because it wasn't that good.

Revisiting this journey has been a spiritual practice in itself. I'm so happy to be able to share it with you.

Jay Michaelson
Brooklyn, July 7, 2019

Part One

Uncoiling

Loneliness and Faith

There are so many walls in the world. I thought that when I came out of the closet, to myself and to others, the weights would be lifted off of my shoulders and the boundaries lowered. This did happen. But what also happened is that I became aware of dozens of nested closets which maintain themselves in my life, and maybe other people's lives also. Even if it was okay to be openly gay in my religious contexts, I found it was rarely okay to be openly religious in gay contexts. And the closets are wider than sexual ones. I realized that I was a closeted rock & roll fan at trance parties, a closeted (ex-)lawyer at Rainbow gatherings, a closeted contemplative at poetry slams. I began to see that I had internalized dozens of lines of demarcation, of 'appropriateness', even ones that probably didn't exist outside of my own insecurity.

By far the tightest-shut closet door is that guarding my spiritual life. No one wants to hear about it, and I don't want to talk about it. Words devolve into clichés—love of God, the unfolding now, Be Here Now, awareness of what Is. Or they slide into alienating conceptualizations—immanence, transcendence, radical amazement, a dwelling place for the infinite in the finite (or, perhaps, a recognition that the finite is only illusion). I believe in, and I feel, that all of these concepts approximate a reality that is real and that is a central part of my consciousness. To take one example, I believe, and feel, the sacredness of eating, and believe—when I remember—that my patterns of diet cause that sanctity to be heightened in my mind and in my relation to the substances, supposedly other-than-me, that I choose to make part of my body. I think there is not only quality but also holiness in the delights and loves and arts that humans are able to create and experience.

But I try not to talk about it. After all, that is 'private'. Too intimate, like the parts of our bodies that we hide and call 'privates', as if acknowledging that whatever matters too much for us to share in the ordinary exchange of human pleasantries, whatever is too close to our essence, must be hidden.

And yet, as I experienced last week at a silent meditation retreat, the unfolding of God is most freely experienced when it is open. There is nothing but God. Our acts of concealment are God too—but they are acts that can lead to the only thing that is evil (which, of course, is also part of God): namely, the illusion that there is anything other than the one reality that is. Our 'evil inclination' is that erroneous belief that something we are doing is not connected to now; that, for example, the world is okay but I am not; or the world is okay but I know better; or, these thoughts, doubts, fears, loves, forms that I have are mine and not a part of the vast emptiness.

So, each act of constriction is a danger. In meditation, I perceived this almost viscerally. Each act of doubt or judgment, I *felt*, brought me back down, back in, out of the *samadhi* state and into small mind. It's not that judgment is bad—judgment is important, and essential for moral behavior and aesthetic originality. But when one is in a contemplative place, and at one with being, judgment causes the ego to arise and assert its illusionary individuality; it shuts us off into critical mode, where we comment on style rather than being mindful first of truth. It is the 'I' that judges, the same 'I' that forgets that it is only a convention, that really the molecules of my body and brain are in no discernible way distinct from the other molecules of the universe. They happen to be gathered here, and have given rise to consciousness. But surely the greatest error of 'spiritual' dualism is to suppose that our souls are separate from the world.

That illusion of separation, and the pain it causes, is healed by awareness, or religion, as some people understand it. The sorrow caused by being a lonely ego can be healed by realizing that one is not a lonely ego. For many, this realization occurs in love, when the 'I' and the 'you' are bridged. For others, this happens in contemplative practice, when the 'I' and the 'you' are bridged, or when the 'I' ceases to exist as a separate entity at all.

Langston Hughes wrote, in the poem "Luck":

> Sometimes a crumb falls
> From the tables of joy,
> Sometimes a bone
> Is flung.
> To some people
> Love is given,
> To others
> Only heaven.

And so, my own doubt, possibly the greatest one of my recent intro-spection: that religion is a balm, or a salve. Possibly more substantial (a bone) than love (a crumb), but ultimately an all-too-wished-for substi-tute. That I want to dissolve my own ego in the All primarily because I don't like myself. (Just as my favorite fun activities are those in which I 'lose myself' in the music or visuals or sensual experience.) That the pro-jection of God is only a projection of our great need to be held, cuddled, loved by our distant or dead parents. Bad enough, I thought, that I seek to overachieve and impress others so that I can earn their love, like my six-year-old self getting love for being clever. My perception that being radiates love, that all human interaction is just a clearer or more obscure exchange of yearnings for love—this awareness makes a void whole. Is it *only* that? Only a consolation?

I had a dream early on in retreat in which I saw the retreat leader, Rabbi David Cooper, arrayed like some guru with flowers and devotees. I tried to communicate with him, but felt myself pulled away, that reality stripped away and replaced with a white liminal space. A spirit guide appeared—who else, for me, but Lou Reed. Lou said, "You think that's reality? I'll show you reality." And I flew through the white space to a primeval scene of cavemen, naked cavemen, fighting some sort of crea-ture. The biggest cavemen were like offensive linemen, guarding against the beast. The nimbler ones were in back, throwing spears. Lou asked me where I fit in. And I realized that I, along with one other effeminate, wimpy, gay cave-fag, was running for cover. We took refuge in a delicate place of women and aesthetes, pathetic excuses for men.

After I woke up, it felt as though this pain, of not being masculine enough, of being gay, of having felt excluded and unloved—this pain was "reality." Under the confident speaking voice I honed in school, behind the knowledge I used to somehow earn the love of others, there remained, at my foundation, this pain.

If it is true that one must be 'sick' for religion to really matter, as Kierkegaard said, I at least took consolation from the company I kept. I thought of Abraham, Isaac, and Jacob, the patriarchs Jews name in their prayers and many other times. Abraham—a man who felt himself called to leave everything that he loved and go to an unknown place. Isaac—who witnessed his father try to kill him and, the Midrash says, was left mute as a result. Jacob, my own namesake and model, who tried so hard to stop his brother from beating him out of the womb, who stayed home cooking while his brother went out and hunted, who was the wimp who had to cheat and deceive his way into stealing (or earning?) his birthright. These forefathers were men in intense pain, "Adam 2" in Rabbi Soloveitchik's term: people who had wounds that created space for compassion, love, and God to flow in.

Jacob becomes Isra-el. He wrestles with God, as I do. And Jews say twice a day: Listen, Israel, listen: God, the Presence (Y-H-V-H, the only way to say "Is" in Hebrew), our god, to whom we submit even as we wrestle, is One. All of being, all of now—not the yesterdays or tomorrow in our imagination, but the real now in front of us—is one with you, because there is no you, only the One. The Torah doesn't say that Jacob won the wrestling match, by the way.

I can understand my pain as teaching me the compassion I need to better divest myself of egocentricity and help, as I can, to ease the suffering of others. I can see the demons as angels, and bring all of myself, with all of my history, to every moment of experience, not losing myself like on a good drug trip, but engaging myself, sublimating myself, recognizing that these bits I call 'myself' are not really a self, but are only expressions of the presence. Mostly, I know that I am not positing any ontological structure, any pearly gates or old men in the sky, and that the world I experience is not different in that way from the world of someone who calls herself an atheist. But none of this understanding can convincingly quiet doubt. At least I am comforted by knowing I have no answers.

Ultimately, the only path forward may be for me to trust the yearning and surrender to it. Let the practices work. (They do work.) Be here now. Surrender the criticism and doubt, allow myself to feel faith. I have no answer other than my own awareness to point to the reality, rather than fantasy, of being. I can point only to the beauty of lightning bugs in fog, or the coincidences, or the complexity of a single mosquito. I can only gesture, and be silent in the all that I know is true.

July 2002

Go as Far as Possible

On the subway the other day, I saw a School of Visual Arts ad which exhorted me to "Go As Far As Possible" (and presumably take a photography class). How far? I've been asking myself that question for fifteen years.

In college, when I was busily exploring—and, more often, only hoping to explore—the boundaries of my own possibility, I became obsessed for a semester or two with how 'far' could one wander into the wilderness, away from safe, bourgeois places of respectability and convention, before one had gone 'too far'? At some point, with all boundaries destroyed, in a place where all is permitted, there is only a sort of anarchy of the self where nothing can be trusted. But to stay within too narrow a range is barely to live. Where is the line?

I was guided in these thoughts by Andre Gide's *The Counterfeiters*, in which several characters move farther and farther from bourgeois safety and closer and closer to anarchic, amoral figures whom Gide depicts as linked to (for better or for worse) Satan himself. *The Counterfeiters* follows several of these characters, all teenagers on the cusp of adulthood, as they interact with artists, bohemians, and underground figures who reject all conventional morality. Eventually, most of these characters return, in one way or another, to where they began. All are changed by the quest. Some do not survive it. While Gide suggests that the wandering of the prodigal son is a necessary stage in our human growth, he seems to say that ultimately there must be some sort of in-between zone, or possibly a dynamic oscillation, where zealous living is possible but where there are still some limits to our actions. Among many metaphors in the book that explain the principle, one that always stuck with me is a description of a certain kind of fish that can only survive in brackish water, at the juncture of the fresh water of the river and the salt water of the sea. Too much salt, or too little, and the fish would die.

This question dominated my thinking for a long time. I saw it in Hamlet's "to be or not to be," in Virginia Woolf's *Mrs. Dalloway*, and of course, in my own life. How far was 'too far'? What did it mean to be 'far'? Far from what? How much sensual experience, drug experience, spiritual experience, hedonism, radicalism, and how much stability, grounding, and convention? How much can one 'seize the day' or 'suck the marrow out of life' before, like a mosquito who drinks too much blood, one simply explodes?

Over the years, I've wondered why this question of limit was so important to me back in college. Most people, I suppose, trust their instincts enough to know when flirtation has turned to lifestyle, or experimentation to addiction. Some people just choose danger. But I was always concerned to find that Aristotelian mean between the stultifying conformity of my childhood and... and what? Losing the respect of people whose respect I shouldn't have wanted? Disappointing my mother? Ruining my chances of running for Congress someday?

Or maybe just being gay? For a time, I thought that all my questioning of limits came down to the anxiety of the closet. I thought for a while that all my college term papers about finding the mean between conformity and anarchy were just unconscious code words for fear of coming out. But now that I am out, and now that I did quit my 'real' job to be a writer, I still find myself wrestling with those questions. How 'far' is too far?

The forms the question now takes have shifted, even if the grammar has not. Now I ask whether it's an unhealthy clinging to convention that causes me to live on the Upper West Side instead of a 'cooler' neighborhood, or is it just me really being myself —'myself' being, in part, a person who actually likes the uncool cleanliness and quiet of my neighborhood. Is it timidity that keeps my hair cut conventionally and my clothes relatively normal, or is it an expression of who I am, a person who is, in part, conventional and normal? "Go as far as possible"—or as far as comfortable?

I still hold, it seems, a possibly misplaced belief in mainstream culture, and a place in my heart that still trusts conventional sources of authority and power. For example, I believe that going to a hospital will help alleviate heart disease because lots of seemingly smart people in white coats tell me so. Have I really read up on the science myself? Of course not. And yet I know many people who are certain that going to a hospital will not help any illness, and will likely make matters worse. And while these people and I can debate the merits of angioplasty versus biofeedback and herbal remedies, the fundamental difference is that I still trust the men from Harvard, and they don't.

Which is odd, because I often consider myself a refugee from Harvard (or Yale) culture myself. I felt much more at home dancing at Burning Man than I did in a suit at a company meeting the following week. Teaching Kabbalah in a djellabah felt more like 'me' than writing a law article on climate change ever did. And yet I still believe in the dominant culture's basic decency and the conclusions of its science. Am I still on the fence?

Burning Man, by the way, is a temporary autonomous zone created by 30,000 people in the Nevada desert. Some call it an arts festival, and there certainly is a lot of art—sculpture, music, interactive and video projects, you name it. Other people call it a party, and there is a lot of celebration and bacchanal that goes on. But Burning Man reduces to neither of these things; it is an entire city, complete with post offices and geodesic domes, airplane pilots and ravers, families and yogis, and an ambiguous ritual at the climax of the week featuring the burning of a fifty foot tall effigy of a human being, a signifier whose significance is left deliberately indeterminate. All of it is created and destroyed, leaving no trace, within two weeks.

My burn earlier this year was, in many ways, paradise. I had wonderful artistic experiences, beautiful sex, and was fortunate to meditate and learn Kabbalah with sincere and spiritually aware people. Probably the highlight of the week was late on the night of the burn, when I wandered out to *Leviathan*, an enormous art installation with massive light beams shining into the sky, ethereal ambient music, and several sculptural elements. Standing in the green and black light-cone shining out onto the open desert, I saw in my shadow the contemplative that I want myself to be. As I sat, and as my robes and an electrical apparatus inside my kippa rendered my shape exactly like that of some traditional images of the Buddha, I knew that this was my path—not as a proposition I was convinced of, but as a fundamental truth that I knew at the core of my soul. Like a square having four sides, or a circle being round. Seeing myself as the Buddha may sound like an exercise in egotism, but there was no 'me' sitting in the light; there was only Being manifesting Itself, awareness rising in creation.

Questions of limit presume that there is a reality at a center, a limit drawn around that central point, and an entity that 'goes as far as possible' from that place of origin. But when the limit, the center, and the wanderer are all seen to be transitory manifestations of Being, and unreal in and of themselves, what is left of this diagram of human existence?

The allure of the edge, when one's center is conditioned or constrained, is that it holds the potential for greater self-actualization. There is more to you than your 'box' allows. There is a buzz to exoticism, as the Beats felt in Harlem or Hemingway felt in Africa. It's cool to be extreme, essential to explore the world beyond conventional limits, to learn that all such limits are unnecessary.

Yet when all is really understood to be possible, the romance of wandering is replaced by a confidence of silence. Going as far as possible ceases to be the purpose of life, because once you've effaced the idol of the self, you never really go anywhere, and there is no one to do the going. Leaving the box remains a step along the path, maybe even an essential one. It may be that the quest is, after all, an absolutely necessary stage in seeing that there is no 'there' there, or here, or anywhere. Yet ultimately both the box and the path are seen to be empty of substance. There is no identity that will be lost; every man we believe ourselves to be ultimately will be burnt.

And the miracle that one finds, in this place, is that (to paraphrase

Shelley) silence and solitude do not equal vacancy. Miraculously, silence generates a kind of compassion. This is the secret of ethical monotheism: that Being Loves, or put more traditionally, that our morality matters to God. And it is the source of the compassion that characterizes the Bodhisattva.

Gide is right that there are anarchic elements, 'Satanic' in the Miltonian sense of the word, whenever one strays from safe harbor. If I question everything—authority, tragedy—there are no guideposts. If I accept everything, there is no life. But my answer ought not be an Aristotelian mean where things are 'out there' enough but not too much. Rather than a place of centers and edges, I want to exist in a wide plain of being, with only horizons instead of boundaries, and the confidence to go as far as possible, or be as still as possible, or exist anywhere on the matrix of possibility.

And yet: there are still choices to be made, and all but the most enlightened of us will feel the consequences of our decisions. I turned to one of my meditation teachers for advice. I explained to her that, as I saw it, it was bad faith to deny that, at 32 years old, I am still very much about 'making something of myself' in the conventional sense, as well as playing, having sex, drinking the marrow out of cultural life, etc. To go off and meditate more might help my mind be quieter, but shouldn't I honor the part of me that is still full of *yang*—and young—energy? And, I continued, the reality of my personality is that I like to straddle the fence between convention and non-convention. Yes, I go to Burning Man and believe that everything is God; but I also look 'normal', have a boring two-days-a-week job at a software company, and am very much involved in the mainstream economy and culture. Moreover, I continued, this makes me a good teacher, because, having one foot in each world, I can translate between the two.

My teacher's abridged answer to all of that was: Bullshit. What's holding me in New York City, in my software job that I have increasingly come to hate, and in all of this convention, she said, is fear. My rational mind fears letting go. My ego fears the judgment of people on the grid—judgment I already feel or project onto my many law school friends and colleagues who have become very successful professors, lawyers, and statesmen. They are writing constitutions of other nations, or publishing op-eds in the *New York Times*; I am writing in *Zeek*. Sure, I hate myself every time I get too conventional, but dammit, I want success!

This really is my fatal flaw, I think: that I am a fox and not a hedgehog. The metaphor belongs to Isaiah Berlin, who broke up intellectuals into know-a-little-about-a-lot foxes and know-a-lot-about-one-big-thing hedgehogs. I am a fox; look at this tripartite, schizophrenic article for proof. And yet like many foxes, I wish I were a hedgehog. I wish I could be good, really good, at one thing, and be content with one place on the matrix—not always wondering what someplace else would feel like.

'Feeling' isn't quite right: I don't just 'feel' corporate life when I'm at the office, I become immersed in it. I talk a certain way, relate to other people a certain way—and there's no other way to do it. It isn't skillful or effective to talk to attorneys on the other side of a deal in the same way I talk to the students in my *Embodied Judaism* class; and, after a certain amount of time, I become the attorney.

Deep inside, I prefer the *Embodied Judaism* Jay to the Software Company Founder Jay. Part of me likes that I can move between all these worlds, teaching Kabbalah at Burning Man one moment, preparing affidavits the next, writing nonfiction about logocentrism and then playing my songs on break. But part of me feels unsatisfied living the fox life and deeply prefers being the 'me' I hear when I teach the dharma to teenagers. And I know, all too well, that you can't really be a successful fox; in both dharma and dollar, at a certain point you have to commit. There may be no limits, but there are decisions to be made. If I know that corporate life is a poison to me, why can't I let go of the square world? Am I really a fox, or just chicken?

December 2002

You are God in Drag:
Notes From and After Retreat

1.

The scientific critique says: when you're relaxed, your brain thinks all is one. But really that's just a feature of brain chemistry.

In that state now, I can hold the critique. However, the critique cannot hold the state I am in now.

If I were seeing pixies, the critique might be stronger. But I am just seeing a light, a bed, a computer, etc. It's true that my body and mind are relaxed. But that is neither adding to nor subtracting from theological speculation. What it is doing is letting me absorb the magnitude of the truth.

This truth—that this, just this, where and what and who you are right now, is the One and nothing else—this underlies Western and Eastern metaphysics. Impermanence is true.

Every time you eat, you are eating the sun. All sources of energy on this planet, stored up in plants, long-dead plants, animals—all comes from the sun. This is true even of plastic soda bottles. And every atom in every thing you see was once in a star.

In busy, ordinary, 'small' mind, these truths are just facts. We can evaluate whether they are artfully expressed observations or clichés, or whether we think they are mere diversions. We may have other things which we think are more important.

All relaxation does is allow the truth to be felt. The mind is cleared, like a dirty window wiped clean, and the magnitude of what we might ordinarily take for granted inspires tears. Moreover, the mind is quieted so much that all that's left is its true nature: God. Awareness, radiating love. I have said this before, but what a miracle, that all we have to do to be beautifully loving creatures is just relax and allow.

You don't have to put anything in.

2.

How do we know anything is true? Certain things are logically provable, but many other kinds of truths are not—even 'hard' truths, not just emotional ones. We know something is true because it fully accords inside our minds. There is a sense of knowing. That sense is present now.

Is this knowing related to how a plant 'knows' to grow, so beautifully, intricately?

As the Persian poet Hafiz says, you are God in drag.

3.

I know, too, that I become more compassionate and open this way, which makes the world a better place, albeit in a small way. At this moment, as I write this, I can hear that someone is crying, or at least, something is making a noise that sounds like it. I really want to know, because I don't want to be insensitively typing theology in the presence of pain. I would respect the suffering. Actually I'm pretty sure it's just a noise.

And I become happier. I've noticed that because of the way I'm built, or trained, I am almost unable to simply say, "Even if it's not true, it makes me so happy to believe it." I might be better off if I could do that—if I could set aside truth and just be happy with a comfortable illusion. But I might be better off with the body of a model and the bank account of a millionaire, too; some things are just not my lot. I want to know that what brings me happiness is true.

Sometimes that need manifests as doubt which closes me off from happiness. But other times, I see it as very valuable, because it has led me to become a mystic.

Of course, words like 'mystic' and 'enlightened' are problematic, because they have associations and connotations of boasting. By the same token, it is not inaccurate for you or me to say "I am God," as long as we remember that everyone else is too. But not necessarily skillful.

I love that, as realized as I have been fortunate to become, I am still early on in a long, always-present path of greater and greater realization of true nature. And it will always be Now along the way.

4.

When I think of putting these notes into *Zeek*, the mind races ahead and gets distracted. What happens? Two things. First, it closes itself off from now and goes into someplace else—into the magazine, or the website—someplace that isn't right here. Second, the mind becomes filled with aversive or attractive desire: I want the piece to be like this, I want it to be received like that. The writing of this piece becomes performative, and thus a critical part of myself (as in movie critic) is engaged, ruining the flow of experience. So I have to swear now that this will not be part of *Zeek* without extensive revision later—revision which means that it doesn't matter how artfully I write now. (For example, the phrase 'how artfully', like this parenthetical, was inserted weeks later.)

Breathe. Hold the sensation. Notice the feeling of that. Watch it and eventually let it go.

5.

You can't simultaneously pursue enlightenment and interrogate it.

6.

Back from retreat.

It's such a fragile truth: the simple pantheistic notion that, really, everything is just God. Or, everything is emptiness, if you prefer—that no thing, including the self, has separate existence. It's very easy to write down, and incredibly fragile. Learn it too quickly, and it's a cliché, or doubt arises; or, worse, it inhibits the actual experience (knowledge in the Hebrew sense) of it. Forget it after you really learn it, and you sink right down into the concerns of the small mind. Today, the knowledge is still present for me; I don't have to fake it, just cultivate a calmer mind state to allow it to penetrate. Eventually it may not feel as natural; or maybe it will. But I can dip my toe into either side, feeling the world as it truly is, or as my mind is conditioned to feel it, suffer with it, dread it, love it, etc. All our minds are so self-centered, so self-certain that there is us and them. Without this *yetzer hara*, this will of separation, we could not survive or reproduce. Still it boggles the mind why it had to be so.

And the truth is so easy to forget. So we are told again and again and again: remember, remember, remember. All the Jewish religion does is remember. All the Buddhist path does is remember (in the Jewish sense: i.e., see anew, make real now, remove veils of ignorance).

"Be faithful to me, and I will show you love," God seems to say. What does this mean for me? On retreat I worked with the phrase for a while, but I think I'm only understanding it (or understanding it on a deeper level) now, off retreat. Be faithful to me—know that I am all there is, that 'it's just Me' here. No inside, no outside. It does feel like a kind of faithfulness to keep that consciousness intact, or be reminded often in 'small moments, many times'. However, it is faithfulness to a dear friend, not a principle. Once it becomes a principle... well, all is not lost, but the heart of it is.

Much of the Jewish love language gets lost in what it says God is doing for us lovingly. "You have chosen us with love." Today we wrestle with chosenness and what that means. But I think it's more fruitful to observe how our ancestors felt they were chosen *with love*. Every nation thought they were chosen. The point is that the experience was one of love.

And then every contemplative says they can't really talk about what it is they want to talk about. The Tao that can be named is not the true Tao. The indirect/absurd speech of the Zen koan. The unpronounceable Name. Negative theology. *Neti-neti*. You can just go across the board.

Non-contemplatives may go and say that they know this or that, or perversely, that they don't know anything and therefore they must obey the Bible (or some other text) with literal, intense devotion—all the while trapped in the notion that there is a self obeying a text. But I don't know of any authentic writer of mysticism who can say with certainty that God/Being is this or that.

A funny thing just happened. I was searching for phrases with which to end the previous paragraph, and the first two were "...can say with certainty that 'I know'" and "...can say with certainty that 'This is It.'" Of course, both of those phrases flow immediately from the mystical experience. But what 'It' is, or what the 'knowing' is (it's not really an 'I know')—no one can say. People get frustrated with this. Mystical obscurantism, vagueness. But it is not meant to be some sort of game or deliberate mysteriousness. It really cannot be said.

Secret teachings are not esoteric; they are experiential.

7.

I've noticed a convergence happening between what I thought was esoteric Buddhist wisdom and what is, in fact, the most commonplace of advice. There is a little unease around that, since for many years I have disliked the "be happy and greet each day with a smile" school of self-improvement. I think the reason for that is that it seemed very disingenuous, and also an inauthentic response to a world in which vast suffering exists. If we greet each day with a smile, are we being honest with parents whose children die, or, more importantly, parents whose children are killed in wars that we might have avoided?

Greeting each day with a smile, or 'seeing the good in everybody' also seemed personally dishonest. I am glad that my consciousness is more complex than that—that, some days, it greets the world with a smile, and other days the smile quickly turns into something else. That is my reality, I am glad it is my reality, and there is little that annoys me more than being told to paper over my reality with a banal cliché.

Seeing reality clearly, of course, is why I go on meditation retreats to begin with. It is, for me, the opposite of pabulum.

And yet, as I was sitting today, a thought came up about how much more I have enjoyed seeing people in these few days since the end of retreat than previously. I see them as manifesting God in unique ways. Some are joyful, some mean; others cool, aloof, clueless, wise, caring. I love 'subway practice', which usually takes the form of choiceless awareness, combined with a dropping of the self on the one hand and an allowing of the mind's curiosity on the other. I love looking at people's clothes, imagining what they are doing, sympathizing with those who are stressed out or who look unhappy, loving when a group of kids come on, with their crazy, unruly energy (luckily, they're not my kids). Subway practice depends on dropping my own story—where I am going, how pissed off I am at what happened an hour ago—and it doesn't always work. Particularly when I am running late, I am too anxious to quiet down, and so I give up, reading something on my Palm Pilot instead, or playing a game. Maybe, with deeper practice, I will be able both to drop harder stories, and to allow those stories to be watched as part of the parade of life/God passing by at this moment.

How different is subway practice from 'see the good in everybody'? Seemingly, only one letter different: "good" has an extra 'o'. I don't really mind that I have come full-circle to the advice columnist in *Reader's Digest*, but it is very curious.

Or, more banal wisdom: I had a lot of fears about how things would go with my family. But it has gone more softly than I expected. Maybe, slowly, over time I will indeed learn to trust that things rarely are terrible. Except when they are, which worrying doesn't help in any case.

I suppose there are some differences between me and 'Don't Sweat the Small Stuff'. I don't really enjoy talking as much as I used to, so it's not as if I want to make sparkling conversation with people. (Of course, given how egocentric much of my speech is, this could just be a balancing out to 'normal'.) And the no-self piece is a crucial, radical one. Then again, no-self is just a more extreme version of 'don't think only of yourself'.

Another important difference is internal. I actually feel and believe where I am coming from. It's not 'oughta' compassion—it's natural compassion, or interest, or openness. If I had to sit and repeat to myself "be nice, be nice, be nice," I would not be very nice at all. And I am trying to watch the times when I don't want to be nice, and act as skillfully as possible to respect my own feelings while at the same time not being an asshole.

Probably the most important difference between where I'm at and where the supermarket books are at is this: You can also not sweat the small stuff and yet not look too much inside either. Then you lead a life that may be destructive, or selfish, or, and I guess this is the least important, not quite fully human.

Does the ordinary, plain, good-people world cause suffering? Yes, but it is subterranean. "Just part of life," they say—but it isn't.

Now, I don't think that pantheism is absolutely necessary for the world to save itself—but it would help. I was a radical environmentalist before I was a pantheist, although even then it really came from the experience of the "impulse from a vernal wood." Spirit in nature, not quite the same as spirit manifesting as nature—but close, and close enough to want to excoriate Bush for destroying the Tongass in Alaska.

But if all we are doing is relaxing and feeling good about ourselves, this suffering will continue. We constrict into our selfish needs, which we relax about, and go on hurting the weak, the othered, the planet. If we are being fully open to what is, we will experience the Ground of all being, which radiates compassion, and so we won't go to war unnecessarily or spray everything with pesticides or warm the planet, so the forests die. We won't make an idolatrous god out of convenience. That is the most important difference, then, between really relaxing and opening up into truth, and relaxing like you do at the beach: when you get back from the beach, are you acting to alleviate suffering in the world?

8.

My wind chimes are ringing on a clear winter day, and I've just noticed a few buds coming from a plant that I was sure had died.

All these programs, executing within the mind of God. These hands, clapping in emptiness.

9.

At the Sunday school where I teach, a teacher was trying to teach something about a point of Jewish law, and the kids were misbehaving. They were full of energy. So he got a little upset at them. I suppose if you trace it back, the point of Jewish law eventually leads to God. But those kids, with their energy, *were* God. It was as if people argue about and puzzle over and declare the absence of exactly what they are at the exact moment they are denying it.

10.

I used to carry around a subtle anxiety that meaningful religion will soon disappear from the Earth. Fundamentalisms will survive, and possibly kill us all, and the stupid will likely continue to take refuge in an imagined God. But I worried that the communities in each religious tradition that actively engage with the spiritual and deep-ethical teachings of their tradition seem to grow smaller and smaller in proportion to the hordes at the shopping malls. Now, two changes have occurred in my thinking. First, I have grown to trust the unfolding of God. Even if It evolves in a way that would fill me with great sadness (continued ecocide, continued vulgarization of Western culture), It evolves.

More importantly, I have begun to think of 'God' as a concept that evolves by disappearing. Tribal and regional gods on most continents were very personal, very present, and were represented in images. Beginning with monotheism in the West and monism in Asia, God began to take on a new, less visible form—One God, whose human-like image cannot be represented.

Philosophy pushed the One even further from image, to an unchanging, formless perfection—closer to the One Being of Vedanta and Buddhism in the East, which also supplanted a rich pantheon of personal deities. In both East and West, the older forms have survived to this day, albeit transplanted into an unconvincing new cosmology or theology. Within the last five hundred years, even the concept of the One, or the Formless Being, has begun to be eclipsed by something even *more* removed from concept: the lack of God altogether. And within the last two hundred years, the joining of East and West in some romantic and spiritual circles has spread the doctrine of monism.

If we assume that the One is ultimately unknowable, these later developments are welcome indeed. The gods are idols. Concepts of 'God' are idols. Even the 'belief in God' is a concept. So the most accurate picture we can have of God is no picture at all, which is precisely what most intelligent people today hold.

The less clear the picture, the further the distance feels. A philosophical Jew who believes in the One has a far less rich emotional-religious life than the pious Jew who prays to the God of Abraham, or the Catholic who addresses the Virgin. This is the critical difference between atheism and monism: that for us monists, God is right here, now, in the fingers typing these words, the plants on my desk, the thoughts being sensed by the mind. God is bathing me in love, if I admit it.

For the atheist or agnostic, such nonsense words (nonsense because, having not been experienced, they are implausible, and associated with bad thinking) do not bring comfort. And so we are seeing a turn to religious and spiritual practices, or to more self-aware artistic or cultural ones, on the part of the minority of people in the West who do not have an explicit relationship with the Numinous.

Of course, most Westerners are still quite happy with Christianity, thank you. And not everyone who has no God-concept is close to God—many are serving gods of ego: selfishness, materialism, the dull egoistic kind of hedonism. I am speaking of cultural creatives and people like them—people who are deeply engaged with the Good, be it aesthetic or intellectual or ethical. These people are rediscovering God—only without the concept of God and, they suppose, in explicit opposition to it. In fact, their minds are closer to God than most of the religious.

At the same time, I have nothing but respect and awe for the organizers of organized religion. They are trying to teach to everybody what nobody can understand.

11.

I used to think I knew about everything except God. Now I think I know about nothing except God.

What that means: Of course, I didn't know about *everything*. But I felt that I knew something about most things which interested me. Politics, religion, literature, art. I was learning continuously, and synthesizing information, and it gave me delight. Now I have a small shudder of revulsion that passes through me each time I think of being enticed into some subject or other. More importantly, I don't think I know anything anymore. I don't know how to teach, I don't know how people really work, I just don't know anything. Or at least, if I have ideas, I think they are all tentative and idiosyncratic. I want to say nothing.

February 2004

What the World Is,
and What to Do About It

1. What the world is

The universe is a vast field of matter/energy, sometimes referred to as 'spacetime'. Sometimes spacetime manifests itself as matter (substance) and sometimes as energy (which is not substance, but rather forces which may act upon substance); although these two are ultimately the same, and may be changed one into the other. This single, incomprehensibly large, and ancient field of matter-energy is not uniform: matter has coalesced in some places into galaxies, stars, and so forth, and in other places is relatively absent. All bodies of matter are formed according to certain rules and principles, some of which we know and others of which we do not. These laws determine the shape of Being, causing it to manifest as matter or energy in particular formations all across spacetime, from the cosmic level (galaxy clusters, for example) to the biological (human genetic makeup) to the sub-microscopic (subatomic particles).

In one galaxy that we know of, matter coalesced around a certain star and formed planets, one of which became the site for a manifestation of Being called 'life', an organization of matter/energy governed by the relationships among certain molecules (DNA), and between such molecules and a very large number of environmental factors. Life forms, most of which exist for only brief periods of time, replicate their organizational patterns by reproducing their DNA, and thus take in more and more matter-energy and organizing it according to DNA's patterns, which may often change over time as DNA itself is combined with other DNA, mutated, or changed in some other way. Some genetic patterns, and their resultant traits or behaviors, tend to lead to more reproduction than others; over time, they are 'selected' as more life forms with their patterns reproduce than do life forms with other patterns.

Human beings evolved in this way, and apparently alone among life forms have evolved an ability to think conceptually, as you are doing as you read these words right now. Because of this unique ability, human beings have created enormously complex cultures, artefacts, and even explanations for how the universe came into being.

One such explanation is that God created the universe with Wisdom. Although the term 'God' has frequently meant a sort of super-human personality, for which evidence is lacking, if the term is applied to Being itself, then this explanation has the same meaning as the narrative in the first paragraph.

2. What enlightenment is

Enlightenment is the full knowledge of the foregoing section. Although in one sense this knowledge is quite simple to attain (after all, you have just read it), this knowledge is incomplete; it is an intellectual understanding of what the world is, but not experiential knowledge of it. "Map is not territory." One important example of this distinction is that human beings have evolved the tendency to see themselves as individuals, distinct from Being. Even though this thought is in direct contradiction with our current understanding of spacetime as One, the notion of 'self' in some form is necessary for even the most basic tasks needed for human genetic patterns to be preserved and reproduced, and is thus a fundamental principle of human self-understanding. Thus, to truly experience that one does not exist as an independent entity requires unlearning a basic and primal conception about the nature of the self and the universe. Moreover, because humans' rational faculties generally operate in a dualistic mode (separating the world into objects, and distinguishing between the world 'out there' and the self), they must be somehow set aside in order for accurate, non-dualistic perception to occur. Here too, however, basic principles of human thought, necessary for survival, must be unlearned in order for 'enlightenment' to occur.

One method for unlearning these (and other) basic errors is that of meditation, a process of suspending the mind's ordinary function so that a unitive perception/actualization of Being may occur. Many different practices of meditation exist. These practices do not convey information so much as open the mind to reality by quieting its ordinary function. "If the doors of perception were cleansed, every thing would appear... as it is: Infinite." (Blake)

It may be that the mind's operations may be altered by some other means, e.g., through pharmaceuticals that alter brain chemistry, and enlightened understanding may occur. However, these are just experiences, and they may be unreliable for obtaining an accurate perception of Being.

3. Is Enlightenment Worthwhile?

Humans have evolved many complex and varied ways of gaining satisfaction in life even without passing on their genetic material. Thus it is by no means clear that enlightenment is worth pursuing, if we define *worth* in terms of activities that bring either (a) satisfaction to the individual or (b) benefit to human society and/or Being in general.

There are many other pursuits which may bring satisfaction to the individual, even if such satisfaction is fleeting. These may include raising children, pursuing sensual pleasures, helping others, attaining status or praise, or self-expression. In addition, it might be argued that social/political activism, direct assistance to suffering people, and other such activities may bring more immediate benefit to human society than the pursuit of enlightenment.

There are many reasons why pursuing enlightenment may be worthwhile from an individual's point of view, however. First, even apart from enlightenment, meditation may engender calm, peace with one's life, a sense of purpose, and enjoyable mind states such as rapture and ecstasy. It may also lead one to be a more careful, loving, compassionate person, traits which many individuals see as desirable. Second, insofar as meditation leads to interim truths about oneself and one's world, as well as larger truths about Being, many see truth itself as worthwhile in the sense defined above, or in terms of some general value of human essence. Third, since the experience of Reality as it is removes the veil of separateness that conditions ordinary experience, it is often described in terms of awe/amazement on the one hand and great love on the other. Particularly for those who feel a lack of love in their ordinary lives, or search for an enduring Source of love, deeper than any particular romantic or religious manifestation, a contemplative path may thus be attractive. Finally, many people seem temperamentally attracted to meditation, even considering it tied to their own identities and their purpose on Earth.

At the same time, pursuing enlightenment carries certain costs to the individual. Many people derive satisfaction from 'making a mark' or 'making something of themselves', or from certain kinds of loving relationships, or from the gaining of sensual pleasures. However, the long retreat process necessary for undoing the error of self, and the resultant self-abnegation, may undermine these efforts (efforts and values which may be naturally 'selected', even though many adherents of contemplative paths say they are doomed to fail). In addition, meditation may also uncover fear, anxieties, and other difficult emotions that are ordinarily buried by the conventional self; although some may claim these will eventually become visible in any case, certainly meditation is a difficult path of self-confrontation.

From the non-individual point of view, there are likewise many reasons for and against seeking enlightenment. On the negative side, many claim that meditation takes people away from practices which may reduce suffering or counteract selfishly-motivated activities which threaten the health of the planet. Proponents of meditation counter that the contemplative path gradually leads to more compassion and less selfishness on the part of humanity in general. Empirically, this claim appears to be true, although it is impossible to measure whether non-contemplative activism or the contemplative path yields more overall good.

Meditation does promote several non-individual values. First, if suffering is seen as something to be minimized, then meditation is good because it promotes gentleness and compassion in its practitioners. Second, while it is not certain that life is preferable to non-life (although most humans believe it to be), to the extent that it is, then having more people engaged in meditation is likely good for all life forms because contemplative practice tends to lead to less destruction of life and more gentleness with respect to it. Third, even apart from the welfare of sentient life, some have noted that Being in general has tended to evolve across time toward the direction of greater knowledge of Itself from undifferentiated spacetime, to organized inanimate matter, to life forms, to human beings, and through human history toward a direction of greater understanding of Being. If this trajectory is true, then each attainment of enlightenment is a further development of Being itself.

In some religious traditions, this last benefit is sometimes expressed as "The purpose of life is to serve God and know God."

4. What to do about it

It is a very simple matter to know intellectually that all of spacetime is one field of matter/energy; that the individual self does not have any existence independent from the One; and that all creatures, matter, and energy are but fleeting manifestations of Being, organized according to Being's 'transcendent wisdom'. However, to truly know it—that is, to experience this truth (to 'Be Here Now')—is to know one's real nature, to end the selfish desires which cause one's own and others' suffering, and to experience a peaceful yet indescribably, achingly beautiful sense of spaciousness in the One that Is, here, now, everywhere, and always. The factors which hold each individual back from this path vary from individual to individual, according to the values and fears residing in each mind. Yet the end of the path is the same: an end to desire and suffering, an experience of unbounded love and peace, the merging with the One.

February 2003

Meditation and Sensuality

I have only just started meditating, and yet I've already noticed what a profound effect it has on my traditional religious practice. It's like getting the answer key. "Aha! This is what they were talking about when they said that God is everywhere!" The attention brought to mundane objects renders them everyday miracles, and an opened heart makes davening a cathartic, healing experience. Suddenly simple phrases that seem like clichés—"Be Here Now"—are full not only of truth, but of invitation. They cease to sound like pop psychology ("Remember, bourgeois busy people, if you just become *present* you can do all sorts of things and be a more successful businessman/lover/person.") and instead sound like a call to the One.

To some degree, this spiritual dimension is not surprising, even if to those who have never experienced it may sound dubious. People who meditate often talk about rapturous union with Being, or dissolution in the Divine. But I didn't expect how meditation would affect my sensual life. I suppose I imagined it to be a 'spiritual' practice, forgetting that all meditation really is, is being present with what's going on right now. And what's going on right now is, usually, an embodied experience. We eat and use the bathroom a lot more often than we pray, and God is everywhere. So perhaps it should have been obvious.

Of course, meditation is not primarily a sensual path. Nor is it limited to the individual spirit. It also enhances those communal aspects of worldly existence which Judaism seeks to maximize. It nurtures compassion, caring, and gentleness. It makes greed and social injustice viscerally hard to bear. But here are four new lessons that I've learned about sensuality and meditation:

1. Why people who use drugs like meditation

When you're stoned, or rolling, or tripping, or on any number of drugs, certain sensual sensations get enhanced. You can see and feel music when you're on ecstasy. The taste of some kinds of food on marijuana is, as a stoner would say, "intense." Everybody knows this, and it's why many people use drugs. There are, I know, people who smoke pot just to get wasted, and not to have heightened visual, tactile, or other sensual experiences. But for me, and for my friends, drugs are not an escape from reality; they are a magnifying glass held up to it. Intimate details of how the mind works, of how fabric feels, of music. Drugs can make every potato chip a delicate, crispy, greasy delight.

Meditation is about the same process of 'intensifying' daily experience, not by pursuing increasingly visceral thrills, but by quieting the mind enough to—in the words of Warren Zevon—"appreciate every sandwich." (Zevon coined that phrase when David Letterman asked him what effect his diagnosis of terminal illness had on his day-to-day life.) I used to see a contradiction between the ethos of "seizing the day," living as fully as possible, and the contemplative life, which I associated with a withdrawal from much of human experience. On retreat recently, though, I realized that there is no contradiction, and that in fact a contemplative path is the logical extension of living deliberately. There are, really, only two choices available to someone who wants to 'suck the marrow' out of life: either continually seek more extreme experiences, or make *every* experience 'extreme'. Some people can apparently do the former, but I find that tiring. Meditation allows me to 'suck the marrow' out of this tree, table, soda, or breath. By simply eliminating signal noise and stopping thought, the true colors of the phenomenal universe become revealed in ever-increasing brilliance. It's not like being stoned all the time, because there is not the disorientation and tripping up of the rational mind that occurs on pot. But it is like being stoned in the sense of tastes, touches, smells, sounds, and sights all becoming enhanced, kinesthetically interchanged, and—simply in their non-conceptual presence—enough reason to live.

A second point of similarity between drug use and meditation is that both lead to states of consciousness that are different from the ordinary. A lot of people like to take vacations in foreign countries. Some like exotic foods. And many others like vacations from their ordinary modes of consciousness into a different 'mind-space' where new insights can occur and even ordinary stimuli can be experienced in a whole new way.

Many people deeply fear altered states of consciousness, I think because they are overly afraid of their own non-rational minds. Subscribing to a worldview in which 'rational' rules of decency, propriety, etc., govern every aspect of life means relying on our capacities of rational judgment for every important decision. And so different mindstates are scary. Now, I'm all for using rational judgment to make most decisions in the world, and certainly all of those which seriously affect other people. But is it a rational judgment to dance? To let go of the self in orgasm? To fall in love? Come on. Some of our most transcendent moments come when the rational mind is quieted and something... else takes its place. In some aspects of life, being in touch with the nonrational is essential to being human.

Meditation, like drugs, leads to a state of mind in which the ordinary rational mind is not dominant in our experience of self. Of course, there are critical differences between (some) drug states and meditation, most importantly what Ken Wilber calls the "pre/trans" distinction: the rational mind does not become suppressed in meditation as it can in some kinds of drug use. Rather, its incessant train of ideas, thoughts, judgments, decisions—stops. Or, if it continues, it is seen for what it is, rather than as "me" thinking these thoughts. Direct perception of what is, rather than thinking about it; that's what happens.

So, drugs and meditation share two essentially sensual phenomena: enhanced sensual experience of the world, and non-ordinary consciousness. And, of course, meditation has none of the potentially damaging side effects or addictions of drugs. If anything, its side effects are more compassion, less anger, and greater gentleness. What a trip!

2. Meditation and sex

Once in a while, we in our culture hear about the Kama Sutra, but, in general, I think our image of a meditator is a desexualized figure sitting in some sort of robe. Yet even in the short time I have been meditating, I have found it to tremendously improve both the pleasure of sex and its ethical/religious valence.

On the simplest level, you've probably noticed how even the most mundane (and consequently hilariously inappropriate) thoughts can come up during sex: taxes, conference rooms, laundry. Or, perhaps, more problematic thoughts arise: of other people, or pornography, or one's own insecurities. In any case, these "foreign thoughts" (to use the Jewish term for them) take me out of the sensual pleasure and emotional delight, and into some other place that is not as much of a turn-on. In meditation, I have begun to learn how to notice these thoughts, and let them drop. It doesn't usually work, in meditation or sex, to push the thoughts away: the pushing is itself too much an action of the mind. "Dammit, why can't I focus!" is not an aphrodisiac. So these thoughts have to just be allowed to drop—mid-sentence, mid-articulation—and the attention guided gently to what is happening right now. In meditation, there are a number of ways in which the attention is turned: sometimes to one-pointed concentration on the breath or another subject, sometimes to open awareness toward whatever is happening now, etc. In sex, one-pointed concentration can lead to intense experiences of sexual release, and open awareness can tune us into the needs and desires of our partners. Both practices bring us back to what's hot, what's real.

In what Jewish mystics call 'small mind' (*mochin d'katnut*), I can be so distracted or neurotic that it's almost like the sex isn't happening at all. I have also been in sexual situations with people whose pleasure I ignored, because I was too lost in my own story to 'tune in' to what the other person was feeling. Why even bother with sex like this?

But in 'expanded mind' (*mochin d'gadlut*), when my concentration is focused just on the sexual pleasure I am feeling (usually on only one part of my body, but sometimes more generalized), I can keep the mind present during the ecstatic release for seconds at a time. Mere seconds—I can only imagine what experienced meditators can manage, floating in the physical pleasure for ten? twenty? thirty? seconds before a single thought or judgment arises. And I can only imagine tantric practitioners extending, through their mindful concentration, the period of orgasm itself to last—so we hear—for minutes and hours.

Finally, since meditation teaches us to let go of the natural identification most us have with our thoughts (I am hungry, I am greedy, I am insecure), it reduces self-consciousness. "I'm not the sort of person to shout/moan/sigh during sex," the small mind might say, identified as it is with a certain person and personality. That small mind can be discarded, and just as we can *daven* with an open heart, crying and laughing and singing beyond tears, so too is it possible to access parts of our sexual being that our personalities might otherwise put out of reach.

3. Meditation and love

The second major shift related to my sexual life that has come about through meditation is a change in how I regard it from a religious point of view. As a gay, single, sexually active man in New York City, my personal life bothers fundamentalists. But no one who grew up in a homophobic society can escape internalized homophobia, or voices that say things like being gay is wrong; being sexually active is unholy; decency and modesty are important religious values. And once again, trying to blot out these unwelcome thoughts does not work.

All of them, though, are thoughts rather than perceptions. An idea of right and wrong, rather than a perception of it; a concept of the holy, rather than a sensation of it; a confusion of social norms with ahistorical rules of behavior. When the mind is quieted, an openness to what actually *is* takes over, and all is seen to be nothing but God.

Now, many, many times, 'openness' leads to very negative sensations, because to expose ourselves to what is means opening up to cruelty, suffering, objectification, unhealthfulness, destruction of the body or Earth, and so on. It becomes viscerally painful to see an SUV belching climate-changing gases into the atmosphere for no good reason. The suffering of innocent people because of war becomes harder to endure. I often used to think that 'spiritual' people were just oversensitive. Now, I see that authentic spiritual practice makes one oversensitive, at least as measured by our own callous society.

So openness is not all sweetness—but delight is. When the conceptual mind shuts up, it's clear that the expression of love, of life, of carnal energy—these God-given pleasures and emotional connections—all are holy. It's obvious, not as dogma, but as experience.

Of course, there is still doubt in my *katnut* mind about whether I can truly judge what is holy, or whether I simply want to label what I enjoy as such. Yet one thing I have noticed about doubt: you always doubt your happiness, but you never doubt your sadness. So maybe a good use of doubt is to doubt the doubt: is doubt really the objective objection it pretends to be?

4. Why all this is actually very Jewish

In a way, Judaism is a tantric path. By this I mean that there is a choice in the contemplative life between living in the fullness of the world (and, if able, to see God in that world) or living in less-full environments which allow concentration and contemplation to take place more easily. The latter choice, asceticism, is not masochism; it is a tool to enable the ascetic's mental-emotional-spiritual processes.

Yet asceticism is not usually the Jewish way. There are exceptions— most of the inventors of the Kabbalah, people like Abraham Abulafia, the German Pietists, etc., for example. In the main, however, the Jewish path is one of sanctification of the sensual and material worlds. Food, sex, business—these are to be engaged in, lived in, and sanctified. From a contemporary perspective, Jewish restrictions on these areas of life may seem, well, restricting. However, they can also be seen as elevating to the holy every aspect of human life. In contrast to early Christianity, which saw certain parts of life as inherently evil (even if necessarily so) Rabbinic Judaism developed an attitude of "build a fence and honor what's inside." Kashrut laws govern food, and eating properly is seen as holy. All kinds of laws govern sex, and sex, too, is seen as holy. Jewish law is based upon a communal model of responsibility, and assumes people are engaged with the world. The way of renunciation, though practiced by many Jewish mystics, is not the mainstream.

In that context, enjoying the sorts of sensual benefits of meditation which I have discussed here are in line with this Jewish sensuality-affirming path. Obviously, it is neither a traditional nor Orthodox interpretation of 'affirming sensuality'. But more broadly, I think the application of spiritual attention to physical life is very Jewish indeed. We are taking our religious consciousness and practices, and joining them to the sensual world in which we live. This, on a fundamental level, is the unity of *shamayim* and *aretz* (heaven and earth, spirit and matter, soul and body) that so much of Judaism is about.

And it enhances love. When I am in a relationship, my mind begins to race as fast as my heart. The more I fall in love, the more anxiety rises: he doesn't love me as much as I love him, what can I do to keep him, how are things going, what does this mean, what do I want it to mean. The neuroses, and the words themselves, get in the way both of sexual expression and of meaningful relationship. When I quiet the mind, though, I learn to let go of the fear. God is not in the future, when my lover will or will not conform to my dreams and expectations. God is Here and Now, manifesting in this way, conditioned by an infinite chain of causes that goes back to *yehi ohr* ("let there by light"). The idolatrous false gods of my wants are set aside, and the One That Is As It Is (*ehyeh asher ehyeh*) fills my divine soul, my animal soul, and the ties that bind the two together.

July 2003

Thinking Despite Doubt
and Feeling Despite Truth

"Whatever God is, It must be closely related to truth." This is one of the few mottos that I adopted ten or fifteen years ago and still hold today. Most others have fallen by the wayside, or been outgrown like an old set of clothing. But I have long defended my idiosyncratic 'spiritual' beliefs—to myself, first and foremost, but also to others—on the grounds that they are not selections or evasions of the truth, but consequences of the pursuit of it. I do not fear inquiry; it is, for me, part of the process. So, although often labeled as religious, my ideas about the world are the opposite of what some people mean when they say "faith." They are part of the project of trying to get the most accurate picture of the universe, by whatever means, and living in accord with it.

For this reason, I have a lot of trouble with teachings like "thinking won't get you anywhere." In the contemplative world, it's something one hears a lot—but with two very different meanings, as Ken Wilber frequently discusses in his work. Some teachers mean it the way it probably sounds: don't think, feel; your truth will come to you through emotional, or spiritual, paths. Your intuition, or mysterious magical forces, or your 'inner truth'—these are the ways to enlightenment. For Wilber, and for me, this is very problematic. First, although they may be possessed of poetic genius, our 'inner children' are also self-centered, self-interested babies; even if we do need to acknowledge and express them at times, surely they do not have *all* the answers. They won't tell you how to be tolerant, or how to give CPR. They're a piece of the puzzle, not the solution.

Moreover, if spiritual practice is about regression, then those who practice it deserve all the snickers they get from the contemptuous intelligentsia. Why not just take drugs?

A lot of teachers, however, mean something very different when they say that thinking won't get you anywhere. They mean that there are faculties higher—not lower—than rational thought. What is meant by "higher"? For Wilber, that which is higher "transcends and includes" what is below it in what he calls a "holarchy." To take an easy example, the unit of daughter-family-community is a holarchy. Unlike a hierarchy, a holarchy does not imply priority: the family is not necessarily more important or more valuable than the individual member, and a community is not more important than a family. But communities transcend and include families, in a way that families do not include communities; families transcend and include family-members, in a way the individual members do not include families. Likewise, contemplatives want to say, 'higher' faculties of the individual transcend and include the rational mind— they are not 'pre-rational' but 'trans-rational.' They include reason—and something more.

Wilber wants to say, and has spent thousands of pages saying, that much of human mental-emotional-spiritual experience of the world can be mapped onto a holarchy that proceeds along a number of levels of the body, mind, soul, and spirit, beginning with the sensorimotor world (bodies, matter, physics) through emotional-sexual, magical, mythic, and rational, on to levels which are only accessed through meditation, contemplation, mystical experience, art, or the host of other human practices that are 'transpersonal' in nature, i.e., that move us into something which *seems* (a critical word to which I will return) to be greater than ourselves.

Wilber hates the fact that so many people confuse the pre-rational and trans-rational. He calls it the "pre/trans fallacy," and blames it for much New Age and related spiritualist confusion. Much New Age *mishegas* is magical or mythical in nature, for example, but because it is *non*-rational, it can easily be confused with being *trans*-rational. Yet magical practice does not include rational thought at all; in fact, it often denies it.

Critically, the 'higher' levels on the human-experiential holarchy (I'll stop scarequoting words like 'higher' now, but continue to mean them in holarchical terms, not hierarchical ones) do embrace the lower ones. There aren't many ways to test this except through personal experience, but having had a few peak and plateau experiences of the psychic (nature mysticism, 'cosmic consciousness'); subtle (deity mysticism); causal (the Witness, mystical union); and nondual levels myself, I can agree with Wilber on the basis of my own experience: these levels do not deny the thinking mind, but include it within something more. The thinking mind is present, and can be watched by the Witness as it goes through the motions of thought. You don't have to set it aside, or check your reason at the door. However it is very clear that there is also something watching the mind, embracing it, more than it.

Curiously, I happen to have progressed through these stages chronologically in my own life, before knowing that any of them existed. In college and before, I was a part-time, sometimes-wannabe nature mystic, an amateur Wordsworth entranced by the light of the setting sun, and the motion and spirit that runs through all things. It is easy to laugh at my Romantic self, but I cherish it; solitary times, alone in nature, were my first taste of God.

Following college, I began studying mysticism, and recognized within the Jewish tradition some of what I had found attractive in my brief Zen practice, and my study of Asian religions. I was attracted primarily to the mystical aspects of both Judaism and Buddhism, and chose the Jewish path because I knew it better: I knew the language, the customs, and the community; I was part of the culture. It fit. In davening and Torah study, being in holy places and among holy people, I occasionally was fortunate to have *peak experiences* of the Divine, on what Wilber calls the *subtle* level, and came to see my Jewish practice as both a path to such experiences and, as Heschel wrote, a response to them. (I have written an entire book on the complexities of that last sentence, and so it is difficult to just let them sit there. I'll restrict myself to an aside that the Hasidic model sees the *mitzvot* as a way toward *devekut*, cleaving to the Divine, whereas the Mitnagdic model sees them as a response to the existence of the Divine. I think we can integrate both.)

Only in the last two years have I cultivated the sort of practices that lead to causal and nondual awareness. I had glimpses of the numinous before, but they were flickers of light, and not more than that. I studied, read, and wrote about *unio mystica*, and puzzled through its implications. How could we be sure that our experience is an experience of union? What if this is all the mere buzzing of neurons in our own individual minds? How do the mystics themselves evaluate their experiences? But I didn't really know what I was talking about, because I had only been there in elusive and allusive ways. I am still very much a student of these practices today—not a teacher. I write about them in *Zeek* partly because I think a student's perspective—still uncertain, still with one foot in the normal, finite world that questions all of this—is valuable. My beginner's mind is valuable for what it is. Where I often find myself, though, is in a flux of belief and doubt.

Today is the first clear sky after two solid days of snow. It is cold, and clear, and I am staying inside. An old, old doubt keeps nagging me. I get the whole Wilberian map, I understand it, and I have been there. But I still wonder, despite myself, if it isn't all just a good buzz. "Flatland"— the view that there is nothing in the world that cannot be explained through fully materialistic science—is so compelling! I read about Wilber's years of working with the mantra *mu*, and it sounds to me like going downwards, not upwards. It sounds like the mind is being, if not repressed, then effaced, eroded. Sure, repeat *mu* to yourself a thousand times and you'll think you're one with everything. It doesn't mean it's true. Just because it seems like God doesn't mean it is God.

And *emet* (truth) remains too much of a value for me to let go. I am learning that there are reasons to let go of the nagging cognitive apparatus that doubts and checks and re-checks whether something is true. But the only reason I embrace it is to do so in the service of more truth. "Wait—you doubt your peak experiences?!" my friend David Ingber once asked me, incredulously. Well, yes, I do, because… truth.

This morning, while I was thinking about this, three things happened. First, I noticed how when I am in doubt, the position of belief seems wildly implausible. Come on—of course mysticism is just buzzing neurons. Wilber is a flake. Next, I calmed down a little, and, remaining calm, tried to remember what I actually think. I remembered that, within the scientific worldview as I understand it, there really is no place for the chief delusion of Western thought: the reality of the individual *I*. What is this ego, with *free will* that somehow exists separate from everything else? Look around you right now—what is not part of the One? All the matter and energy around you can be changed into something else; at this moment, it is, of course, real in its present form. But it is not ultimately separate from anything. And that includes the stuff in your brain.

The irony is that, for me, science and intellection are one of the most useful paths away from doubt and toward remembering.

This was transcending and including: watching the billions of forces at work in the complexity/chaos of the motes of dust; seeing and feeling the beauty of the currents and the reflection of the light; being a little grossed out by the dead skin that makes up most dust; recognizing, yes, the cliché of watching motes of dust in a sunbeam, but recognizing also the beauty beyond the cliché; and seeing all the cultural factors that determine the cliché and avoid it. All of Wilber's quadrants (I, we, it, its) were present. The universe was in a few grains of sand. And no fuzzy thinking was required.

There is a sort of neo-Pascalian wager that colors my contemplative practice these days. The contemplative path is a series of self-fulfilling prophecies. You do become kinder, you do become more open. The world does not change, but your attitude toward it does. Really, there is just this—just the same world that is in front of everyone else. But, without being sickly sweet, it can be seen and felt as the living skin of God. Both the flatland view and the mystical view seem internally consistent on a rational level (although flatland has trouble explaining the certainty associated with direct mystical experience, a certainty as sure and as clear as your perception of your hands or feet right now; and meditation allows greater cognitive *experience* of rationally-verifiable truths). So why not choose the option that leads to expanded compassion, love, and peace?

The fear that arises with Pascal's wager is that it is actually a choice—with consequences.

On the one hand, I can see the world from the good, humanistic, skeptical, liberal perspective—what, for shorthand, I think of as the New Yorker view. In this world, certain things are clear. The great variety of human experience, from ballet shoes to the terrible complexities of Afghanistan, is a wonderful, rich, dazzling symphony. Culture is essential, beautiful, and real; people like Ken Wilber are weirdos. Religion, for its part, is sometimes beautiful, sometimes horrible. Meditation is good to relax, as part of a complete, humanistic life, but anything more than that is closely related to delusion. Restaurants, operas, political debates, the joys of family and friends—all of this is accessible, to read, experience, even possibly to contribute a verse. It is all part of a world that, if you have the right education and political liberalism and privileges of class, you have an invitation to enjoy.

From the perspective of *mochin d'gadlut* (the "expanded mind"), on the other hand, all of these worlds are, essentially, manifestations of the One. They exist, they are beautiful, but the reality is that they are just ripples on the ocean. In theory, all the beauty remains—but it's not so easy.

Here is how it is supposed to work. The highest of Wilber's 'levels' is the nondual, the tantric path in which the world is fully engaged, yet simultaneously known to be a manifestation of the One. Now, Wilber doesn't engage much with the Jewish tradition's tantric path, because he probably doesn't see it as such. Neither do most Jews, who, if anything, associate tantra with exotic sexual practices. But halachic Judaism is integral—it seeks to marry *shamayim* and *aretz*, to make in our finite world either a tabernacle for the holy (in the dualistic view) or an embodiment of it (in the nondualistic one). It is tantric because it engages with the stuff of the world, even while knowing that all the *yesh* is but a manifestation of the *ayin*. It is an embrace both of the fact that we are all ripples on the ocean *and* the beauty of the ripples.

How does this play out? Wilber says, in *One Taste* and other books, that he is as at home in pop culture, postmodernist theory, and political discourse as in the world of meditation. In fact, it is essential for his integral philosophy that he be so. Wilber wants you to meditate, but also

Enlightenment by Trial and Error

listen to music, follow an athletic discipline of some kind, be in therapy or some other psychoanalytic work, and develop on "all quadrants, all levels." You can be culturally developed as a businessman or basket-maker, but be culturally developed; you can ride motorcycles or go to raves, but get your groove on somehow.

That's how it's supposed to work. But to me, it feels like a choice with consequences. First, the reorientation of *mochin d'gadlut* changes how I experience the finite world. Continuing the analogy to water, the unified "wetness of all the waves" (Wilber's term) seems to eclipse their particular properties and beauties. The opera and the sound of a cricket are both heard as the voice of God. This is a beautiful truth to experience. But it tends to flatten the opera into no more than a more complex version of the cricket. More intricate, yes; a higher level on the holarchy, yes; but that is all. At the end of the day, it's just one face of God or another. And when you have seen the face of God, as your own Original Face, how exciting can anything else really be?

Second, great art, great tragedy—these exist precisely because of the bounds of finitude. The world is beautiful precisely because we do not have the answers, because suffering is real, and pain is part of life. By transcending suffering, we 'transcend' much of the vitality of human art. Meditation does enliven the experience of this moment, but I have also felt, in the last two years, a whole lot less invested in New Yorker culture, and even in my own personal trials and travails. Not as much feels at stake. Wilber himself analogizes it to being at the movies. "With meditation, you begin to relax in your seat and just watch the movie of life." Now, I know he includes working, caring, and loving in what he means by the "movie of life." But is this disengaged Witnessing really living?

For me, the tantric path only works by forgetting. While I am on retreat, I have to forget what I know to be true in order to drink deep from Shakespeare—and I want to drink deep from Shakespeare! Maybe this forgetting is not unlike our forgetting during the suspension of disbelief while reading fiction. Or maybe it's not so different from feeling moved by poetry despite other manifest truths—that people are starving as you are reading, or that the Earth is being destroyed because of greed. Or this forgetting could just be an uninteresting question of balance: how much escapism do we need to keep going?

It's ironic that the twin challenges of an integral, Jewish, tantric life-in-finitude—entering into the thinking, rational world despite the risk of doubt, and trying to feel finitude viscerally despite the truth that it is not ultimately real—are addressed with opposite remedies: remembering, in the case of doubt; forgetting, in the case of feeling. When I am lost, I sit, and it is not hard to remember. And when I feel an urge to become lost, it is easy to forget.

Admittedly, though, this all sits uncomfortably. Judaism is so much a practice of remembering—in an active way, that makes real today that which is remembered from the past. Is forgetting really a value? And on the complementary side, perhaps oscillation is the nature of my path, yet when I am angry and impatient in my constricted mind, I don't seem or feel very enlightened. Yet what other way is there? World-renunciation is not my path, just out of karma. But to care authentically about the world of finitude—not only out of compassion, but out of direct, personal involvement—is to guarantee desire, suffering, anger, all of it.

The first time I heard this problem expressed remains, for me, the best expression of it: Thornton Wilder's *Our Town*. The problem of *Our Town* is the tension between the long view (i.e., of the dead), which is more accurate but lacks life, and the local view, which may forget about the great questions of existence but has a down-to-earth reality that is where we all want to live.

Only the Stage Manager seems to be able to navigate both worlds, with both the wide perspective of the dead and a real caring for the living. When, in Act III, the dead Emily tries to empathize with the world of the living, she can't do it. "They're sort of shut up in little boxes, aren't they?" she says. Yet it is she who cannot adapt. With the knowledge that she has of life's transitory nature, she is confronted by ordinary people, going through their ordinary lives, and she can't bear it. "I can't go on. It goes so fast. We don't have time to look at one another." She asks the stage manager, "Do any human beings ever realize life while they live it?—every, every minute?"

At first the Stage Manager answers "No." Then, after a pause, he says: "The saints and poets, maybe—they do some."

The saints and the poets, and, it seems, the Stage Manager, have the gift of living deliberately and fully in the world, not despite the knowledge that all is evanescent, but, we think, because of it. They are able to embrace this moment fully, in its richness, and not let it disappear. In the best productions of *Our Town*, the Stage Manager is actively engaged with the townspeople, genuinely surprised by what happens to them, interested in the results. He has a perspective—that of "saints and poets"—that both the dead and the townspeople lack, and that perspective allows him a wider understanding than they possess. 'Complex seeing' is what Brecht called this ability to simultaneously care and critique, to be distanced and yet moved at the same time. The ideal for Brecht, and for Wilder, is not some illusory 'golden mean' which supposedly splits the difference. It's more difficult. It's both feeling and thinking, shifting in and out of desire. Perhaps desire is the root of suffering, but sucking the marrow out of life is what we are here on Earth to do. Caring too much, sweating the small stuff, it leads to ulcers and early death—but who wants to live a few more years but be alive fewer?

The small, cosmically insignificant sandcastles we build around ourselves are small and cosmically insignificant, yes, but they are also all we have between ourselves and the tides.

January 2004

Am I "Religious"?

Being religious, in the sense that I understand the term, is not a matter of opinion. It is a matter of love.

For many people, being religious is absolutely about opinions. It means believing in certain ideas (e.g., there is a God) or stories (the Bible is true), and having ideas about one group of people as compared with others. It may mean following rules about how one is to live—according to *hadith*, or *halacha*, etc.—and believing those rules to be absolutely true. For some, these principles cannot even be called opinions: they are truths which must be accepted and fulfilled. But they are opinions in the sense of being ideas which are held about the world.

None of this really matters to me. I have more in common with an atheist who dances than with the supposedly pious men who are asleep in their lives. For me, religion is about being in love with the world, rapturously and fully and deliciously sucking the marrow out of life. How that plays out—painting, Walden, Hinduism, *halacha*—is far less important than that it play out at all. I don't care about the God you don't believe in; I care about what makes you inspired. I care that you *get* inspired. I care that you are so damn alive that you can't help but sing, or pray, or study, or help. I couldn't care less what you think about when the Torah was written, what happens after we die, or whether a deity exists. I want to know only if there is something sacred for you.

Am I 'religious,' then? It depends on whom you ask. I am very religious according to my own definitions, and according to those of Friedrich Schleiermacher, Rabbi Zalman Schachter-Shalomi, and many mystics, nuns, and poets. Here is Schleiermacher, the consummate German Romantic, writing *On Religion* in 1799:

> The universe exists in uninterrupted activity and reveals itself to
> us every moment. Every form that it brings forth, every being to
> which it gives a separate existence according to the fullness of life,

every occurrence that spills forth from its rich, ever-fruitful womb, is an action of the same upon us. Thus to accept everything individual as part of a whole and everything limited as a representation of infinite, is religion.

For Schleiermacher, religion is about cultivating and expressing our intuition of the infinite. And so, he knew, those "cultured despisers" of churches, hierarchies, and dogmas are often more religious than those who uphold them. They just confuse the essence of religion (being fully alive to this moment and seeing it as part of the One) with the structures that some people have chosen to build around it (such as churches, theologies, and power structures). There can be no authentic system of religion, Schleiermacher wrote, any more than there could be a system of intuition.

I am also religious according to the fascinating, obscure volume by Frederick Streng, *Ways of Being Religious*, which includes "Social and Economic Justice as an Ultimate Concern," "The New Life Through Technocracy," and other worldviews of ultimate value which function in religious ways. For each of these ways of being religious, Streng analyzes the problem the system is meant to solve, how it answers that problem, and how it expresses its means to answering it individually and socially. It's an intriguing work, and properly gives the atheistic social worker, toiling in a soup kitchen, far more religious standing than the rhetorically or superficially pious.

Whether I, or Schleiermacher, or Streng, are 'religious' according to someone with a too-narrow definition of the term ought not to matter. And yet, language is meant to communicate. As Lewis Carroll developed with great humor in *Through the Looking Glass*, a language in which words mean only what the speakers want them to mean is not really a language. Nor, to use Buddhist terminology, is it particularly skillful to go around using the word 'religious' if it means something different from what 90% of religious people think it means. I don't want to give people the wrong idea. Finally, going around talking about God to people whose initial associations with that term are dogma, repression, and ignorance—this is not going to draw anyone to open up and inquire. Quite the contrary.

Many contemporary teachers have dropped the word entirely, preferring to call themselves 'spiritual.' With different language, they are drawing essentially the same dichotomy Schleiermacher drew. Spirituality is what religion is really about, they say: an encounter with the numinous; moments of real, rich presence. Religion is what happens after that encounter gets translated back into life—particularly, the lives of people unwilling to undertake transformation necessary for deep spirituality. Religion includes dogmas, theologies, rules, myths, fears, and sins. Some of that is connected to Spirit, some of it isn't. But none of it, for these teachers, is essential. So they leave behind the word 'religious,' or set it up as a foil.

The omnipresence of Spirit is a useful differentiator. Like Schleiermacher and Streng, these teachers see Spirit at work in a surgeon who practices her craft with perfect concentration, a volunteer in the Peace Corps, an actor on the stage. One group I admire, Q-Spirit, has developed ritual that they lead at gay circuit parties around the world. Their aim is not to make these parties spiritual; it is to invite the participants to see that what they are doing is *already* spiritual. Many gay dance clubs are re-enactments of ancient ecstatic rituals: the trance-inducing music and dance, the ingestion of somatic substances, the two-spirit people as shamans. All that's missing is the heart, the spiritual intention.

I have two main concerns about the word 'spiritual.' The first is that it, like 'religious,' has been tainted by its associations—in this case, with cheesy, feel-good New Age stuff, and with an ultimately unethical lifestyle of spiritual hedonism. The second problem is deeper. For many people, being spiritual is about having a certain feeling. But the thing is, there is nothing to get, and no particular feeling to have. Being in love with God is like being in love with a person; sometimes it's ecstasy, sometimes it's laundry (paraphrasing Jack Kornfield here). And sometimes it's intense pain and sadness. The question is not, how do I get away from the ugly or boring bits and into a cool 'spiritual' vibe. But rather, how can I accept everything as what God is like right now. This acceptance does not mean "I accept everything as the will of God" or "God has a plan" or "There is no reason to change anything." It means, just this—whatever is going on for you at this moment, reading, sitting, wondering, worrying: this is it.

This, what is happening now, in the fullness of this moment, is It, the Big It, God, the Friend, Enlightenment, the Now, Being, Awareness. Often we assume that "It" needs to be accompanied by long beards (for men), mountaintops, bells, whistles, perhaps various mindstates that we read about in Abulafia or somewhere else. However, that's clearly not true. On the logical level, if God is everywhere and fills all of creation, God is right here, now, in your mind and outside your mind, in fact there is no inside or outside, no separate self or separate anything, and this moment is arising only within primordial Awareness. On the trans-rational level, that can really be perceived and felt; try it. It is there even if the "this" that's going on involves mindstates we don't much care for. This is It even if no effort is made to appreciate little joys or little pleasures. Even if there are no little joys or little pleasures, even if there are big sadnesses.

So 'spirituality' might be just as misleading as the word 'religion'— even though I routinely go around as a 'spiritual teacher' and do my thing.

I have no vocabulary word to define what I am. But I've always been religious in this way, I realized. When I was seventeen, the most important teacher in the world for me was the film *Dead Poets Society*, which came out that year. I wanted to seize the day, to make my life extraordinary. I also wanted to be roommates with Neil, the beautiful, probably gay character who, like Finny in *A Separate Peace*, is ultimately a tragic figure. (I've maintained my crush on the actor who played him for nearly half my life now.) For a while, this meant being a poet, an artist—and teaching just as Mr. Keating did, right down to the soccer practice with important quotes. (For me it was an ultimate frisbee practice with Edward Gorey, but close enough.) Although I was too timid and closeted to really act on it at the time, I yearned in college and the years right afterward to be one of —Kerouac here—

the mad ones, the ones who are mad to live, mad to talk, mad to be saved, desirous of everything at the same time, the ones who never yawn or say a commonplace thing, but burn like fabulous roman candles exploding like spiders across the stars and in the middle you see the blue center light pop and everybody goes "AWWW!"

Well, it took me a while—a detour through respectable life, a car accident to break me open—but I got there eventually. At least, I'm doing my best at it.

November 2004

I Still Believe
That People Are Good At Heart

Anne Frank is routinely reduced to a cliché. The arc of the story fits cleanly into the Hallmark Tragic Heroes mold: an optimistic, bright-eyed young girl, maintaining her spirit even in the midst of hardship. So, all of us who endure hardship are told to look on the bright side, enjoy our psychological opiates, and keep a smile on our face. Come what may.

But Anne Frank was a much more complicated, thoughtful person than the simplified image suggests. She was not an emotional ostrich, sticking her head in the sand of happy thoughts while the world crumbled and burned around her. She was, as expressed in her diary if not the various film adaptations of it, keenly aware of injustice, paradox, pragmatism, sexuality, sentimentalism, tragedy, irony—the whole range of human complexity. Perhaps her best-known aphorism, which I have chosen as my title here, is actually only the second half of a more complicated sentence: "I keep my ideals, because in spite of everything I still believe that people are really good at heart." She keeps her ideals—but she knows that the world gives good cause to abandon them.

I have no way of knowing whether Anne Frank meant what I mean by saying that people are good at heart. But it certainly startled me to realize that this simple statement is the foundation of my meditation practice, and the way in which I think spirituality is meant to be lived. It also bears, I think, on how I understand difficult times, such as those our country is now entering. So here goes.

Let's distinguish between religion, spirituality, and contemplation. (I dealt with this issue in the previous chapter, and so will only summarize the point briefly here.) Essentially, I see spirituality as being about cultivating certain mind- (or heart-, or soul-) states, for the purpose of transforming the self or having an experience of ultimate reality. It includes practices like dancing, ecstatic prayer, some kinds of meditation, ritual, being with loved ones, and producing art. It gives color, shape, and flavor to ordinary experience.

Religion, in contrast, is a set of social forms and communities that, sometimes, move toward and from spirituality. Toward, in the sense of prescribing attitudes and practices which tend to cultivate good spiritual states; from, in the sense of prescribing ethics and other rules order the rest of life according to the ideal glimpsed in the states. In both cases, religion involves itself with forms—these candles, this holy book—and, as we know very well, can degenerate into fundamentalism, which is a valuing of the form more than the purpose for which the form exists.

Contemplation seems like spirituality, but is actually somewhat different. Both spirituality and contemplation are oriented toward the inner life, in contrast with mainstream religion. But contemplation, often but not only in the form of meditation, is less about cultivating states than quieting the mind enough so that we can see any mindstate in a clear way. Thus, where spirituality naturally prefers mindstates like ecstasy and lovingkindness to boredom and doubt, contemplation does not. Of course, it's more pleasant to be in a state of bliss, but, as one of my Buddhist teachers said during a recent retreat, "It's not what's going on that matters—it's how you relate to it."

Wherever it is found—in Dharmic traditions, in Western philosophical reflection (Stoicism in particular), or in Jewish *hitbonnenut*—contemplative practice is largely about cultivating an equanimous space large enough to accommodate even the most difficult of emotions and circumstances. Equanimity does not mean not feeling the emotion—on my retreat, when I felt anger, I really felt anger. It means relating to the emotion in a way of non-judgment: just allow the anger, or the joy, to exist. Don't hold onto it, or push it away, or wish it would stop, or wish it would never stop. Don't take action in order to get it to stop. Just check it out, try not to judge it (while at the same time not acting on it, since acting is a form of aversion to the feeling itself) be with it, watch it arise and pass.

To quote that same dharma teacher again, the opposite of equanimity is not feeling. It's clinging.

The fact is, I cannot control all the changing conditions of my life, and, chances are, neither can you. So, it's helpful to remember that. Of course, we can and should change *some* conditions—especially those which cause suffering to others or to ourselves. Social justice, environmental justice, doing justice to our own needs—these all remain. But it's helpful to remember that changing the conditions is not what will really bring about lasting happiness, which can only come from how I relate to the transitory conditions of my life. Trying to manage those conditions, or to maintain order, or to only experience happy thoughts—that is likely to make matters worse.

So, if for no other reason, the contemplative practice of seeing clearly—not superimposing moral thinking atop a rotten foundation, but just seeing what is—leads to more justice and more peace. Simply by seeing clearly who or what we are, we become more gentle, more compassionate. Automatically, as it were. We see more clearly our desires, and loosen their hold on us. We can accommodate various mindstates without having to enhance them or be rid of them. It's just not as important to achieve, or compete, or have a certain desirable experience, or grab onto love in a way that, ironically, squelches it.

But look at what else happens.

First, the sense of the sacred arises naturally from presence. How we articulate it—as God, the power of art, Buddha-nature—is up to us. But I can confirm that simply by quieting down the body and mind, the doors of perception do open, and what the mystics of every world tradition say happens—happens. This direct, mystical experience—no faith required—conditions more delight and more certainty than I can put into words. Again: not from putting on a special hat or chanting a magic phrase. But from just quieting down and observing what happens.

And from that sense of the sacred, an inner kindness tends to arise on its own. This is really quite remarkable. Why should it be the case that, if we simply see clearly, the heart opens toward kindness? It could just as well be the case that, when we see clearly, we become more aggressive and destructive. Yet it never actually works that way. Actually, we are good at heart, as we see merely by turning down the noise and observing the heart clearly. Imagine that.

Now, religion or spirituality may filter the contemplative Light through the forms of its own stained glass—in terms of narrative, or concepts, or myth. And some of the shapes of the stained glass may inspire fundamentalism, fear, even violence. But when we're with the light itself... it doesn't happen.

I do want not to misrepresent contemplative practice, which in nearly every system in the world also contains some elements of cultivation. In the Theravada Buddhist world, for example, pure insight meditation is usually leavened with meditation practices which have as their aim precisely the cultivation of certain wholesome mindstates: lovingkindness, compassion, and so on. In the Jewish contemplative world, meditation is accompanied by prayer, or by study of sacred text—both of which arouse thoughts and feelings of God. So it's never completely transparent.

But I can't convey to you how beautiful it was for me to see not merely that "all people are good at heart," but that I am in particular. Me! The clumsy, fumbling, needy me—the ironic, cynical me—underneath, or rather alongside, all those pieces and strategies, is really a very simple loving person who is—gasp—good at heart.

This can be a very embarrassing thing to realize, let alone express. But it's embarrassing because we suppose that the real Anne Frank is the Hallmark Anne Frank—i.e., that knowing people to be good at heart leads to mushy thinking or Pollyannish optimism. But that's not true at all. Knowing that I am good at heart does not cloud my judgment about when I'm too clever, inconsiderate, or *spiritual*—it clarifies it. It does not bring about arrogance; it engenders humility.

And it crucially reframes how I see the political process, which, in recent months, has brought great suffering to people who believe as I do. Unlike those Manicheans who believe themselves to be at war with the intrinsic evil of humanity, I see myself as doing battle with error—with mistake. Evil itself is a mistake—it erroneously supposes that it exists, that real separateness exists, that there is more than one ultimate Being.

Even as I continue to try to see, with hard-nosed clarity, the folly and cruelty of despotic regimes and fundamentalist dogmas, I understand in a deep sense that those who support them are searching for Light, and love—albeit in a deeply confused way. Although interim solutions may include activism, counterculture, even conflict, the real solution is more openness, more honesty, clearer seeing.

Anne Frank was not naive. But imagine her knowing, even as she was victimized and brutalized beyond our capacity to conceive, that what was happening was not the evil essence of humanity, but a mistake. Imagine a surrender not to despair, but to the unfolding of Being itself. Imagine the slightest loving smile, held even amidst tears.

February 2005

Quality of Life

1.

Is my grandmother dying? It's sometimes hard to remember that only a year ago, she could maneuver herself around, was still interested in going out for lunch or dinner, was someone who, although growing old and in need of care, was still a human being, capable of humor and anger and warmth. She had already begun exhibiting some classic signs of dementia: repeating questions asked only minutes before, telling the same stories over and over, etc. Yet she was, until recently, still someone who was aware of her world and her place within it.

No longer. Now she has good days and bad days, as do all sufferers of dementia, but even on the good days she is not the vibrant person she was. Today, for example, was a good day, but that chiefly meant not yelling at the nurse. The less said about the bad days, the better.

Last June, in what may have been her final act of will (and desperation), my grandmother began refusing food. She claimed not to be hungry, even as her strength ebbed and moving from bed to wheelchair tired her out. She would sit through the three daily meals at the assisted living facility where she lives, and simply refuse to eat. The nurses would coax, my mother would coax, and my grandmother would resist. Maybe, some days, she would eat a spoonful of oatmeal.

After some consideration, my mother, sister, and I decided not to force her. My grandmother had always lived life on her own terms, and we would not defy her now. Whose interests would that be serving anyway? There was little quality of life ahead for her, and we all knew it; imposing the indignity of feeding tubes on a strong-willed woman seemed only to serve our own misplaced sense of morality. So the coaxing stopped, the visits from the rabbi increased, and we began to prepare for what seemed to be inevitable.

I paid what I thought would be my final visit during the first week of July. Having just returned from a week of silent meditation, I felt equipped to be fully present with my grandmother's suffering, and my mother's pain in the face of it. Maybe, I thought, I could apply some of the new mindfulness practices I had learned on my grandmother's situation; maybe I could experience directly what my family was going through, and even help to ease their pain. It worked, to a point. I practiced forbearance in the face of my mother's judgments, and practiced patience with my grandmother's barely coherent consciousness. Since I had just spent a week in silence, I was able to endure and even delight in the long lacunae in my grandmother's conversation; I allowed her sentences to unfold at their slow, disjointed pace. I did not shrink from eye contact, which seemed more intimate than her suddenly-unreliable speech. It seemed clear that this was the endgame; this was how a long life would end, in its nineties, in an assisted-living facility in Florida. So I tried to cherish the occasional moments of lucidity that appeared, like lights in a fog, in my grandmother's increasing cloud of fatigue and dementia. I even told her that my sister and I understood what she was doing, and that it was okay with us.

What happened next was an ironic turn: my grandmother's will to die itself dissolved. As she gradually lost the ability to maintain a rational train of thought, she apparently lost the concentration necessary to refuse food. Just as suddenly as it had started, and with just as little explanation, the refusal to eat stopped. My grandmother gained back some of the weight she had lost; while still extremely thin, it seemed like this wouldn't be the end after all. My mother called this an 'improvement,' though I think there was ambivalence in her voice.

And so, a long goodbye has set in. It is unwanted; while there is more time to be spent with my grandmother, there is less of her to spend the time with. And this period of dependence is a betrayal of all that my grandmother stood for. Granny valued three things, she said, in her old age: her independence, her intellect (which she called her "noodle"), and the fact that she was not a burden to my mother. All three of these have been savagely, gradually, taken away. She is no longer able to use the toilet without assistance. She is rarely able to maintain a conversation for more than two or three exchanges. And my mother has become a caregiver, shuttling back and forth, dealing with flareups, meeting with doctors to set the levels of my grandmother's medication.

Really, it is worse than that: my mother has become a prisoner to my grandmother's condition. She is deferring her life: envisioning its next phase (a new home, hip replacement surgery) but postponing any action until after my grandmother dies; planning trips, but worrying about leaving Granny 'on her own'; constantly fielding phone calls from nurses and pharmacists. I wish I could convince my mother not to take each perceived error on the part of the nursing staff so personally, not to take personal responsibility for every aspect of my grandmother's medical care—but I can't. My mother reacts with anger: Who am I to tell her what to do? Who but she is shouldering this burden? More than that, I feel that to make any such suggestion is to confirm my mother's worst opinion of me: that I will not be involved in her convalescence; that it is my sister, not me, on whom she can rely. So I watch helplessly as old age claims two lives instead of one.

2.

It must be a common desire for families in this situation to pretend as though none of it is happening. The method of avoidance that has appeared most readily to me would be to say that "this is not my grandmother." She is barely aware of the passage of time, I tell myself; she hardly knows where she is. Really, she is absent from her suffering; the problem is only an old woman in need of care, and a family stretched to provide it.

There is some truth to this claim, although also strange to set aside the inescapable reality of a person's physical, and familial, identity ("the ineluctable modality of the visible," Stephen Dedalus said) to define life itself, to say that life is essentially about quality, or at least the ability to experience it. This is the familiar debate about the right to die, of course. But we're not there yet; although we all know that in some sense my grandmother is "no longer herself," there are those times of clarity in which she is. These 'good days' are in some ways the worst ones, because they belie our hope that she is oblivious to what has happened to her. We all would like to believe that Granny is gone even though this person remains. Because if there is a part of her that is aware of what has happened, her suffering is unbearable to imagine.

That there is some boundary to suffering seems essential for our ability to exist in the presence of it. Victims of the holocaust, we're told, went "numb" or in some other way lost the ability to feel totally the horror of it. This may have helped them survive. It also helps us. We need them to be numb; if they were lucid in the midst of torture, how can we endure hearing of it? We want victims of car accidents to black out; we want soldiers to be shell-shocked; and I want my grandmother not to know what is happening to her. This is what I want for my grandmother: for the sum of her life's consciousness to be that of an elegant lady, beautiful in her youth, refined in her adulthood, who never in her life wanted what has now come to pass. If equanimity is impossible for her (and I think it would be for me), let her not know what is happening to her, for as long as God requires it to happen. Or at least, let it be over soon.

Seeing what my grandmother never wanted to happen caused me to ask what she *did* want, what she lived for, which in turn caused me to ask the same questions of myself. Here is what was important to my grandmother: her family; prosperity in the New World; the growth and flourishing of the Jewish people; and bourgeois values like respectability, tidiness, and climbing the social ladder. Here is what is important to me: love (whether in a family or not), artistic achievement, spiritual seriousness, joy, integrity. What is important to me but I do not want to admit: prosperity, fame.

One crucial difference was that for my grandmother, born into abject poverty and violence, success, prosperity, and so forth, were all laudable desires. For me, born comfortable, these desires are the root of suffering—their non-fulfillment leads me to see my life as not worth living, even as I sit by my grandmother's sickbed. She never despaired, I don't think; her will to live was always too strong. Come to think of it, maybe it is still. Maybe she *did* choose to start eating again; maybe she knows a bond to life that I, indulgently, do not. Although I claim that my aversion to desire is part of a spiritual practice, I wonder if I envy my grandmother's perseverance. Even lying in bed, terribly weakened by age, she seems to possess a strength I lack.

The medical community is still very generous when defining quality of life—probably as Buddhist as America ever gets. If you can experience life—think it, perceive it, feel it—that is quality of life. Whether what you are experiencing is pleasure or pain—that is not part of the bargain, so to speak. The current debates about physician-assisted suicide seem to be about a divergence from this norm: whether there is a time at which the experience of pain is so great, certain, and unremitting that it is merciful to help someone avoid it. The distinction between assisted suicide at the end of life and suicide in its middle is muddier; it is now one of degree, rather than kind. With the choice in some cases now *between* quality and life, simple distinctions are lost. 'Choose life' becomes ambiguous.

It looked for a while as though my grandmother had chosen quality instead of life, and we assented. Now, she has changed her mind and silently opted not to rush God—or perhaps she lacks the capacity to make the choice. We will not know which is the case. If she has chosen this path, her volition is locked inside a broken mind. If the path chose her, her will is lost. I hope, for so many reasons, that it is the latter. And yet, do I also secretly hope that, even now, she intentionally clings to life—and that I might have inherited her will to live?

I should be a better grandson. I should come more often. But then again, when she forgets my visit within a day or two, what am I providing her? What is the point of this existence? I believe that, with mindfulness, every moment of life can be sacred. But what about when the mind has become damaged, and cannot remember, cannot, in a fundamental way, be mindful? "There is nothing there," my grandmother said at one point, and from the context it seemed to me she was referring to her mind, now stripped of memory, personality, and control.

One of the last things she said to me today was, "I feel pity on you." I asked why. She answered, "Because you come, and this is such an outstanding place. And this is the window. It lets everything in, and lets everything out. But they don't give you any..."

Then the nurse came in.

January 2003

Constriction

1. Cowardice in Sedona

My next stop was the Psychic Expo I'd seen advertised at the Center for the New Age, a bright purple building just outside of town offering any number of spiritual trinkets and people proffering everything from aura cleansings to chakra realignments to pet channeling. I figured this was the place to sample Sedona's mystical wonders. A total disbeliever, I leafed through the binder at the concierge desk, finally requesting an aura cleansing by whomever was free, which turned out to be Renee, a barefoot, barrel-chested woman with spiky orange hair and a rayon dress to match. . .

Somehow, my aura told her I was a stressed-out person who lacks vitamins B and C and doesn't breathe enough. . . that I tend only to use my left brain (true), don't express my emotions to the fullest (true) and that the cleansing had lifted a weight off my energy field (I'll let you know). She warned me I'd have "wacky" dreams that night and suggested a personal affirmation: "I freely and easily release the old and joyfully welcome the new."

Perhaps freaked out by how right-on Renee had seemed or maybe just conveniently taking her last bit of advice, I sped to the local outlet mall and bought four pairs of shoes.

—Hope Reeves, "A Vacation, or Maybe a Quest,"
New York Times Travel Section

When I read Hope Reeves' experience with an aura reader in Sedona, New Mexico, it struck me as very sad. It's got a good punchline, and when I read it, I laughed. But I also felt, almost immediately, a sense that something potentially valuable had been wasted. Reeves had an encounter with something she (and we) expected would be ridiculous. Yet it was surprisingly insightful. These serendipities are gifts, little glimmers of grace in an increasingly worrisome world. And yet she threw it away, instantly seeking solace in the oblivion of consumerism.

It's not that Reeves thought the aura reading was hokum. She admits that she was "freaked out" by its surprising insight. But her reaction was to flee; rather than confront the pain she felt, she immediately recoiled and sought to erase it from her soul, like someone nervously giggling upon revealing too much of a private truth.

Of course, I'm not so serious as to not enjoy her joke, and I recognize the absurdity of a tourist industry devoted to the most self-centered indulgences of the New Age. I've never had my aura read, myself. But I have noticed that when I think honestly about the New Age, especially the parts I find ridiculous, my pulse begins to race. This happens even before I pinpoint what it is that bothers me, which suggests that the explanation is more rationale than anything else. Now, I can eventually articulate what about the self-centered aspects of the New Age are so problematic for me. But that isn't my first response. The first response is resistance, constriction, anger. I am repulsed. Or is the first response actually—fear? What is that quickening of my heart if not nervousness? Am I afraid of the New Age because the nonsense might make me uncomfortable?

Well, why else? Hold that thought.

Last month, I was labeled a "Torah-bashing gay radical," because I suggested that the Conservative movement should read as narrowly as possible Leviticus' prohibition on anal sex between men. I was, in the context of a heated debate, publicly vilified by a man who claims to be a "reformed homosexual"—he now calls himself a celibate bisexual—and who has spoken out in favor of maintaining exclusionary policies at Jewish educational institutions. Because of the particular context in which the debate took place, no one came to my aid.

By coincidence, that same week, a project I was working on for a university—editing a book of songs and prayers—ran into a snag: some Orthodox college students became so incensed at the addition of an egalitarian liturgical phrase (even though it was asterisked, smaller-fonted, and prefaced with "some add") that they threatened not to eat at the college's kosher kitchen. Only after I and my editorial board caved in to the Orthodox demands did the project move forward.

The combination of these two events drove me to tears. All this Jewish ethnocentrism, Jewish insensitivity, and Jewish fear of change. I felt a pull toward the freer, less doctrinal atmosphere of Buddhist practice, in which what is, is. Simply.

Halacha, the Jewish 'way to walk,' is a dual-focused spiritual path. One of its trajectories is toward the Ultimate, orienting the individual toward the One by refocusing consciousness in every mundane act of human existence. The other trajectory is toward the ordinary, imprinting upon our lives a structure that reflects the Divine will as we, in all our flawed humanity, understand it, which may be quite distinct from how we feel, or how our spirit is moved at any particular time. Most observant Jews choose one modality or the other, practicing *halacha* either because it makes them 'feel spiritual' or because it is a yoke that they have taken on. The former group has the contemplative path of the Hasidim and the mystical literature of the Kabbalah; the latter the active path of the halachic process and the legal reasoning of the Talmud. Often the two groups come to blows.

Sometimes, *halacha* becomes an attachment, a perverse and idolatrous pathology of Jewish religious consciousness. There is, particularly in the legal-categorical camp, great pain and great fear. While this fear may be grounded in Jewish survivalism, or neurosis, it is supported by Jewish religious frameworks. There is within what is called "Torah Judaism" a fierce desire to ascertain and follow the Right Way, which (to reiterate) is trans-subjective, which does not depend on what makes us feel spiritual or not, but which is, in its objectivity, the recipe for living in a way that is larger than ourselves. And yet, despite all the effort to get beyond the ego, the self does intrude—a self which yells, fights, asserts itself.

One would hope, or I would hope anyway, that Jewish practice is meant to open us up. Every blessing we recite is supposed to take us beyond the phenomenon of this apple, or this occasion, and toward the unified Source of all apples, times, and people—either by orienting our consciousness toward It (Hasidic) or conforming our will to It (mitnagdic). Some interpret the language of Jewish godtalk dualistically (God created the apple), some non-dualistically (the apple is nothing but God), but in either case, God-consciousness of some type is invited at least one hundred times a day.

And yet, there is often in this path the opposite of expansion: a particularly Jewish mode of constriction, of tightness. It is a collapsing into the self's deepest fears, which uses the practice of Judaism much as the outlet mall in Reeves' article. Instead of clinging to the transcendence of ourselves, we cling to our fear.

Hope Reeves ran to buy shoes because she was scared of something: scared that her notions of truth, those of a well-adjusted, acculturated *New York Times* travel writer, might be off the mark. She was scared to confront herself and be confronted by someone with spiky orange hair. The discomfort seems almost palpable in her writing (particularly when, later in the article, she describes being moved to tears by a psychic who tells her that her current husband is not her true love—an emotional intensity she 'cures' by getting a massage). And the Orthodox Jews were scared of the change represented by egalitarian liturgy, as if to allow the slightest of cracks in their rigid practice would cause the whole edifice to shake. I won't pretend that I met their myopia with boundless compassion. I got pissed off. But I was acutely aware of a deep fear that they seemed to be expressing, as if something very close to themselves was being threatened.

Right before his best known solo album, *Imagine*, John Lennon recorded *Plastic Ono Band*, a work filled with searing personal revelations and examinations of pain. Under the influence of primal-scream therapist Arthur Janov, John and Yoko were confronting their childhood demons and the pain they had endured over three years of hyper-scrutinized celebrity. After seven years of being in the most famous pop group ever, Lennon said, in connection with the album, "I was never really wanted when I was a child. The only reason I am a star is because of my repressions. The only reason I went for that goal is that I wanted to say: 'Now, Mummy, Daddy, will you love me?'"

Lennon later said that *Plastic Ono Band* was as much a peace album as *Imagine*, because you've got to have inner peace in order to make outer peace. For a long time, I thought that idea was nonsense. What you need for outer peace isn't for everyone to love their inner child; you need structures in place to stop people from hurting each other, stop the most powerful from oppressing the least powerful. You need people to stop using violence—period.

But now, as America marches off to war again, Lennon seems right. Of course, Saddam Hussein is an evil man, who has tortured and murdered hundreds of thousands of innocent people, and who might have dangerous weapons in development. But what is happening is more primal: anger, fear, lust for revenge, a tightness in the heart. We have been wounded—we strike back. Constriction.

Some might suggest that those who agitate for war actually hate themselves, and that they have learned to live with that self-hatred by projecting it onto anyone and anything that threatens to undo their myths of selfhood. I hate myself; you threaten the story I tell myself to avoid confronting my self-hatred, so I hate you. But I don't know about that. I don't think we need that pathologization of the oppressor. Even for people who don't have an unusual amount of self-loathing, boundaries around the self arise all the time. Hope Reeves doesn't necessarily hate herself, I don't think. I think she, like most people, has constructed an idea of herself that works, and is too afraid of its extinction to allow anything to disturb it. But until the Hope Reeveses of the world allow themselves to be affected by the aura reading—at least for a little while, before rushing off to the mall—we won't get anywhere. Forget stopping the war against our enemies; we won't stop hating each other. In order to really put up with difference, there has to be genuine openness to the possibilities of changing the self that exist in every moment, even in the midst of what we might ordinarily prefer to ignore.

2. Sadness in the Desert

There is a miracle at the core of constriction: that when it is dropped, all the peacefulness that we are striving for just appears. Right action requires cultivation, and a remembering that I certainly do not yet possess. But the core of goodness—it just is. When I stop thinking and allow myself to be with whatever is when I'm just *here*, there is no cause for violence. What a miracle—that the natural state of the human being is not to hurt other human beings.

The procedure is very simple to describe: simply let what matters go, and remember where you are: in the presence of Being. Set down these important, self-defining attachments—even matters of ultimate concern, like halacha. Stop thinking, breathe, and remember.

Simple in principle, but very difficult in practice. Even remembering to remember is very hard. Who is able to remember the miraculousness of breath when some asshole is flaming you on an email list? Sometimes I think that enlightenment is less about the attainment of a truth than about the remembering of it. I can be in a state of wonderful equanimity, smiling at the vanity of human striving, yet mindful of the pain it causes, aware of details I ordinarily am too blind to notice. And yet, I quickly cloud over this clarity with stories. Reasons why such-and-such is wrong, and why it *matters* that they are wrong, and why it matters that I express how wrong they are. I send a hostile email. Thoughts of violence enter my mind. My jaw clenches. Like Hope Reeves running to the mall, I run to the comforts of angry rhetoric against my backward enemies. I become furious at these half-wits who cause suffering, at their cruelty. I forget what I know. I become part of the problem.

Now, political opinions do not disappear with contemplation, and true openness is not a policy prescription. And yet, it is worth noticing that hardly any contemplatives are conservative. Is this because they take an oath of liberalism together with their vow of silence? No. It is because the aims of conservative politics are hindrances along the contemplative path. You just can't 'let go' if you are invested in a view of human beings as selfish creatures in need of toughness, discipline, and order. It's too tight. Kindness, on the other hand, flows naturally. Giving opens the channels of the heart, makes it easier to let go. And it is the unforced result of quiet. It's part of the same miracle: if we shut up long enough to listen deeply to whatever is happening right now, we suddenly become very gentle, good people. It really is quite amazing; do you see the miracle? That if we just get ourselves quiet, *goodness* appears?

The problem is not that we have ideas. The problem is that we take them personally. A debate is not about a word of liturgy; it's about me and my sense of rightness, my sense of place in the world. We mix ideas up with the ego, and the ego wants. It wants to impress, to be large, to be loved, to be right. It is the worst possible thing to mix up with a debate about ideas, which ought to be about non-egoic topics like correctness, prudence, compassion, and security. And a closed, hard picture of the self leads to closed, hard behavior.

On the retreat I went on in January, one of my co-retreatants had a large crystal geode that she would sometimes hold during meditation. She left it lying around one time, and out of curiosity I picked it up. I had chuckled a little, inwardly, when I had first seen the thing, crystals being an egregious New Age cliché. But one of my teachers had recently told me that my rational doubts about the New Age—in particular, about the existence of energy channels within the body—were, in her words, "bullshit." So I was gently trying to notice how I judged crazy ideas. I tried to hold the rock with an open mind.

The crystal was a lot heavier than I expected. I found it to be very centering, holding something so old and so beautiful, something that had retained its form for millennia, while I was working with much 'effortless effort' to be still. I held the heavy rock and thought, this rock doesn't give half a damn whether it's a cliché. All the constriction, all the ideas, all the mockery (and self-criticism because of the mockery)—drop it. It's a rock. Get over it.

And then the rock was a miracle.

That was going to be the end of the essay: me holding a rock, feeling the doubt melt away into openness and acceptance. But I think that to end on that purely individualistic note feels dishonest.

I don't usually go in for apocalyptic thinking. Yet today, in the shadow of September 11, the turning of the tide of world opinion against the United States, many of us—myself included—have begun to entertain thoughts of apocalyptic change we never took seriously before. Yes, every generation has been sure that the end is nigh. In 1648, Christians thought the apocalypse was near because of the Thirty Years' War; Jews thought so because of the Chmielnicki Massacres (not long after, up to one third of European Jews would be attracted to the messiah Sabbetai Zevi). And the feelings were similar, across different Western cultures, in 1300, 1492, 1945, 1999, 1666, 70, 138, and many other years.

But that's my rational mind. On a more emotional or somatic level, I have come to feel that we are indeed in the end-time of Western culture as we know it. We have demolished the biosphere's delicate balance, and now await a century of ecocide. America is determined to provoke hatred, and it seems just a matter of time before the city I love is seriously harmed by some form of biological, nuclear, or conventional attack. You can feel the foreboding in the air.

I often feel despair, like I am living in a dystopic society where the most powerful, privileged elites are taking away everyone else's civil liberties, stealing their money, and plunging them into a dark time of fear and distrust. I have no faith in the earnest chants of the anti-war movement or other Leftist movements, of people who believe that repeating the morally correct argument will somehow get it adopted. It won't.

In other words, I think constriction has won, that the Dick Cheneys of the world have solidified their power, have so consolidated and perfected the ability to confuse the ignorant, that we will never defeat them. Is it possible to soften those who are seduced? I know that I was once much tougher and tighter-wound than I am today. But what kind of intervention is required?

Just a few days ago, I saw Gus van Sant's elliptical new film *Gerry*, which consists of ninety minutes of Matt Damon and Casey Affleck walking and getting lost in a vast desert. There is little dialogue, and lots of time-lapse cinematography of clouds. I walked out of the film refreshed—I like slow film—and also feeling like I had just seen the best 9/11 art yet produced. The movie doesn't mention September 11, or any current events. But it captured the inexpressible sadness of our times: the hopelessness of the characters, the expanse of the desert, the sense that all is soon to be destroyed.

Being open to this sadness is the opposite of constriction. Hope Reeves was afraid of tears, like the repressed gay Jews, and all those who seek a simple answer to our collective pain. The answers, if there are any, are complex. I still think there is nothing we can do, but I know that to try to avoid the pain, to close ourselves to it, to pretend it isn't there, is only going to make it worse. What is real? That life is suffering, and we are in for a whole lot more of it.

March 2003

How I Finally Learned
to Accept Christ in my Heart

When I was about five years old, living in suburban Long Island, I answered the telephone and heard a voice I didn't know. If memory serves, it was a woman's voice. She began to ask me a series of questions, which I dutifully answered, about the subject of religion. She said that she was doing a study, and that I was helping her. "Would you like to continue?" she asked me. I, of course, answered yes. And then she said, "Great, just repeat after me: I accept the Lord Jesus Christ as my personal savior."

These were words I did not understand, and yet for some reason my body was tingling. I must have known that I was doing something wrong, that a Jewish boy was not supposed to say these things. The Christians were the other people; they were the ones with the holidays we didn't celebrate, the big churches we didn't enter. But the woman seemed nice, and I listened to her, and began to repeat the line.

As if by providence, my mother entered the room just as I said it. She grabbed the phone, angrily—it was all my fault, I knew—and shouted into it, accusatorily, "Who is this? What is this?" She hung up the phone. I knew that the nice lady, and the tingly feeling I'd gotten, were evil. I had made a big mistake. I was terrified.

I'm not sure if this early traumatic experience is a symptom or a cause of my longtime aversion to Christianity. I'm also not sure what kind of missionary theology holds that by simply reciting a phrase, a child can accept Christ and be saved. But as a child, and as an adolescent, the proselytizing phone call, the deceptively sweet voice, the erotic charge, all of it hung together with what I believed was the world's stupidest religion. Who on Earth could believe that God had a son? We learned in first grade that God didn't have a body, that God wasn't a person like you or me. What could a "son" mean in such a context? And who couldn't see that Jesus had, obviously, failed in his mission, if he was indeed supposed to be the messiah? After all, he was supposed to be our Messiah. The King of the Jews, not the Christians. And we had certain texts which told us what the Messiah was supposed to do: end war, usher in an era of universal love, cause the lamb to sleep with the lion, all of that. This whole business of a "Second Coming" was such an obvious weasel move to excuse a "First Coming" that hadn't quite worked.

My relationship to Christianity—I didn't really understand the difference between Catholicism and Protestantism until college—was fraught with complexity, contempt, and jealousy. To me, Christians were stupid, popular, lucky, saved, loved, idiotic, ignorant, anti-Semitic, athletic, and, most importantly, Other. I formally learned about the concept of alienation in my senior year of high school, but I had experienced years of it already. Even on Long Island, but especially after my family moved to Florida, we were aliens in our own country, like visitors, almost, or spies. I had a secret which only a few other people had. For a while, I went to secret schools. Then, when I mingled with the Christians, it was my own personal secret, which became painfully exposed every September, when I missed school for funny-sounding holidays.

As I grew a little older, my initial doubts about Christian myth ripened into astonishment at how so many millions of people could believe this stuff. Did people really believe that every baby was born guilty of Original Sin? And that a person who was crucified 1900 years ago could somehow atone for it? And if so, why bother with trying to be a good person now? I remember thinking that if Christ died for my sins anyway, I sure wouldn't be wasting time at church. And yet, it seemed that everyone believed these things. The Trinity? And the idea of hell? The Virgin Mary, the Resurrection of Jesus, the whole idea of a mostly-naked tortured man nailed to a cross becoming a religious icon that people wore around their neck—I just couldn't believe that people bought this stuff.

Sure, Judaism had its myths, but they weren't really that important. I learned early on that whether the stories in the Bible were literally true or not was less important than how you lived—even though, of course, many people thought they were literally true, and would fight anyone who didn't.

So—a fair amount of constriction. Which, itself, became predominant: the fear, judgment, anger, insecurity. Could there be another way to relate to the dominant religion in my country of origin?

I started by assuming that Christ, like other charismatic spiritual teachers, was a realized being. Historically, there were many itinerant, anti-establishment, warning-of-impending-doom teachers wandering around Palestine in the days of Herod; Jesus was one of many. But we've lost most of their teachings, so I want to compare Christ's teachings to those of enlightened teachers from other traditions. What would realization look like in first century Palestine?

How do you explain enlightenment to Jews? You invert the laws of purity, and touch the leper. Everything is holy.

How do you practice the Path in Rome? You accept suffering, and explain that the suffering is that of the world, not of any particular individual. Suffering is suffering; you might say: I am giving myself for you.

How do you preach pantheism to people who've never heard it before? You say, this bread is my body; this wine is my blood. You call the disciples' full attention to every act of eating and drinking.

I want to take this a step further, though. I'm not sure I like the explicit translation of the Gospels into the Vedantic monism that holds sway today. It is too similar to the Christian Scientists, who saw the Gospels as nothing more than 19th century science and medicine, or the many others who sought to syncretize what Jesus said with whatever belief happened to be dominant at a particular time, from transcendentalism to fascism and everything in between. It's even a little similar to the Jewish "appreciation" of Jesus—it seems to say that we contemplatives know him even better than the Christians do.

So I want to return to the question of Jesus h/Himself. I want to say: Take pantheism (or panentheism) seriously. If everything is God, or is, essentially, nothing but a radiant manifestation of the One, then the only distinction between an enlightened being and a less-enlightened one is realization. Actually, everyone and everything is fully enlightened, because you and this leaf are God. The only reason why you suffer is that you don't realize it; you don't actually believe that your true reality is God. There is a part of God, manifesting as your ego, which says, "I don't get it." Or which says "I." What's more, even if you fully grant the ontological/epistemological truth of monism, if you've only "bought it" with your rational mind, you haven't really gotten it. Map is not territory. You have to feel it in your body to know it, and in your heart, mind, and spirit. (Conversely, it's not enough just to "feel spiritual" without articulation; leaving behind the mind is no less mistaken than leaving behind the heart.)

Notice that this realization is not spirituality in the conventional sense. The trouble with spirituality is that there really is nothing special you have to feel, and the trouble with esoterism (such as Kabbalah) is that there really is nothing special you have to get. But you don't have to feel a certain way to be fully realized. You do not need to know the zodiac or the enneagram to be enlightened. In fact, supposing that enlightenment is related to such mindstates or such special knowledge is an error. You are already enlightened. You just have to realize it—to realize the truth of what already is.

If Jesus was a fully realized being, then whether we translate his teachings one way or another is less important than coming to terms with who He was to begin with. A fully realized being is God, knows S/He is God, knows that Everything else is also God. Of course, this being is also human too—so, if male, he is both man and God.

It may be useful to mythologize this Being in terms which people can easily understand—it may be useful to call him the "son of God." And so it will be easy to get carried away. But the core principle—that Jesus is both Man and God—is tenable, and reconcilable, and non-problematic for a truly believing contemplative Jew.

To be sure, there is plenty of "the Christians have it wrong" left in this reading of the Gospels. But at least they have it no more wrong than Jews do when they talk about being the chosen people, or Buddhists do when they offer sacrifices to *Bodhisattvas*, or Muslims do when they kill.

In fact, amid all our diversity of myth, we've all got it wrong in basically the same way. We mistake the finger pointing at the moon for the moon itself.

There is a great wisdom in the particular myth of Jesus's incarnation. The cross, I've learned from a wise queer theologian friend, is often seen as a metaphor for uniting the immanent and the transcendent—much as is the six-pointed star. The horizontal line is the world of the finite, the human, the place of yearning and separation. The vertical line is the transcendent, the infinite, the Divine reality. (In Jewish symbolism, this is equivalent to the downward-pointing and upward-pointing triangles.) I've always seen Christ's movement as an upward one: realization proceeds from the individual to the All. This, after all, is the mystic path.

However, the incarnation myth has it better. God is becoming one with God. This is the second error, one might say, of paganism as seen from a monotheist's perspective: that praxis is a magnification of the individual. Two days ago, when I was standing atop an empty, tall mountain in the desert, holding my arms up in the wind, I felt power. It was easy to feel powerful, as if it were my power, as if, to juxtapose the sublime and the ridiculous, I were "king of the world." That is the great error—to suppose that the power belongs to me. In fact, "I" belong to the Power. Practice does not aggrandize the self; it erases the self and discovers the One.

In this view, Christ is a myth of God's becoming. At this moment, six billion humans and countless billion other creatures are participating in the evolution of God. The myth of Christ thus invites, in a personal way for Jews, Christians, Muslims, Hindus, and everyone else in this beautiful, threatened universe, the question of ethics and humanism, and of human flowering itself: what is God becoming through you?

June 2004

Discipline

1.   The fox

I generally think of myself as undisciplined. This often surprises my friends, who see that I edit a magazine, write for a newspaper, teach Kabbalah, have written four books, and, oh right, also work as general counsel for a software company I founded a few years ago. But I see these multiple activities as evidence, not refutation. Together, they are proof that I'm still not able to rein myself in, that I still haven't really chosen the one thing that I'm going to do in my life, and, at this point, I've essentially given up on trying.

Being an intellectual, I've invented several models and rationalizations for why "reining in" shouldn't really be necessary anyway. Why, after all, focus on one thing? Why not live as widely and richly as circumstances allow? Here's what Isaiah Berlin has to say on the subject, from his 1953 essay (alluded to in an earlier essay), "The Hedgehog and the Fox." Although it's a long paragraph, I'll quote it in its entirety because it's such an astute observation:

> There is a line among the fragments of the Greek poet Archilochus which says: "The fox knows many things, but the hedgehog knows one big thing." Scholars have differed about the correct interpretation of these dark words, which may mean no more than that the fox, for all his cunning, is defeated by the hedgehog's one defense. But, taken figuratively, the words can be made to yield a sense in which they mark one of the deepest differences which divide writers and thinkers, and, it may be, human beings in general. For there exists a great chasm between those, on one side, who relate everything to a single central vision, one system less or more coherent or articulate, in terms of which they understand, think and feel—a single, uni-

versal, organizing principle in terms of which alone all that they are and say has significance—and, on the other side, those who pursue many ends, often unrelated and even contradictory, connected, if at all, only in some de facto way, for some psychological or physiological cause, related by no moral or aesthetic principle; these last lead lives, perform acts, and entertain ideas that are centrifugal rather than centripetal, their thought is scattered or diffused, moving on many levels, seizing upon the essence of a vast variety of experiences and objects for what they are in themselves, without consciously or unconsciously, seeking to fit them into, or exclude them from, any one unchanging, all-embracing, sometimes self-contradictory and incomplete, at times fanatical, unitary inner vision. The first kind of intellectual and artistic personality belongs to the hedgehogs, the second to the foxes; and without insisting on a rigid classification, we may, without too much fear of contradiction, say that, in this sense, Dante belongs to the first category, Shakespeare to the second; Plato, Lucretius, Pascal, Hegel, Dostoevsky, Nietzsche, Ibsen, Proust are, in varying degrees, hedgehogs; Herodotus, Aristotle, Montaigne, Erasmus, Molière, Goethe, Pushkin, Balzak, Joyce are foxes.

Berlin himself was a "fox," and no doubt was involved in the same sort of self-explanation as I am, albeit in a more refined way. Certainly, I fear that reading of Archilochus which holds that you can't really do more than one thing really well; that while it's fine to have hobbies and side-projects, specialization is a prerequisite for excellence. Naturally, there are exceptions to this commonplace observation, but I've seen in my own experience the qualitative difference between work that was, at least for its duration, the primary focus of my attention, occupying my waking hours in a way that no single project has done in quite some time, and work which was put together with care, but amidst thirty other items on the to-do list.

So why not focus? Lack of discipline. Not merely in the simple sense of turning off the TV to get back to the writing, but in the larger sense of letting go of choices foregone. I'm good at deciding to do things, but awful at deciding what not to do. I so often find myself looking for the angle in which I don't have to let go of anything—in which I can be a lawyer and a writer, live in the city and the country, be religious, in my way, and also say yes to the material world. When it comes to the big questions, I don't want to answer them. Or rather, I'll answer—but always with a yes.

This is fundamentally a lack of discipline—an inability to say no, relinquish, and focus. But what is discipline, essentially? How does it operate? How does it feel? And why can't I have more of it?

2.   Yoking, caging, taming

All of us are familiar with discipline on the "micro" level: staying focused, working diligently, restraining those impulses which might take us astray or cause us to act carelessly, unskillfully, or unkindly. In spiritual practice, those who practice meditation learn early on that clarity is actually a subtractive property: what we take for granted in our perception is actually clouded by thousands of thoughts, judgments, and assumptions. In the metaphor I frequently use, it's like a radio station that we can barely hear through the static. Removing that static in order to hear clearly is the essence of contemplative practice.

In practice, this involves a disciplined attention to and auditing of countless habits, thoughts, and emotions. It's neither simple nor easy, especially for the anti-disciplined. Each time the mind is brought back to the object of attention, there is a bit of discipline—bringing it back from its pleasant daydreams, saying no to the thoughts that beg to be thought. Just getting up and going to the meditation sits takes discipline, too, especially when it's cold and the sun hasn't yet risen. There were times, on a recent retreat, that felt like reform school. I felt like some kind of yoked animal, being forced to drag a burden that was not of my own making. Other times I felt more caged than burdened—restrained, held back, like Rilke's famous panther, pacing around in circles:

Enlightenment by Trial and Error

From seeing the bars, his seeing is so exhausted
that it no longer holds anything anymore.
To him the world is bars, a hundred thousand
bars, and behind the bars, nothing.
The lithe swinging of that rhythmical easy stride
which circles down to the tiniest hub
is like a dance of energy around a point
in which a great will stands stunned and numb.
Only at times the curtains of the pupil rise
without a sound . . . then a shape enters,
slips though the tightened silence of the shoulders,
reaches the heart, and dies.

There's an aspect of the melodramatic in Rilke's poem (written in 1902, here translated by Robert Bly) which matches the way I overdramatize even the simplest acts of discipline. Surely, a privileged young man on a voluntary meditation retreat is different from a caged panther. But on a non-rational, emotional level, the melodrama gets it exactly right: the itch to break free, the resentment of the scolding voice that tells me no.

And then the doubt. *Why are you doing this? What's the point? Why don't you just do whatever it is you want?* The stories of doubt are so compelling; they seem to be purely reasonable responses, when in fact, they are like snakes in the service of selfishness. Mystical Judaism links doubt with Amalek (the words have the same *gematria* value), the arch-enemy of Israel. You're supposed to cut off its head, slaughter its descendants. In its way, insight meditation cuts off the head of doubt too—by seeing it for what it is. But doubt is much more insidious than these simple images suggest. I cut off its head, but it's a hydra. "This is stupid," says the voice of Doubt, and so I cut it off. And so it becomes replaced by lacerating self-criticism: "No, you are stupid. You have no discipline. That's why you have accomplished so little. Your friends are on the covers of magazines, and publishing successful novels. Where are you?" And of course,

Jay Michaelson

I have my response: "Discipline is repression. We need more freedom, more life. Why 'accomplish' anything?" And then back and back and forth until I've finally worn myself out.

It's easy to see that the cycle of discipline stories is more than merely tedious; it is also filled with hostility. There's something in the process of self-discipline itself, I think, that elicits anger, and that anger seeps into the way these tales are told. It's as if the situation of discipline is inherently one of conflict—notice the metaphors of yoking an animal, cutting off heads. Sometimes it feels like an internal wrestling match, or actual battle, between the id and the superego—and in many models self-discipline is described, approvingly, in such ways.

Personally, my own inner battles have progressed well past wrestling. My feelings now have weapons. My id has grown up and gotten a degree, so now it's armed with volumes of Allen Ginsberg and the slogans of sexual liberation. My superego, not to be outdone, has ditched its paternalistic "I said so" and now beats me over the head with envy and desire. "Don't you want to be like _____?"

Such conflict seems opposed to feeling 'spiritual,' doesn't it? Spirituality is about feeling liberated, pleasant, and at peace, right? No wonder so many spiritual seekers throw aside rules and discipline as one of their first steps toward liberation.

But only as one the first steps. Actually, any spiritual aim worth pursuing requires discipline. Spiritual practice is just like any other kind of practice—it takes practice. So even if we do junk some of the codes and strictures of our native religions, we can't imagine doing without the entire notion of discipline itself if we want to actually get anywhere along the spiritual path, or even show up in a given moment.

My highly over-simplified Freudian model doesn't do justice to the ways in which discipline unfolds in the individual. So, at the risk of losing some readers, I'd like to suggest a look at a different model of what discipline is, and how it can be reconciled with a life of rich experience: Kabbalah.

3. Why be subtle?

In the Kabbalistic worldview, discipline is actually an amalgam of two very different internal processes. Internally, discipline comes from the aspect of *gevurah*, or strength. *Gevurah* is that which reins us in. It sets limits and boundaries. It's that aspect of the self that keeps you from telling off your coworker, smothering your relationship partner, or eating the second piece of cheesecake. Too much *gevurah*, and you're a repressed authoritarian. Too little *gevurah*, and you're an indulgent flake.

Gevurah, though, is only half of the story. The other half is *netzach*, literally "eternity" but also sometimes rendered as "endurance." *Netzach* is *gevurah*'s complement on the plane of external manifestation. This process (which we might understand psychologically instead of theologically) is *gevurah* in action, you might say; it's what channels not our feelings or desires but our actions into a form that actually leads to results. *Netzach* is the aspect of our behavior that does the laundry, gets to work on time, meets our partners at the airport. *Gevurah*'s complement is *hesed*, lovingkindess; *netzach*'s is *hod*, inspiration, splendor, wonder. It's really not that splendid to do the laundry. But if your life is only peak experiences, how does it endure?

These Kabbalistic motives do not map onto a traditional psychotherapeutic map. Sometimes it is the principle of *gevurah* that is selfish—*this is mine!*—and its complement of *hesed* which is more aligned with super egoic principles of sharing, morality, and so on. Other times, it is the reverse: *hesed* is selfish—*look what I can do!*—and *gevurah* feels like respect for boundaries and other people. Each flavor of emotional reality has its function, and each can fall out of balance.

I like this Kabbalistic language for its experiential benefits. The distinction between *netzach* and *gevurah* can be perceived through experience and attention. Doing walking meditation one day, for example, I saw how I was treating each step as requiring *gevurah*: my rhythm was something like restraint, plod, restraint, plod, doubt, restraint, anger, plod. But with a little more attention to the actual feeling of discipline in the body (tightness in the chest, or constriction in the arms, or a bobbing of the head), it became clearer to me that there was actually a wealth of feeling-tones going on beneath my notice. There was *netzach*, moving me along, but it wasn't just restraint and plodding; it was more complex than that. It became interesting to try to characterize and categorize these feeling tones, rather like a sommelier attempts to discern and describe the notes of flavor in wine. *Discipline* was too broad. It was a label, and not a particularly helpful one, for a multitude of phenomena operating within the self.

By labeling what was actually a complicated network of phenomena simply as discipline, I was flattening my experience, and turning it into something monotonous and unpleasant. There would be a constraining of a desire to do something, and an almost immediate response of "un-pleasant—don't want that—find a distraction or a way out." And then the stories ("This is stupid..."). But actually much more was going on, in much more complicated detail.

A second feature of this Kabbalistic language is that each of the ten *sefirot* contains each of the other ten. There is a form of judgment that contains lovingkindness, as when a truly loving parent disciplines a child. And there is a form of endurance which contains inspiration, as when the seed of wonder is tended, and watered, so that it might germinate into something alive. So too, in the case of discipline: it's not merely restraint or determination corralling the selfish id and yoking it to a task. Rather, the restraint contains within it all sorts of other energies: compassion for myself (why was I on meditation retreat anyway?), which the Kabbalists call *tiferet*; the wisdom of the teachings (*hochmah*), and so forth. Real-ly, within every constraining moment of *gevurah*, I could, with enough attention, feel in the body, heart, and mind the movements of other en-ergies.

On the simplest level, this is no more novel than "keeping your eyes on the prize," remembering why you're doing all those pushups, or slaving away at the cubicle. In such situations, one simply recalls that there's a reason for the discipline, and one focuses on the reason rather than the energy of the discipline itself. In so doing—by moving away from the momentary experience—we feel happier. On a somewhat deeper level, the practice is to be so attentive to the energy itself that we can notice in the act of disciplining itself—not as its external motive, but in the feel of the discipline—notes of kindness, foundations of action, and so forth. Observing closely the nature of discipline is not focusing on happy thoughts instead of what's happening now. It's not about separating the prize from the process. Rather, it's about creating a rich taxonomy of emotional life.

Finally, it's useful to tease apart the emotional state from the seemingly immediate reaction to it. Usually, these two aspects are so tightly laminated one to the other that we don't even realize they are separate. You touch a hot stove, you pull your hand away. Feel a feeling you don't like, and you want to push it away too. But this is a childish way of being. It's like a boy refusing to eat mushrooms because the taste is unfamiliar, and thus "gross." A worthwhile emotional life will present a wide spectrum of feeling-tones, which we can observe, notice, and not push away according to some learned habit or instinct. To reduce this wide range to "like/don't like" and then try to get rid of everything on the wrong side is a cheapening of experience. Nor is it likely to work. Of course, we'd all rather have pleasant feelings than unpleasant ones, but is arranging one's life in this way really going to succeed?

Psychological lamination notwithstanding, there is a space between the energy and the response—and therein lie possibilities of freedom. Even during the simple act of revising this essay, I experienced a twitchiness and restlessness that I'm sure is familiar to many people. Emails came in, and I *had to* look. I thought of having a snack, surfing the web, cleaning up the house. Why? Aversion—the desire to push away a particular mindstate, in this case an amalgam of *gevurah*, *netzach*, *yesod*, and *binah*, flattened and simplified into *discipline*. The aversion seems so immediate that it's hard to imagine any other way of relating to its object. But by pausing, noticing how I'd clenched my jaw, noticing how rapid my breathing had become—these phenomena began to loosen, and the aversion began to decrease.

Our culture's general assumption is that the good life has more of the good stuff and less of the lousy. So, when confronted with lots of lousy stuff—inboxes, project plans—I often experience aversion, and suffering, and suppose, "If only I were _____, there would be less lousy stuff and so I would be happier." But since the lousiness is intrinsic to life itself, that won't work. So we have to change the way we relate to the lousy. As Sharon Salzberg, one of my teachers, likes to say, "It's not what's going on, it's how you relate to it." Meaning: the contemplative path is not about having certain feelings, seeing certain sights, and being in certain places. It's about relating to whatever feelings, sights, or places one encounters in a way that is mindful and skillful.

The Kabbalistic contribution to working with discipline is similar to the Buddhist-psychological one—it teases it apart into its many component pieces—but very different from our ordinary Western pop psychology, which sees it as a force constraining desire. As Foucault observed, discipline and desire enjoy a much richer relationship than mere repression and expression; often the latter creates the former.

I'm still not particularly mindful or skillful in regard to self-discipline. I still face choices that require decision, and still avoid some of them. And I still, exasperatingly, experience regret over paths not taken, and feel envious of my friends who have taken them to success and fame. And when sitting down to work, there is still the old dyadic thinking (want to do this / don't want to do this) and imprecision of attention to what qualities of mind are actually being engaged. I still leap to the story, the counter-story, and the variously violent struggles between them, even though I know, as I like to say to my students, that kicking your own ass is not the way to liberation.

It takes time.

Yet one paradox of contemplative practice is that the less you want to be rid of something, the more it slips away on its own. I've found that the less I resent the energy of discipline, the less that energy arises in the first place. Discipline itself is still required to stay on task, but the tension around the discipline does lessen a bit. When I just accept and explore the energies of discipline for their own sake, without expectation—they shift. This is what the Hasidim like to call *hamtaka*, sweetening, and it's what we always ask of the aspect of *gevurah*. Not disappearing, not resolving, and, not becoming any simpler either. But just the slightest note of honey in a tannin-rich red wine.

July 2005

Does Mysticism
Prove the Existence of God?

What can we learn from mystical experience?

Mystics from around the world report encounters with the Divine, as well as experiences of body and mind that are highly unusual. They report a certainty of knowing, deeper and surer than any ordinary perception. They claim to receive insights into the truth of reality. But what do we make of their claims? How can we tell whether the experiences are truthful or delusional, without simply repeating our own preset opinions as to the existence or non-existence of God?

These questions long fascinated me, particularly in college and in grad school. I read testimonies, tracts, and accounts of mystic quests; accounts of visionary ascents, ecstatic unions, and divine theophanies. I was entranced by the possibility that 'God,' that being or reality whose existence or non-existence seemed to be such a critical issue—after all, some people made it the center of their lives, while others denied its very existence—could be directly perceived, and, by extension, proven.

Scholars and philosophers have spent a fair amount of time trying to arrive at criteria for evaluating the mystics' subjective, hard-to-verify claims. On a superficial level, the details of mystical experience, naturally, vary from tradition to tradition: Catholic nuns have visions of Christ, Hindus of Krishna. Perhaps some of those experiences are false, or projection—or perhaps God manifests in a variety of forms, or certain ineffable core experiences are interpreted in religious language by the mystics. Even beyond the details of what is experienced, however, the subjective experience itself—the so-called *universal* experience of nearness of union, of knowledge that transcends verbal articulation—even this experience is difficult to verify. How do we know that what the mystic says happens, happens? And how do we know that it isn't all delusion?

In the last several years, I have moved beyond the college and grad school readings of books like *Mysticism and Philosophical Analysis* and have tried the techniques of the mystics myself. Truthfully, what impelled me to do so probably has more to do with love and yearning than with a search for empirical data. However, I have not left behind my empirical mind, sometimes to the detriment of my contemplative practice, and so I have collected evidence myself—necessarily subjective, but, at least for myself, evidence nonetheless.

Here is what I can report. I can say, in my own limited and subjective experience, that if you do what some mystics and contemplatives say, you can experience the results they promise. Obviously, I haven't tried every contemplative path. But I have tried more than one, and have discovered that they do deliver what is promised in mystical and contemplative texts. It is possible to slow down the mind so much that literally watching paint dry (even if it's already dry) is fascinating, beautiful, and interesting. It is possible to scramble the mind with letter permutations and free associations so much that the thinking mind seems to let go and a strong sense of union with the All arises. And it is possible to refine awareness itself so much that the emptiness of things, and the role mental construction plays, becomes a directly apprehended reality.

Moreover, there is a sense of presence in these experiences that is more than a sensation of having one's mind altered. A great love arises, and an obvious certainty that the love is not just arising within the self. Rather than the self containing the feeling of love, the love seems to contain the self and everything else within it. When my thinking mind and desiring mind are slowed down enough, this love and compassion arise naturally, without any prodding or effort from me. (I'm very bad at prodding myself to be nicer; for me, the only way that works is to actually become more loving, sincerely.)

In other words, in highly concentrated mental states, I have had experiences that conform almost exactly to mystical testimonies and descriptions—including many I had not yet read when I had the experience. A sense of union; a feeling of peace; a sense of proximity to the Divine or the Universal. It is all exquisitely beautiful, and it is all experienceable, with only a few weeks of effort.

For many contemporary mystics and "spiritual people," this is enough. It's the answer. Trustworthy, experienced writers promise a glimpse of Ultimate Reality, and an upwelling of authentic love—and there it is. And for many religious people, it is painfully obvious that what is happening here is an encounter with God—it fits all the criteria, it leads to expressions of love; what more could one possibly want?

But I was raised a skeptic. The process of education is, fundamentally, that of acquiring the cognitive skills of doubt, of learning to take apart assumptions more critically and carefully, and I have honed these skills for many years. This process encourages doubt, and thus can undermine some contemplative practice—but surely it is better than the alternative: naive people (including many public figures in our times) convinced that the values they were taught as a child, by people in authority, are absolutely correct—or so useful for society that we should regard them as such. The power of faith in such contexts is remarkably destructive; even though many once-certain ideas—that white people are superior, that men are superior—have been undermined and relegated, in some circles, to the intellectual dust heap, the premise that fundamental values should still guide our public lives endures. Education, as I understand it, is the slow process of awakening from this delusion into a more mature, critical stance toward values and claims of authority.

Applied to subjective, mystical experience, critical thinking can be a dangerous tool. Certain kinds of doubt are necessary to get the process underway in the first place: doubt that chasing riches in the rat-race will really bring you lasting happiness, for example. And along the way, doubt remains a crucial ally, making sure the conceptual mind, or simple desire, isn't filling in the gaps of experience in a way that suits our preferences. For example, there are many, many spiritual seekers who use their own mystical experience as a foundation for all kinds of belief systems. A sense of intimacy, or love, leads to vast conclusions about the nature of reality ("We're all One," for example). But just because you've had an experience that feels really true to you doesn't mean it actually is true—and while it's easy to dismiss the New Age seeker as harmless, the unjustified leap she is making is not so different from that of fundamentalists.

But doubt can also undermine the contemplative process itself, because its appearance of rigor can actually mask unjustified assumptions, and leave us perpetually sitting on the fence. An example: recently, at a Seder table, I had occasion to mention the six-week retreat I sat last fall. Before I even finished my first sentence, someone interrupted and said, sharply, "You're deluding yourself." "Okay," I said, and proceeded to explain that what meditation practice is, essentially, is seeing clearly. If I could show that I was indeed seeing clearly into the nature of my own emotional makeup, or problems facing me, then isn't it odd that I was seeing so un-clearly into this one aspect of life? "I don't know," he replied, "but you're deluding yourself." I tried again. "Really? For six weeks?" "Well, you're deluding yourself for six weeks."

It was a fascinating, short exchange that illustrates what is often really going on underneath the patina of healthy skepticism. It's just doubt—not justified, not useful, just stuck to some beliefs or desires about the world and not admitting that any alternative is possible. There was no dialogue at the Seder table, just a blanket refusal to admit that any meditation practice could yield anything other than delusion. I didn't prod into why, exactly, this belief was so important to my conversation partner. Frankly, I didn't care. But it was clear from the way he interrupted me, and from his categorical refusal to address anything I said, that he had something more at stake than mere intellectual inquiry. In any case, his blind skepticism is as unappealing as blind faith.

Thus, in posing the questions of what we can know about mystical experience, it is critical to also question the questioner, proceeding carefully between blind skepticism and blind faith. With this in mind, I ask again: How do we know that mystical experience is real? And if we can't know, what do we do with it?

The first step is remembering what we do know. I know that what the mystics promise, happens. I have experienced what they have described, by proceeding along their recommended practices. Thus, if my experience is wrong, it's not just that I'm deluded—it's that all mystics are deluded. This is a critical distinction, because there are thousands upon thousands of mystics who, across history, have devoted their entire lives to contemplative practice, with plenty of doubt and self-examination along the way. Thus, if I am in delusion, so are thousands of other contemplatives across history.

Second, and relatedly, this testimony is "expert" testimony. Contemplatives are precisely those people who have devoted the most attention to the mind and the spirit. I wonder what would have happened if, at the Seder table, I had doubted the foundations of modern dentistry to my conversation partner, who was a dentist for thirty years. "Nope, you're deluding yourself. Flossing does not prevent gum disease." He would presumably point to studies, but I could point to counter-studies—only, I suspect his data would be a lot more reliable than mine, because it was compiled by experts whose life work was the field in question. Likewise, the reports of monks and nuns and mystics are "expert" testimony. Who are you inclined to believe more—the doubter who has never once explored these pathways, or the expert who has spent her life doing so?

Third, and more subjectively, there is a sense of certainty during the experience of mystical union that is, in my experience at least, almost unparalleled. It doesn't just seem true; it feels truer than anything I've ever felt before. It is neither an inference nor a vague sense of the sublime; it is more certain than knowing your name, or knowing that you're seeing these words. It feels like "Yes, this is it. This is the core truth. This is what you have been looking for your whole life." Sometimes it carries a sense of amazement; sometimes it doesn't. At times, it feels calm; other times, it's actually very funny. But the degree of certainty it carries is beyond description.

Now, the sense of certainty is not enough. Everyone's been certain of something that turned out to be wrong—e.g., he loves me, he loves me not. Religious people in particular hate to hear this, because their "rock of faith" is the foundation of their whole lives, and they deeply don't want to question it. But as one politician said last fall, you can be both certain and wrong.

In the case of mystical experience, though, it's worth refining the inquiry a bit more, and asking what we are really certain about, and what is constructed around it. Of this I am certain of my mystical experiences: There is a real love that arises, there is only *this moment*. There is no separate self. That which is called the world is really arising only in Awareness—not my awareness, or yours, but your real awareness; that of the real you, which is Who you really are.

There are already a lot of concepts in there, of course—but note that the *God* concept is not yet one of them. This is a critical point. Suppose we were to say, for the moment, that the directly perceived effects are all there is, without drawing any conclusions as to their source. In fact, if done without indulging in too much doubt, doing so has several benefits.

First, one can see even the most wonderful, rapturous mystical states as just a mindstate. Granted, it is a very pleasant mindstate, but, like all very pleasant things, it can turn sour with too much attachment—and it passes, and it's devoid of separate reality, just like everything else. If we are operating within a theistic worldview, the Infinite is really Infinite; although naturally more delightful, a mindstate of union with God ought not create the false belief that God is not here, in this moment, as well. So, even if the mindstate is one of *devekut*, of cleaving to God, it will pass, and too much yearning for one kind of encounter with God can cause one to devalue all the others. Of course, if we are operating within a non-theistic worldview, not reifying the experience, or inferring stories about it, is a crucial step toward discerning the truth. In either case, simply letting the experience be—without any attempt to prove anything—allows a relaxation into the experience that allows it to be appreciated for what it is, rather than for what the ego may want it to be.

Thus the attitude of "the effects are all there is" leads one to more carefully notice those effects, rather than jump into a story about what is happening vis-à-vis the Divine. This leads to a second benefit, which is a revaluing of the experience itself. This mindstate (*devekut*, *samadhi*, perhaps *unio mystica*) isn't significant because of a story about what it represents; it's significant because it engenders more compassion and more wisdom. Conversely, a mindstate which may have felt very "mystical" but which brings about cruelty or unskillful behavior is easily judged by its fruits, rather than by the supposedly mystical feeling that accompanied it. And one finds in almost every contemplative tradition, theistic and non-theistic, precisely this metric for evaluating truth. The stories cannot be verified, but the effects can.

Third, because there is no attribution of *God* to the mystical experience, certain forms of doubt—i.e., the doubts throughout this entire essay as to whether the experience is "real"—simply do not arise. Of course the experience is real; it is happening. Without a *God* concept, what else does there need to be? One problem with the *God* concept is that it simultaneously carries no attributes and many attributes. I provide an account of a sense of union, and it is read as a union with God. But it doesn't stop there: it's a God which is presumably omnipotent, omnipresent, and so on. Yet are these attributes present in the experience? What do I really know about the experience of union? I don't know that it's with an omnipotent Being, let alone one who gave his only begotten son to redeem the sins of mankind, or who liberated the Israelites from Egypt. Those are ascriptions onto the experience; projections, connections. Myth resonates—but it also can insinuate itself into an experience which, on its own, is bare of such story. And since mystical experience is powerful, with a strong sense of certainty, it generates strong attachment. When mystical attachment gets married to a myth, dangerous results can occur. Passion plus myth equals extremism.

But it's not just Lockean prudence that keeps me from ascribing too much to my mystical experience. That would, I think, be rather dry. Don't we want to dance with God? To sing poems and chant hymns? This isn't just some Buddhist 'mindstate'—this is God! So, no, it isn't just being politically correct; rather, I think that if we keep our mystical experience free from theological associations, we can come to love God even more.

Why? Because mystical theology, hewing closely to experience, actually turns out to be more careful theology. If we strip *God* of associations and concepts, we are being more faithful not only to our experience, and not only to our ethics, but to God as well. Any concept we have of God is not God; it is a finite concept, tied to the finite mind, conceptualized in terms of finite substances and ideas which, in their limitation, are not God-in-godself (a concept which itself is inaccurate, because it is a concept). If you have an idea of God, God negates your idea.

So any idea or concept imposed upon the ineffable mystical experience actually takes us further from the Divine. Perhaps this is why mystics are notoriously reticent about describing their experiences, even in reliable religious-mythic terms: because every term is a diminution. Think of something you'd like to say about a mystical experience—that it was truly of God, for example—and you'll see that it is actually about a concept. It is wrongly finitizing the Infinite.

Samadhi, *devekut*, other mindstates—these are mindstates. They do exist, as mindstates. The only time we get into the whole question of "Is this real? Am I deluded?" is when we are claiming an experience of something outside the self. And that is error. From a negative-theological perspective, the claim is always going to be false, because it is a claim about something. And from a nondual perspective, the claim is false because it is a claim of something outside the self. Either way, the less said, the better.

Delusion, in a nondual perspective, has nothing to do with God. It only has to do with mistaken utterances about the world of appearance.

Mysticism does give experiential access to the nondual truth, but that truth could be deduced from logic anyway, as Spinoza did and Vedantists did, and many Kabbalists did as well. In this light, rather than see contemplative practice as *proving* something to be true, we might see it as *showing* something to be true—something that can be proven apart from experience, but whose power is not really felt until it is experienced. For example, it is possible to see, directly, that even one's longest-held, deepest-felt desires—the parts of ourselves we really want to call our *self*—are actually merely *arisings*. They appear, they disappear, and while we may conventionally refer to their agglomeration as the *self*, there's nothing really there that constitutes this *self*. And once that illusion is seen—not argued or proven, but directly seen—to be illusory, there is no separate self left to be uniting or not uniting with the One. There is only the One. And the anxieties, about what mystical experience does or doesn't prove, subside. There is the knowing of all of these experiences, is there not? So who is doing the knowing, if there is no separate self?

Get this: if there isn't someone doing all that knowing, if there's just the epiphenomenon of knowing itself—well, that's exactly right. Because we've moved away from a concept of *someone* and toward the ineffable. After all, God doesn't have a self either. We tend to say *Being* as if a gerund were really a noun, but in that statement is a mistaken ascription of self-ness. This contradicts both Buddhist and Jewish dogma (everything is empty) and the idea of the Infinite (*Ein Sof*) itself. There is nothing more than all of these composites of experience. There is not a *Knower* if by *Knower* we mean some separate thing out there. God is not something in addition to the universe (if God is, then that part is by definition completely unsayable, unknowable and unthinkable). But there is a *Knower* in a more refined sense, a sense free of concepts and anthropomorphism.

There's this persistent thought that there is some tangible God-consciousness that stands apart from all the strands of reality, and that either does or does not exist. But that is bad theology. It is yet again to make an error of selfhood, this time on a huge theological scale. God, also, is Empty—indeed, God is the Emptiness itself.

This is what mysticism shows. It proves nothing, but it provides a direct experience of the Knowing that is without a conventional Knower. It is surer than dogma or syllogism, and it leads to abundant love.

If we suppose that mysticism can prove the mythic assertions of the Bible, we are mistaken. Myth is its own language, not a poor form of theology. When we ask "Does mysticism really prove there's a God?" or "How do you know your experience is real?" we are misusing mythical language, and it shows. At this extreme, the mythic language collapses, and seems to be full of mistaken assumptions about what God is or isn't. In fact, these assumptions were never really there to begin with; we're asking myth to do something it isn't trying to do. The Bible isn't a theological cookbook; it's an account of eating and drinking.

Mystical experience is as the mystics say. That much I can relate to you. And the more carefully we think about our theology, the less else it could or should evince. Just one last illustration: A Buddhist might report, after a mystical experience: "I feel love." A Jew might report "I love you, God." The more we can dissolve the difference between those statements, the closer we are to heaven.

July 2005

Part Two

Unraveling

Fresh Baked Bread

The Insight Meditation Society in Barre, Massachusetts, occupies the site of a former Catholic retreat center. The meditation hall was once a chapel, and although the founders of IMS removed most of the stained glass windows long ago, they left two of the windows in the vestibule (now used for walking meditation) intact. One of the windows depicts Christ in the wilderness, crying as if in desperation for the Lord. The other, directly across the room, depicts a scene from the Last Supper, with Christ distributing the bread of the meal, and, as every Catholic would know, initiating the first communion rite. One of the disciples, probably John, is looking on with rapt attention and a subtle smile on his face as he prepares to receive the flesh of God. There is love in his eyes, and he is resting on Jesus's shoulder. It is an exquisitely tender scene which can be appreciated by Christians, Buddhists, and, I hope, Jews alike.

Toward the end of a retreat I was sitting at IMS, someone stuck a yellow post-it note next to John's face, with the words "Fresh Baked Bread" written on it, and a small drawing of a heart. It was funny, if a bit impudent, and it underscored the gap between the ornate mythology of Jesus and the clean, no-bullshit air of *vipassana*. The bread, after all, was symbolically contentious: I thought of all those raging Christian debates about transubstantiation, consubstantiation, and the ultimate significance of communion; about whether soda crackers really did turn into meat (to use Kurt Vonnegut's paraphrase of the ritual) and whether, as a result, Christians were engaging in ritual cannibalism. Maybe it was a metaphor; maybe it was a figure of speech; maybe it was magic. I remembered how Jesus was re-signifying the symbols of the Passover Seder, and how the Talmudic rabbis would attempt to steal them back. All these stories in the air, contrasted with the simple delight of fresh baked bread. I came to see the note less as a satire on the window than as a complement to it—an alternative reading. To a Catholic, the significance of the scene is its mythic and theological context. But to a Buddhist, it's about fresh baked bread.

And not because bread is insignificant. On the contrary, I remember reading at some point a Buddhist-Christian reading of the Last Supper, which translated it in the same way as the Post-It joke, although in more reverent terms. The writer—I can't remember who it was—interpreted Jesus's words "This bread is my body" as meaning, "I am God, just as you are, just as this bread is. Understand that there is only the One; only Being; only God. This bread, this bread is my body. This wine, this wine is my blood. If you can eat this bread with total attention to it, it will taste to you as the flesh of the Divine. And so it is—there is no distinction, really, between it and Me."

About a year ago, in the print issue of *Zeek* magazine, I wrote an essay with a similar trajectory. It became a bit controversial—at one well-known Jewish learning conference, a disgusted reader took all the copies of *Zeek* in the bookstore and threw them on the floor, demanding that the store stop selling such trash. Maybe it was just that the title was "How I Finally Came to Accept Christ in My Heart." Or maybe it was that what the essay discussed—my own Jewish fear of Jesus is still alive and well in the Jewish community. Really, though, all I was trying to do was understand Jesus on his own terms, and on the terms of nondual theology. My claim was that if Christ were a fully enlightened being, then he knows that his separate self—the small mind, the ego, the *yetzer hara* of Joshua son of Joseph—is not separate at all. And then Jesus's God-language makes a lot of sense, because, without the illusion of separation, who else are we, anyway? There's all this activity, all this knowing, but no separate self is really doing or knowing anything; we're just temporary agglomerations of the same atoms that once were inside a star. Our brains produce the useful illusion of separate consciousness, but we're not separate at all; we're just earth, air, fire, and water—or subatomic particles, in more recent science—soon to be re-scattered and re-formed. Moreover, since the enlightenment of Christ is really a shedding of the separate identity of Jesus, it makes more sense to speak of Jesus as being an incarnation of

God than to speak of God-consciousness as something Jesus "attained." Enlightenment is something that happens—not something you get.

So maybe there is a convergence between the communion and the dharma. Communion is like a mindfulness practice, and a contemplation. Mindfulness practice insofar as the attention is meant to be wholly focused on this moment—all the bells and whistles, all the ceremony, really makes it seem *Important*, and so the mind, if it takes the ritual seriously, is far more attentive than usual. And contemplation insofar as communion invites the consideration of an important theological idea: that every cracker, every drop of wine, is really the flesh and blood of God. Fresh baked bread is God, and communion makes that known experientially and intellectually.

Still, there is a fundamental difference between the Jewish and Christian moves on the one hand, and the Buddhist one on the other. In Judaism, we eat fresh baked bread all the time: challah, matza, you name it. Bread is the *halachic* requirement for a religious feast, and, of course, the rabbis carefully measure out exactly how much you have to eat. Yet despite all the focus on the materiality of bread, its use in ritual frequently ignores how delightful fresh baked bread is, in favor of some theological, symbolic, or legal construct. This is the critical move of most Western religion, whether "spiritual" or not: away from the thing itself, and toward a web of significance.

In the mystical, Kabbalistic model, the bread is significant because of its specific symbolic meanings: two loaves representing masculine and feminine, the numerical equivalents of "matza," and so on. Ideas about the thing, not the thing itself. Of course, the Kabbalists themselves would dispute that "the thing itself" is its true reality; for them, the word "matza" is more real than the actual cracker. But I wonder if I agree.

In the *halachic* model, the move takes place in the realm of law. For example, Rabbi Joseph Soloveitchik, in *Halakhic Man*, describes the importance of a sunset inhering in its status as a legal signifier:

When halakhic man looks to the western horizon and sees the fading rays of the setting sun or to the eastern horizon and sees the fast light of dawn and the glowing rays of the rising sun, he knows that this sunset or sunrise imposes upon him anew obligations and commandments.

Here, too: ideas about the thing, not the thing itself. Personally, my relationship to this bit of Soloveitchik has evolved, from an initial horror to a deep appreciation of *halacha*'s groundedness: Hasidism and Romanticism take us to inspiration, and *halacha* brings us back; every act is capable of sanctification, regardless of how we feel about it. And probably back to a bit of horror.

In both the mystical and non-mystical models, there is a move away from concrete reality toward an alleged deeper reality, or a conceptual map. And to me, this pull away from the materiality of bread toward either the myth (Christian) or the law (Jewish) or the symbolism (Kabbalistic) of bread seems like a pull away from God Itself. If I wash my hands with the right amount of water, make that blessing, then silently return to the bread, and make the blessing then, and then eat the bread without much consciousness, I have, indeed, contextualized the bread into a system of holy, legal signification. But have I made proper use of the world which God has created? Have I appreciated the body, the bread, and the miracle of eating? Or have I, in the name of following a Divine precept, actually moved *away* from the Divinity inherent in the fresh baked bread?

I've heard *halacha* described, by at least one rabbi interested in syncretizing it with the nondual, integral philosophy of Ken Wilber and others, as the true nondual path. It is a return to the world, an acceptance that the One exists, and a return to the Many as a manifestation of the One. Notice that there are at least three stages in this progression. First, there is holiness in nature—this is the stage of paganism, which sees the sacred everywhere. Second, there is the holiness beyond nature, the one God which unifies all—this is the stage of monotheism, of salvation, and of the attainment of Nirvana as an escape from the wheel of Samsara.

But then there is the path of unification, of seeing the downward-pointing triangle of the Jewish star (i.e., this world) and the upward-pointing triangle (i.e., God) as being the same. Thus we return to the world neither denying the holiness of the manifest nor denying the sacredness of the hidden.

In theory.

In practice, I have come to hold great doubts about the way *halacha* engenders the appreciation, delight, awe, and wonder that is a precondition for an individual's authentic spiritual evolution. Indeed, in much of traditional Jewish practice, there is a fear of enjoying the bread too much, lest we lose sight of its central significance, which is legal. (I'm reminded of the Church authorities who tried to stop Gregorian chant because its beauty was distracting people from the texts being sung.) And in the Kabbalistic model, there are all kinds of spooky suppositions that need to be accepted before the symbolic bread has any meaning deeper than a vague spiritual feeling. Sometimes the web of signification enhances the experience of eating bread, but sometimes it deadens it.

And of course this isn't about bread. The more dangerous "breads" of art, music, sensual pleasure—even beauty itself—these are feared, banned, marginalized, and mythologized into cosmic forces of evil. Obviously, it's only the fundamentalists who reject beauty. But the pull is there even in the mainstream, away from the act of fasting to the "reason why we fast," away from the simple beauty of candlelight to the "reason why we light candles." It's like we're looking for a text to link this act to God, when God is right here in the beauty of the act itself.

Finally, *halacha*, and religious signification more generally, can create attachments to a particular bread, land, and tribe. What's liberating about "Fresh Baked Bread" instead of "This is My Body" is that it doesn't depend on a particular myth. It's the opposite of what I called, last month, "fetishizing the trigger" because its trigger is not Christ, or Gaza, or a *kezayit* of challah, but any bread, any breeze, any moment. Any trigger will do—and indeed, the point of meditation practice is gradually to expand the boundaries of what will do, including times and places which may be very unpleasant, or even awful. Of course, it doesn't happen automatically; practice takes practice. But it can happen. That, for me, is the goal: to live so richly that every crumb of bread has the importance of communion.

It seems like every contemplative tradition eventually translates itself into a similar kind of religion. Buddhism as practiced in Asia has very little to do with paying attention to bread, and very much to do with fixed ritual, symbolic omens, offerings at shrines, praying to *bodhisattvas*, and acquiring merit through particularly defined acts. And the contemplative Judaism of a few elites—whether it's Maimonides' philosophical ecstasy, the Kabbalists' pan-symbolization of the world, or the Hasidim's pantheism—inevitably gets turned into dogma, magic, and code. Likewise in countless other traditions which begin with a mystic in the wilderness and end with fundamentalists enforcing dogma with violence. It's like we make the same mistake over and over again, around the world, as we try to translate a disruptive and individualistic practice (transforming experience, grounding ethics in wonder, etc.) into a system that maintains the status quo, binds together a community of householders, and offers a little bit of God's mojo to people without the luxury, taste, or karma for mystical practice. Perhaps it's the necessary mistake of religion.

Some would say that this 'mistake' is the only thing keeping us from fascism. Once we start exciting the passions, they claim, the zealotry of the hilltop youth (who are mostly spiritual, guitar-playing hippies) is inevitable. But that's only true if a certain hilltop matters. If fresh baked bread is just bread—not this specific God-given magic—then, it seems to me, it's nonsensical to fight over which finger better points at the moon, or where one has to stand to see it. One needn't choose between fundamentalist spirituality, disembodied mythical religion, and desacralized humanism, because the simplest, and most obvious, realities of our experience are also the ways beyond myths of God to realities of God, and the ways away from concepts and back to reality.

That's the kicker: that fresh baked bread, with no ornamentation, is simultaneously the deepest mystical path and the simplest material one.

It's where the *here and now* of the contemplative meets the *here and now* of the Epicurean, leaving dogmatists with their dusty books and stories. It's so simple—if we can just clear the cobwebs out of the way and enjoy it.

November 2005

Guilt and Groundedness

If tomorrow, you could completely free yourself from guilt—if you'd never feel guilty again, no matter what you did—would you do it?

Much contemporary discourse about guilt is conflicted. On one side, there are those who value guilt as an essential check on our selfish desires. No guilt: no shame, no morality, they say; this view is particularly prevalent among conservative religious and political circles. In contrast, others see guilt as a childish form of ethics at best. If you cultivate the right qualities, developing your conscience and becoming more sensitive to suffering, you don't need guilt to keep you behaving properly, like a schoolmarm or parent scolding you with her forefinger. At a certain point in moral development, most liberals say or imply, you get beyond guilt and into a place of moral maturity and responsibility.

What's more, many progressives say, guilt actually holds you back. Guilt is unreflective; it's something that we are taught as small children, and is thus tied to the specific norms of childhood. This learned aspect of guilt is particularly noticeable in religion. Someone raised to keep kosher, for example, may feel guilty for years—even a lifetime—when she eats a cheeseburger, even after she has long since given up on the practice of kashrut. The rational mind knows there is nothing wrong with eating a cheeseburger, and the attraction of a religious lifestyle may have long since evaporated—but somewhere in the recesses of the heart there remains that pang of guilt. Eventually it lessens, or even disappears, depending on the 'sin.' But for some—and I am thinking here primarily of sexuality—the emotive response of guilt remains long after the mind, heart, and spirit have all reconciled themselves to the reality of sexual expression, and of love.

In traditional Jewish discourse, shame and guilt are regarded as invaluable allies. The voice of guilt is really the voice of conscience, the spark of Divinity that endures even after the desiring self has rationalized its way into getting what it wants. Cultivated by proper fear (or 'awe' in more politically correct circles) of the Divine, the attitudes of obedience and guilt inspire right action. That little spark remains, traditional discourse says, even among the most recondite of sinners. And so no one is really lost.

In modern psychology, this 'spark' is a vestige of neurosis that just has to be accommodated. It would be better to be healthy and guilt-free, self-accepting and at ease, when guilt is attached to a non-ethically-valenced action like a cheeseburger or sex. Guilt can help us avoid stealing and harming, but when it gets mucked up with ritual law and angry gods, it's best to just see it, accept it, and try to let it go.

I wonder how much of Jewish practice really depends on guilt; I'd guess, more than most people let on. I can explain the *mitzvot* with the best of 'em, I think. I can talk about trans-subjective morality, the value of the written law, the bonds of community, and the holy act of building a *mishkan*, a dwelling place for the Divine created by our acts and our bodies. I can tell stories about the beautiful spiritual moments brought on by observing a law which may, at other times, seem tedious. Or I can relate tales of Shabbat rest that was only made possible because choices were made due to the boundaries set by *halacha*. Or, if you prefer, although it's not really my theology, I can speak of the sense of being commanded, of the covenant, and of cultivating a relationship with a Divine lawgiver.

But I wonder if that's all just intellectual window dressing for guilt. Libraries have been written explaining the beauty of the Jewish religious path. Are they to convince others—or the authors? Intelligent, rational men (mostly men) find themselves inexplicably attached to bizarre codes of diet, behavior, and dress—and so they are at pains to offer an explanation. This effort is a mirror image of the sinner's rationale: to provide reasons why it's good to do what we want. Whereas we're really doing these things because we were taught either when we were very young, or when we were at some impressionable period in our lives (e.g., yeshiva, post-trauma, etc.), that doing them is good, and not doing them is bad.

I don't mean to overstate the power of guilt. The cheeseburger-eater in the earlier example may feel a twinge of guilt, but she may easily recognize it as a leftover from her childhood—and enjoy the burger. It's no big deal, or at least not enough of a deal to overcome simple desire and the powers of rationalization.

Some 'sins,' though, are a big deal. Religious gays and lesbians, if we are fortunate, know that sexual orientation is much more than the anatomy of same-sex activity. It creates identity, and brings us to love and to a place where, if anywhere, the Divine is more readily experienced. But getting to that place, and remaining religious, requires a revolution in thinking because of the power of guilt. At first, one loves religion and thus hates oneself. Then, there is a choice among three alternatives. One may affirm the self and hate religion; here guilt is but a vestige of a past life that is essential to purge. Or one may continue to repress the self, and love religion; here, guilt is essential. Or, somehow, one may affirm the self and reconcile religion with the reality of love and sexual expression. And here, guilt is ambiguous.

I quote this story perhaps a bit too much, but the situation religious gays face is like that faced by Huck Finn in Mark Twain's novel. Huck has been taught that if he helps escaped slaves, he will go to hell. But he has befriended Jim, the runaway slave, and cannot turn him in. "Well, I guess I'll go to hell, then," Huck decides at a pivotal moment in the book. That moment, the Huck Finn moment, is precisely the birth of mature conscience out of immature rules-and-religion. Huck's conscience evolves: he makes ethical decisions for himself, and is willing to "go to hell" in order to save his friend.

Gays and lesbians born into religious communities all must face the Huck Finn moment. Unlike heterosexuals, we have no choice but to develop an independent conscience—to decide either to "go to hell, then," and live rich emotional/sexual lives; or turn in our inner Jim; or somehow try to have it both ways. This choice, perhaps unlike keeping kosher or observing the sabbath, is a big deal. For those who reject religion because it has taught them a lie, that the way they have been engineered to love is "wrong," it may often mean severing ties with family or renouncing a connection that was once beloved. For those who reject their independent desires and side with religion, it means a lifetime of repression, sublimation, and striving to do right in the eyes of an inexplicable God—a God who has provided them a uniquely onerous burden. And for those who refuse to choose between religion and love, it means having to develop a new religious consciousness, which is no easy task, and facing occasional contention with those who hold fast to the old.

Gay religious consciousness is thus necessarily different from straight religious consciousness. It is inherently distrustful, because it has seen—and, more importantly, felt—how rules, codes, and even the operation of conscience itself can actually be tools of oppression and self-repression. Of course, straight people may come to this realization also. But religious gay people must.

Yet guilt remains, because it is a conditioned emotional response, not a rational, ethical one. Guilt is not a turn-on, and so few gay men openly admit to feeling guilty when they have sex. But how could we not? We—at least those of us raised in homophobic cultures—were told for ten, fifteen, perhaps forty or fifty years that this act is wrong. Does the emotive pang of guilt simply disappear because the ethical mind has made peace? As time passes, the strength of the pang diminishes, and the strength of the conviction of love and the rightness of love grows. For me, guilt only arises now and then. But it still arises.

What is the significance of that guilt? That is the question that has haunted me. I know that guilt is an emotional response that is, essentially, content-neutral. The substantive elements of guilt are learned, and so if the presence or absence of guilt is itself used as a barometer for ethics, you don't get anywhere. However, there is still a sense that deep guilt is, somehow, an indicator of what we really know to be true, even if only for ourselves. We have a conventional geology of the self, in which some things are deep down, and others are just on the surface, and when you feel something deep down, it feels more real than that which is on the surface. I came to see the falsity of this model during a long retreat I sat last year. An intense feeling of self-hatred had been triggered by a remark made by one of the teachers: He had said, in a dharma talk, that "you can change anything about yourself," and I angrily responded, inside, "No you can't!" Over the course of several days, I came to see how attached I was to the belief that sexuality can't be changed—because, I realized, I might still change it if I could.

At first, I interpreted this feeling according to the conventional geology of the self. This is what I felt deep down. The doubt and guilt told me that this is was what I really believed, despite all the rationale I'd proffered to myself and to others. But then I came to see that the entire geology is flawed—deep down inside what? Really believed *how*? All that was actually present in my experience were different beliefs. One belief (gay is bad) had the character—the 'feeling tone' in Buddhist language—of being long-held. Another belief (gay is good) didn't have the same character, even though I knew it made more sense, and had led me to more happiness and more spiritual capacity. The former belief wasn't really deeper or truer. It was merely its character—its feeling—that was being interpreted as 'deep.'

To suppose the belief, or the guilt, will simply disappear makes light of the depth of homophobia and homophobic acculturation. Being gay, when I was growing up, wasn't just an unfortunate characteristic, or a disfavored choice—it was a curse, and I believed it. So, it's unrealistic to suppose that all traces of the belief will simply vanish. Instead, what I, and I think many LGBT people, have learned to do is, as above—recognize the guilt and know that its foundation is not true.

I've noticed, though, that the pang of conscience I feel around unethical acts, and the alienation I feel around failing to perform ritual religious acts, is almost exactly identical to this guilt. And, because of my sexuality, I know that the facile belief that "your conscience should be your guide" is untrue. Your conscience is conditioned by all sorts of social expectations and other phenomena. The conscience of someone raised vegetarian recoils at the thought of eating meat; a carnivore's doesn't. My conscience recoils at eating shrimp, but not at drinking non-kosher wine—primarily because that was my family's practice, only secondarily because I think it makes sense. The conscience of someone from an older culture might be quite at peace with war and killing in the name of honor or tribe; yours might not. There is no rhyme or reason to the operation of conscience; guilt adheres equally to the sublime and ridiculous.

Where, then, is guilt? One might like to say: use it when it's useful, ignore it when it isn't, but don't let it do the deciding. Make your decision based on introspection, examination, consideration—but don't "listen to your heart." Or rather: Cultivate the process of heart-listening, but know that the substance of its speech will always be conditioned.

But what about religious practice? Let's look at actions between humans and God first—*mitzvot bein adam l'makom*. If I admit that I'm keeping kosher mainly because of guilt, as I think I and many religious people would have to do if we were intellectually honest, then shouldn't I reevaluate my practice? Of course, keeping kosher is mostly harmless. It gets in the way of my enjoying myself in restaurants, but it doesn't hurt anyone. Still, enjoying myself in restaurants is a (small) part of a more important value: celebrating the beauty of life, drinking deep from the world's well, sampling the varieties of experience. Why am I passing this up—guilt? And it's not just the restaurants—given how guilt can cause us to repress and distort ourselves, shouldn't it be thrown out entirely?

More significant, of course, are ethical actions—actions *bein adam l'havero* in the Jewish formulation. Here, guilt can actually cause harm, as we favor some people over others, some land over others, and some values (e.g., freedom to make as much money as possible) over others (e.g., equality). Usually it's the political Left that gets accused of acting based on "liberal guilt." But the Right also acts according to guilt, insofar as its ethical choices are based on values which, more than anything else, just feel right. And, of course, since the Right's guilt is conditioned by preset social structures, it does not extend to those beyond those structures' concern—marginalized groups, the environment, and so on. Thus guilt harms by its absence as well.

The phenomenon of groundedness illuminates something about guilt. At first blush, these may seem like two completely different states of being. Yet in my experience, they are intimately connected. I have found that the less I listen to guilt, the less grounded I am in a root tradition. When I let go of guilt, I feel a bit more like Huck Finn, on my own, on a raft, outside of civilization and its comforts. The traditionalists are right: guilt keeps us moored, grounded in traditional ethics and feeling secure.

It's that feeling of groundedness that is so important, I think, for many religious people. Some would say this feeling is merely one of safety in a time of uncertainty and insecurity. But I think it is deeper than wanting to be safe. I think groundedness is a primal need, underlying the strongest bonds we have, like those of family and relationship. We may romanticize the wandering gypsy, but on an emotional, if not a physical level, most of us want to have roots.

Mystical, spiritual religion is often set up as the opposite of ethical, traditional religion. It's supposed that the former values experience and spiritual states, whereas the latter is less about how you feel than whether you are acting correctly. But how does acting correctly make you feel? In contrast, what does it feel like for a traditional religious person to disobey God's command?

Really, traditional Judaism is every bit as experiential and individualistic as mystical religion. It just values different experiences, particularly that of feeling grounded. And guilt is, I think, the primary tool of maintaining that experience.

It's notable, in this light, that most of the world's mystical traditions require lots of groundedness before the destabilizing work of mystical practice may be undertaken. As a teacher of Kabbalah, I've encountered many students who ask whether it's OK to learn (let alone teach) Kabbalah before you're forty years old and fully learned in Bible and Talmud, as is customary. Other traditions have similar restrictions.

What these restrictions are saying is: be grounded. The spiritual practitioner is like a tree: If the branches are not broad enough, the tree will not be nourished. But if the branches are too broad for the roots, the tree will blow over. So, know the Ten Commandments before the ten *sefirot*; learn about suffering before you say that all is perfect.

At the same time as I appreciate this wisdom, I used to think, with regard to the Kabbalah in particular, that these groundedness-restrictions were more or less about guilt. Forty, in the Jewish tradition, denotes completion. It means you've lived a life. You've had children, you've built a home—you're not going to jump off a cliff because you've experienced that all is One and you don't exist as a really separate entity. And you're not going to stop keeping Shabbat either. Just as something holds you back from jumping off the cliff (love of family, or the norm of preserving life, or just a deep instinct for self-preservation), something also holds you back from transgressing the law. Observance is part of your infra-structure; you're grounded.

So the Kabbalah is reserved for those who won't sin as a result of study-ing it. At the far reaches of Jewish mystical practice is antinomian heresy: the followers of Sabbetai Zevi who wanted to sin in order to uplift sparks of divinity, for example. But a bit nearer are the Hasidic rabbis, such as R. Aaron of Staroselye or R. Mordechai Lainer of Izbica, who grasped the contradiction between the concept of sin and the reality of God's omni-presence. The Ishbitzer created a worldview in which one becomes fully Divine by becoming fully oneself, refining the individual conscience and even, on rare occasions, transgressing the superficial law in favor of the deeper. What separates the heretics from the Hasidim is their practice— the Hasidim never strayed from pious observance, even as their meta-physics allowed them to do so. Why? We don't exactly know—but surely guilt played a role.

I want to be clear that, in the mystical moment itself, the energy of guilt and the energy of groundedness are almost identical. Why not jump off the cliff? All is God—do it! Go farther... sin... unite the opposites... cross the boundary that separates the sheep from the shaman. What calls me back, in such moments, are thoughts of home, and attachments to precisely the illusory self that gets effaced by contemplative work.

But there is another kind of groundedness.

Unlike the groundedness that is attachment, that so closely resembles guilt, and that is tied to specific norms and behaviors, I have experienced a form of resting—that is the operative word—in consciousness itself, and in a mode of consciousness that is ever-present. The phrase "resting in the present moment" carries a slight whiff of the New Age, but what it means is that the mind has been practiced upon enough that it can stop worrying, stop thinking so many thoughts, and stop rewinding and fast-forwarding to times other than now. "Resting in now" is a form of relaxed concentration. The mind witnesses the arising and passing of desires, it sees them clearly, and it holds to commitments without the tightness of guilt. And, as such—here is the crucial turn—it allows a wider, deeper journey to unfold. Without a practice of being grounded in the present moment, I experience fear—and it's a good thing, too, because otherwise I might well jump off the proverbial cliffs. (Indeed, the possibility of doing so itself creates more fear.) I feel called back, restrained, rooted—but with the sense of "I haven't yet made it." On the other hand, with the practice of concentration and grounding in the present, I can allow myself to cut loose, and be almost fearless. Images, energies, emotions, ideas—all can arise and pass, and I am resting, watching, feeling. Amazing trips happen when you're free from fear.

What if, instead of reserving mysticism for those who won't transgress, the restrictions on Kabbalah study are meant to reserve it for those who can truly take such journeys?

Without this form of groundedness—the content-less kind, the kind that comes from concentration and practice and lots of hard work on the mind (*effortless effort*, it's called in the Buddhist world)—you can't go anywhere. You'll see a vision, and be afraid. In the terms of the Talmudic warning of those who engage in mystical practice, you'll cry, "Water, water!" when you visit the palaces of pure marble, and you will be destroyed. Or you'll think too much, creating stories of apostasy. Only the grounded one—Akiva in the Talmudic story—is able to journey to the heights and the depths.

Again, the crucial difference is that the groundedness is not a groundedness-in-something. It is not tied to a specific code or text or feeling. And it's not a puerile sense of guilt. Rather, it is a form of stability of mind that, in my experience, allows all kinds of wonder to be held. There is more to heaven and Earth than is measured in Horatio's philosophy—but without the preparation of mind, fear will get in the way.

The practice of grounding the mind in the present—experiencing whatever arises, remaining with the fact of experience rather than becoming trapped by fears—also cuts through the recursive circuits of guilt. It is a paradoxical state—one holds onto it by letting go, again and again and again. Guilt works by fighting, but this practice works by surrendering. Yet it leads to the same, grounded, secure, trusting place. *Hinei el yeshuati, eftach v'lo efchad*: here, God is my salvation, I will trust and not fear.

As one of my teachers said on a recent retreat, "Stopping the war has no limits." It takes a lot of work, and I am a beginner who makes many mistakes. I get trapped, and it's not like meditation is a cure-all that dispenses with problems. I have no way of knowing whether I've really cleared my mind of biases, guilt, and fear, or whether some still remain, so it's not as though I can just breathe a few times and then make the right ethical choice. And I still get driven crazy by annoyances. But every so often, I remember to stop judging, stop preferring, stop fighting. And then a real groundedness appears, one conditioned not by social norms but by a state of mind which arises through practice. Trusting in that one attachment, the attachment to whatever is happening now, real concentration: this is what is meant by "stopping the war."

From the perspective of this witnessing mind, guilt is just a conditioned phenomenon like everything else. It isn't a still small voice, or the internalized voice of the patriarchy, or anything personal at all. It's mechanistic. Play with a dog, and he'll want to play more. Give a man enough drinks, and he'll get drunk. Transgress old boundaries, and there will be guilt. It's been my karma to have been conditioned in a certain way, where some bad things (like theft) give me guilt, some good things (like sex) give me guilt, and some completely neutral things (like *treif*) give me guilt. Sometimes guilt obstructs love, and sometimes, let's be honest, it helps love grow by constraining our behavior, either with respect to other people or, in religious life, with regard to the One. Guilt works well in an identity constructed out of fears and desires, and since I still mostly live in that identity, I am learning to accept it and appreciate it for just what it is. Would I rather it be gone from my life? It depends. I would let it go, but only if it were replaced by concentration.

Only, that is, if the groundedness in inherited truths might be supplanted by groundedness in the real truth—to cleave only to what Buddhist sages call the one fortunate attachment.

September 2005

Fetishizing the Trigger

> There was once a prisoner who yearned for freedom. One day, the
> prophet Mohammed appeared to him, and gave him a set of keys
> to his cell, saying, "Your piety has been rewarded. Allah has set
> you free." So the prisoner took the set of keys, mounted them on
> the wall, and prayed to them five times a day.
> — Sufi tale

Since moving to Jerusalem three months ago, the most disturbing aspect of living in Israel again has been the congruence of religion and
politics. In the days leading up to the disengagement from Gaza, the vast
majority of the religious public was staunchly opposed—and the majority of those opposed were religious. Wearing a kippa became synonymous
with wearing an orange (anti-disengagement) ribbon, and those few of
us (almost all Americans) who were both religious and pro-disengage-
ment were left in a very lonely place.

Now, it might be expected that the Israeli religious public generally
was anti-disengagement, pro-"greater Israel," and against the Palestinians. This is true around the world. Populations that are more religious,
particularly more fundamentalist, tend to be more conservative and more
patriotic. Islamists in Pakistan or Saudi Arabia; Christian fundamentalists in America; Hindu nationalists in India—it stands to reason that
people who are extreme about their religious particularism tend to adopt
political positions that are equally ethnocentric, and often equally extreme. While we in the Jewish community seem unable to label our own
fundamentalists and terrorists as such—witness the silence in the Orthodox community around Rabbi Ovadia Yosef's statements that Hur-
ricane Katrina was punishment for American support of disengagement,
or for Jerusalem Mayor Uri Lupolianski's statements that the Jerusalem
gay pride parade was like "bringing a pig to the Al Aqsa mosque"—it
should still not be surprising that those who are 'extreme' or 'ardent' in

their religious fervor are equally so politically.

What was most unsettling when I first arrived, though, was not this community's zealous patriotism. It was that the 'peace and love' crowd, the hippies who are most likely to meditate, sing songs, and smoke marijuana before davening—these people were not only anti-disengagement, they were some of its most hard-core opponents in the country, even more so than the ordinary national-religious camp. To Israelis and others who live here, this is not so surprising; we are all familiar with the sight of shaggy-looking, floppy-kippa-wearing settler youth who play guitars and carry M-16s. But to outsiders, the cognitive dissonance can be shocking. In America, we're used to hippies being for peace and love not just rhetorically, but politically as well. The only debate among the dreadlocked crowd in the states is whether to vote Democrat, Green, or not vote at all. In Israel, I heard one Anglo immigrant hang up the phone by saying "peace," and then reveal that he lives in the territories and can't believe that "our" government was committing national suicide by leaving Gaza.

What's going on? How is it possible that a population that says it loves peace is actually so vehemently against the most rudimentary steps toward achieving it? There are two uninteresting possibilities in play, I think, and a few other elements which are fascinating.

The first possibility is that the religious-hippie-settler crowd—and their Amen corner in the Carlebach community in Israel—is simply lying, or in delusion. They say they want peace, but they don't really; really, they just want to indulge in their narcissistic spirituality, and if it comes at the expense of Arabs they hate, then so be it. Having lived with some of these people for three months, I don't think this is fair. Some, surely, just want to play their guitars, and own their land, and precisely the same obliviousness to reality that enables them to go on great spiritual trips also enables them to ignore the demographic problem of two million people who don't want Israel to rule over them. (None of this crowd, when pressed, has ever offered a solution to the crisis other than Divine intervention or ethnic cleansing. In fact, one hears the former so much that one suspects it is but a cover for the latter.) Many, though, at least from my own anecdotal experience and from reading their literature, seem sincere both in their desire for peace and in their opposition to the peace process. They're not lying. So, the situation seems more complicated than mere hypocrisy.

Another possibility is that the religious-hippie-settler crowd is right, and that the peace process as it is currently unfolding really will not bring peace. As with the first possibility, there is some truth to that. Much of the American Jewish Left seems to regard the Palestinians as noble victims of Israeli aggression, a proud, gentle people to whom we must extend an arm of peace and reconciliation. In reality, though, a large percentage of the Palestinian population supports armed violence against Israeli civilians, and an erasure not just of the occupation but of Israel itself. Any arm that's extended might well be cut off. After all, this is an occupied and subjugated people, and subjugated peoples can hardly be expected to offer olive branches of peace, love, and understanding. Of course, much of the Right then proceeds with a racist and absurd claim that this is due to something about the people as an ethnic group, rather than the conditions of living under occupation. But on the surface level, the phenomena are certainly there.

So it's not that the hippie Right is incorrect about some of Palestinian society. But what do they propose to do about it? The total absence of any right-wing alternative to the current process—which, it may be recalled, is itself a Center-Right alternative to a more negotiated solution—belies the rightists' claim that it's only the current process that they oppose. Since they have no alternative, one can only assume that they oppose *any* process: land for peace, economic development, unilateral withdrawal, whatever. The hippie-Right's view of the Left, moreover, is a straw man. Sure, there are probably some dovish Lefties who still buy into the myth of the noble, suffering Palestinians. But most Israelis are pragmatic; they just want this problem to be solved. Were there another option, one that didn't involve perpetually subjugating (or exiling) two million people, I would certainly be happy to hear it—as would many other people. But there isn't one, at least not one that the Right has proposed. And you can't say you're pro-peace and have absolutely no suggestion as to how to pursue it.

So, what is going on? How can people who are sincerely open-hearted, who sincerely do their spiritual practice, and who in almost any other social context could be counted on for ardent progressive views, take such oddly militaristic positions?

Part of the answer is surely emotional, rather than rational. First, this is a traumatized community, shell-shocked by terrorist attacks, and wounded by the failure of the Oslo process. Second, those with friends or relatives in the territories—probably a majority of the hippie-Right/ Carlebach crowd—also experience first-hand the beauty of the government-subsidized settler lifestyle, and the pain of its partial destruction. Whereas very few of them know anything about daily life in Arab Palestine. One spiritual teacher sent a glowing report, pre-disengagement, of how lovely and open the Gush Katif community actually is, and how the media has it all wrong—seemingly oblivious to the fact that the community only exists because of the tanks parked outside, and to the fact that its sprawling suburban houses were a government-contrived injustice next to the packed slums of Khan Yunis. So there is trauma, pain, the love of the settler lifestyle, and obliviousness to the suffering of others. And of course, the "others" are demonized. Most Israelis, certainly most religious Israelis, do not go to peace gatherings where rabbis do zikr with Sufi sheikhs; they get hustled by Arab merchants or laborers, and confirm their fears and prejudices on the selective evidence they admit.

Another part of the answer is that Judaism lends itself to right-wing positions. In the contemplative world these days, you see many statements like "Judaism is a set of mindfulness practices" or "The point of religion is to connect us to God." These are very nice things to say, and they do apply to religion as practiced by some. However, they certainly do not describe the Jewish religion as practiced by most of its ardent adherents. For some people, Judaism is a set of ethical practices designed to make us less cruel to one another. For others, it is a set of required behaviors, mandated by an all-powerful God, whom we obey regardless of whether the behaviors make us feel good, or "spiritual." (For many others, of course, Judaism is not a religion at all but a nationality and culture; however, I am concerned here only with those who practice Judaism as a religion.) There are dozens of possible points to Jewish religious practice, and it is both specious and arrogant to claim that one or another is the main one. Moreover, all of us can look to proof-texts in the Bible or the Talmud to support our positions, from the rationalist-covenantalists to the magical-Kabbalists to the secular-humanists and the anarchists. But the fact is that no text is both unambiguous and determinative as to what the point of it all is. Hillel's Golden Rule? The first of the ten commandments? The Shema? These yield different points. And what about the general thrust of the Torah's legislation—is it to create a just society based on law? What about the Priestly Codes and rules regarding sacrifices and temple architecture? Maybe it's about "peoplehood"—maybe it's just about tribe.

This multiplicity of points may be one of Judaism's great strengths, particularly as compared with religions of creed. It has long been observed that Judaism is less about beliefs than about practices—it's not what you think, but what you do, that counts. And so, I can stand next to an ardent and (in)famous Kach supporter in shul, and pray with him—as I did recently—even though I think we probably disagree on every point of what holiness, morality, Israel, and God are about. To be sure, there are plenty of disagreements on practice, but they're still less contentious than arguments over ideas.

However, the multiplicity of points does mean that everyone can find a text to support their position—including ethnic cleansing, not trusting non-Jews, not trusting Ishmaelites in particular, and ardent right-wing nationalism. Personally, I see the practices of Judaism as engendering and then expressing a certain form of God-consciousness. But I also see, as Maimonides did, that Jewish law functions on a number of levels, in a way that seems to be intentional. The same practices work with different theologies, and different purposes.

But I want to go a few steps further, because it's not just those who think Judaism is about the Holy Land who have espoused far-Right views lately—it's the contemplatives too. Even for those who agree with me that Judaism is a path of spiritual enrichment—even these people—can end up with extreme Right-wing political views. The ones who are meditating; the ones who think this is about spiritual practice; the ones who are striving to be in the Divine Presence—these are precisely the ones who are the among most ardent pro-settler, anti-peace-process Jews in Israel.

I do not want to say, "Well, they've got God wrong." I don't think that's true, and of course it's arrogant to say so. Rather, I want to give the Carlebach Right full credit. I want to say that, in their davening, they really are reaching an exalted spiritual place. Not delusion, as the secular Left would say—but really, a place of spirituality and holiness. I want to agree with them that they are doing this Jewish work to reach a state of closeness to the Divine, and that it is working. Some may be mere freaks or weirdos—but some are authentic mystics, with serious contemplative practice and far more knowledge than I have of the Jewish mystical tradition. What is happening is real. These people are pulling a trigger, and experiencing the Divine. But then they fetishize the trigger.

"Fetishizing the trigger"—a phrase that comes from my friend Tamuz—is when a trigger (e.g. the holy land, *halacha*, whatever) gives you a real spiritual experience, but you then make the mistake of thinking it's all about the trigger. The finger points at the moon, but wow, how about that finger! And fetishizing means: It's only this trigger, this trigger is the point, this trigger is better than others. Or: It's these words. It's this Torah, written by God. It's this Zohar, written by Shimon bar Yochai. These codes, this land, this holy people. This spirituality, these souls—on a higher level than any other. It's that turn, that move—that fetishizing of the trigger—that causes the distortion. Now the entire world is seen through the prism of the trigger (Torah, Israel, etc.). Now the trigger is reified into an objectively real reality. *The* reality.

And then the trigger has to hold everything. The Torah has to say

everything we want it to say; the Jewish tradition has to hint at everything we want it to do; and so we take thousands of years of interpretive
traditions, and marshal them to find in our sacred texts precisely what
we need to find. And we will find what we need, because of Judaism's
many voices. But if we are looking with Romantic, non-rational, or mystical eyes, we are in trouble. Mysticism (as I have written in *Zeek* before)
excites the passions, stimulates the soul. But when it is tied to myth, it
becomes toxic, because while the passions are universal, the myth is par-
ticularistic. Combine the particularism of myth with the excitement of
mystical practice—and violence often results.

I don't know what's kept me immune from hippie-Right fundamentalism. Maybe it's because, due to my own life circumstances, I know
that the "Torah is everything" approach will never work for me, at least
if Torah is interpreted by hetero Orthodox men with no understanding
of the Others they create. Or maybe it's because, having had powerful
experiences not just on the Jewish path but on other paths as well, I see
Jewish forms as forms—nothing more, and nothing less. They are to be
respected, if we want them to work. But they are forms, not the substance that fills the forms.

Personally, I love the Torah. But I don't need to make it say everything
I believe. I love that the Jewish path can lead me to *devekut*. But I don't
need to prove that *devekut* is better than *samadhi*. In short, I don't need
my group to own the mojo. I'm happy to share it with the rest of the
world's religious traditions, to learn from them, and not to assume that
the choice I've made—to follow the Jewish path—is necessarily the right
or the best choice. Most of the religious-hippie crowd are *baalei tshuvah*;
they became religious later in life, usually after experiencing many other
paths. So now they've found the best one. Really, the only one.

I love the Sufi tale with which I started this essay, because it seems to
capture the dilemma, and its humanity, so perfectly. It's not that the Jewish fundamentalists are confused in a way that the rest of us aren't. We all
make this mistake—it's natural and human to do so. You feel good after
doing something, so you value the something that brought you there,

whether it's a meditation practice, a territory, or a car. We fetishize our own triggers all the time, which is why we're constantly trying to arrange the conditions for our happiness.

But this act of fetishizing the trigger, as universal as it may be, is also the cause of the great evils of nationalism, extremism, ethnocentrism, and worse. When the gifts of my people, nation, or land possess are mistakenly seen to be intrinsically better than those of other peoples, nations, or lands, naturally I will resort to extreme measures to protect them. I will divide up the world into 'us' and 'them.' I will dehumanize my enemy. I will grasp ever harder onto the possessions and security of my people.

The danger of fetishization grows the more powerful the trigger is. If your religiosity or sense of tribal belonging is soft and thin, you're less likely to fight to the death for it. But if you chant Jewish niggunim in the Judean desert and feel the vitality of Jewish spiritual practice flowing through your veins, then even if you've got your hair in white-person dreadlocks, you're going to cling to this thing that makes you happy, that gives your life meaning, with an ardency that will cloud your better judgment. It's just how humans are. We don't choose our political beliefs. We feel them.

This is how ordinarily rational human beings can lose their senses of logic and reason: because of their profound love of that which brings them joy, connection, identity, family, security, or whatever it is they get from their religion, people, or land. And the more intensely they feel those things, the less compassionate they become.

Lately I've become so suspicious of zeal. No, I haven't given up on seizing the day, or living intensely, or pursuing spiritual and sensual experiences. But I have started appreciating quieter pleasures, if only because it feels like fewer people would want to fight or die for them. It's funny, in some religious and spiritual communities, one often hears a kind of pity for 'normal' people, who lack the sense of meaning, or energy, or connection that religion can bring to one's life. But maybe a little less energy would be a good thing. These days, when someone expresses a profound, zealous love of their spirituality, I get nervous.

The great irony, in the end, is that there's nothing more universal than particularism. Hindu fundamentalists are sure that Hinduism is the only true (universal!) religion, Christian fundamentalists are sure that everyone who doesn't accept Christ will burn in hell, and Jewish fundamentalists are sure that the chosen .5% of the population are God's favorites, operating on a higher level than everyone else. And so with every other religious group. Ironically, in fetishizing the trigger of one's own spiritual practice, one becomes the most like everyone else.

If only we could all remember: *other paths lead here too... other paths lead here too...* If only we knew that the lock has many keys.

October 2005

Star Wars, Conservatives, Judaism and the Penis

Is it better to be tough or sensitive?

This simple question, which I probably first wrestled with around age ten, seems to still divide liberals and conservatives, feminists and anti-feminists—and the Jedi and the Sith. And it has ramifications far beyond political divisions, extending to fundamental questions of what it is to live a full, human life.

"So this is how liberty dies: to thunderous applause," Senator Amidala says as the Senate votes Chancellor/Emperor Palpatine imperial power in the *Star Wars* saga's latest, *Revenge of the Sith*. That line has been widely quoted in the press, with George Lucas agreeing that it is a political allegory for our own times. In fact, the allegories began earlier in the series: a phony war waged in order to raise an army, suppress dissent, and arrogate power; blaming everything on the enemy; a republic to voting away its liberty in the name of security. Sound familiar?

In the first *Star Wars* films (i.e., episodes four, five, and six) the Empire is a fascist state, maintaining control by means of military might. But now we see that, in the beginning at least, this fascism had popular support. Many members of the Republic/Empire think that good, strong government is just what the unruly galactic federation needs, and that Palpatine is the strong leader who will protect it from a host of enemies. When fear is exploited, the spiritual is political. The people are not being terrorized—they are being manipulated.

Moreover, the Emperor is not just an evil sorcerer who shoots lightning from his fingers. He's a man with values: power, the individual, strength, and the expression of violent emotions. The appeal of the "Dark Side" of the force is not mysterious; it is power. What is called the "dark side," Palpatine explains, is really the application of power to those aspects of the self labeled as "dark" by the timid and the meek: anger, fear, rage. This is our nature, Palpatine explains, and it is good to express it fully. The liberal Jedi are non-violent, pop-Buddhist and gentle. The conservative Sith are violent, Ayn-Randist, and fierce. The Jedi say that the real enemy isn't the person you think is your enemy; it's your inner capacity to hate. The Sith say your enemy is your enemy.

The Right also says: believe in yourself, and your values, enough to force others to believe them. Kill if necessary. Strength and toughness define the well-made man (sic), and, if necessary, freedom must be sacrificed in order for our values to endure; dissent is to be quashed. "Strength is not only safety—it is our essence," says the Right. It's a dog-eat-dog world out there, the Right says, and people are out for themselves. So, we need strong, secure values and leaders to keep us safe—and a strong moral compass to keep our own animal natures under control. It's entirely consistent: the strong morals, the individualistic achievement, the use of power—all cohere within a worldview in which we are selfish animals, bent on power. And, the Right and the Sith say, "everyone knows this is true." We all know, underneath the phony patina of liberal ethics, that the guy with the bigger house, bigger penis, and bigger bankbook is the guy who is winning. Darth Sidious says that even the Jedi want power—they're just in too much self-deception to even realize it.

The Left, in contrast, says: believe in the Force, i.e., cultivate compassion, and do not attach to your own emotions. Thich Nhat Hanh, Yoda, and the Dalai Lama agree that indulging one's fear, hate, and rage is not a sign of beautiful human expression—it's a sad distortion of what humanity should be. The good society, in turn, is one which cares for the weakest, and which respects difference of opinion. In fact, we don't all "know it to be true" that might makes right—we only feel it to be true at times, when our individual dark sides are allowed to predominate. Bigger is not better. The Left says that, actually, humans are naturally compassionate, albeit often corrupted by a dysfunctional society. So, the advice is different: go work on yourself, develop your better self... and you'll see how happy you can be. What's more, our political culture ought to encourage the better parts of humanity to work together, sharing the world, preserving it for our children. Yes, we can be selfish—but we can also be noble. So the Left, too, coheres: the greater reliance on individual conscience rather than fixed moral codes, the communitarian focus, and the cultivation of mercy all fit within a structure of compassion.

The debate arises in a thousand everyday choices. Do you buy the SUV, or do your part to save the environment? Do you "sell out" and make plenty of money (if you have the option to do so), or pursue a less lucrative line of work, all the while telling yourself that you're the "real success"? Do you aim high and work hard to achieve your ambition, or cultivate humility and a virtue of smallness? Do you work within established values, upholding generations of inherited wisdom, or follow your own heart even if that's not what they teach you in school?

Who is right, and how to tell? History is little guide. In our own world, as in Star Wars, conservative and liberal societies have each thrived and fallen, at least since Athens and Sparta. What about ethics, then? Well, it depends which ethics. On the Right, remarkably, the Empire is getting some good notices. "The truth is that from the beginning, Lucas confused the good guys with the bad," Jonathan Last wrote in the *Weekly Standard*. "The deep lesson of Star Wars is that the Empire is good."

But what about Darth Vader killing all the young Jedi students? What about the Death Star annihilating an entire, peaceful planet? Just like "collateral damage" in Iraq, these details tend to get brushed off in the Right's rush to the moral high ground. This is not a mere oversight; it's a moral choice, with the ends of conservative values justifying the nasty means of genocide, avoidable war, poverty, and death.

An example: recently, a conservative colleague of mine said that, in his opinion, "we're going to mix it up in Iran, too, before this thing is over." Mix it up? Is that how we understand making widows and orphans out of innocent human beings? Well, if we're tough, it is. You want to make an omelet; gotta break some eggs. Yes, war is hell, but you've got to be tough about it. Don't tell me about your bleeding heart. Whereas, it seems obvious to liberal Jedis that the suffering of war should be avoided at all costs. To say "mix it up" is, to me, part of the problem.

Maybe happiness, then? Personally, I have tried life on both sides of the fence. Admittedly, I have never lived as a pro-life, pro-war Republican, but I did spend some time pursuing wealth and, in my way, power. It felt inauthentic. I don't really like the side of myself that is angry, demanding, and rude. I prefer to cultivate the parts that are caring, loving, expressive, nurturing. Jedi philosophy feels right, seems right. I've made my choice—but probably on grounds that are psychological and subjective. I can't generalize from my tastes.

I really do believe that these questions ultimately boil down to questions of fundamental value. Are we to be strong, or kind? Selfish, or generous? How are we to be most fully human?

When Israelite religion developed, the dominant model in the Ancient Near East was that of the Sith: one in which bravery, virtue, and violence were celebrated. God-kings, eldest sons, rule of the powerful; pagan rituals, eros, Dionysian violence. Speaking very broadly, and, as a caveat, primarily based on texts written by their opponents, Canaanite, Moabite, and Assyrian religious systems celebrated strength and virtue, together with ecstatic, erotic religious experience. The sacred marriages of Baal and Asherah, the Gilgamesh cycle, the slaying of Tiamat by El the sky god—these went hand in hand with a highly-charged religiosity of sacrifice (including child sacrifice) and what is sometimes, anachronistically, labeled as paganism. (The "paganism" label is quite unhelpful here, as it applies both to feminine-centered Earth religions and masculine-centered cults of war and thunder. Both may be nature-based, but the differences seem as large as the commonalities.) In other words, be strong and get tough.

Judaism rejected that. Israelite religion was, as Nietzsche said, the slave revolt in morality: as in so many Biblical narratives, the younger, wimpier son triumphs over the older, stronger one. Humble leaders and even humble mountains merit leadership of the Israelite tribes—themselves humbler and smaller than their enemies. Of course, there is powerful-phallic-sky-god language in the Bible—God as "man of war" or descending on earth in thunderstorms, not to mention the maintenance of sacrificial cults. Yet the trajectory of Jewish ethics seems to be about clothing the naked, caring for the weakest, and subverting those systems in which might makes right.

Today, of course, one often finds Jewish rhetoric married to an ideology of strength, "personal responsibility," power, and militarism. Israeli conservatives, Jewish neocons, Jewish nationalists, and others minimize the narrative of empathy in favor of selected "Old Testament" pronouncements of moral absolutism. The Book of Joshua more than the Book of Isaiah, holiness codes more than the Golden Rule, the powerful more than the dispossessed. It seems to me that these iterations of Jewish power are in tension with fundamental Jewish values, but the fact is, there are lots of fundamental Jewish values, and conservatives can pick the ones they agree with. The Book of Joshua does exist, after all.

Finally, it's impossible to omit the gendered nature of this entire discussion. This is about masculinity—all this valorizing of power and strength and virtue (lit., manliness). Values of meekness, of submissiveness, of inclusion—these are "feminine." The "masculine" wants to take over, divide, organize, rationalize, and conquer. The "feminine" seeks to include, co-exist, nurture. No wonder the Talmudic rabbis valued "cunning" over virtue, as Daniel Boyarin has discussed at length. No wonder Ann Coulter writes adoring Op-Ed pieces about the how large the president's penis is. No wonder many contemporary spiritual teachers see the work they are doing as restoring the exiled Divine Feminine, the aspect of God which is yin instead of yang, cyclical instead of linear, holistic and inclusive, loving instead of tough. (I've long been uneasy with this gender essentialism, both for queer reasons and for justice reasons: talking about the "feminine" is just too close to essentialism and reductivism. But we seem stuck with it for now.)

Of course, the ideal must be some balance between toughness/ construction/authority/phallus/yang on the one hand, and suppleness/ naturalness/autonomy/womb/yin on the other. But everyone preaches a rhetoric of balance. So the question is what *type* of balance we want.

For the Jedi Left, balance means balance within the self. If you're a man, but you've only developed your yang qualities (strength, confidence, toughness), you're incomplete. You may have big muscles, but your yin side (suppleness, sensitivity) is a spiritual 98-pound weakling. This is why the wise, orientalist sages in karate movies always talk about inner strength rather than brute force. Real strength comes from internal mastery.

For the Sith Right, balance is external. Society needs men to be macho, strong, and powerful, balanced externally by sensitive, emotional women. One sees this logic all the time in anti-gay and anti-feminist rhetoric; "gender complementarity," it's called. But it's implicit in any male narrative that celebrates (male) heroism, toughness, and "reality."

With this in mind, I can offer a few arguments for my Jedi values.

First, personally, I prefer a mode of being in which I can be macho and tough sometimes (more steak and rock climbing than light-saber fights, but still) and sensitive other times. It seems like a real shame to diminish the range of our sensitivities. Why hold back from experiencing life in as rich and diverse and flavorful a way as possible? Why not really suck the marrow out of life, feeling its energies fully, radiating yang and yin, exploring toughness and sensitivity? I want to taste Baal energy, Kali energy, Yahweh energy, Shechinah energy; I don't want to limit myself to those flavors deemed to be gender-appropriate.

Second, the model of external balance—men are men, women are women—is more likely to be oppressive than one of internal balance, because not everyone fits into boxes. This under-inclusive model has oppressed women, queer people, and gender-non-conforming people for generations. The Popeye/Olive Oyl model of gender is woefully inadequate. And violent: making wars, destroying the earth, destroying Alderaan. The omelet is not good news for the broken eggs.

Third, shutting down empathy is incompatible with spiritual practice. To get the benefits (relational, personal, mystical) of spirituality, you have to open up. You can't do it if you're shut down, encased, like Darth Vader, in a suit of armor. Empathy is both the result of and prerequisite for spiritual practice. The tough do not awaken.

It would take Anakin twenty-five years to break through the armor, literally and figuratively. But he did do it. It makes me reconsider the exteriors of those who seem not to care. It asks of me a lot of patience, and trust. And it gives me a certain kind of hope.

June 2005

My Journey to Flexidoxy—
or, At Home on the Slippery Slope

1.   Weaving

When I was in my twenties, I wrote a book on the philosophy of *halacha*, as I had come to understand it over a half-decade of being a *baal tshuva*, one who takes on religious observance later in life. Like many a convert, I was zealous about my new faith, but my zeal was accompanied by a combination of intellectual anger and relief—anger that no one had explained the point of Judaism to me, and relief that I'd finally been given the chance to figure it out.

Periodically I look back on that manuscript, even though the certainty of it and the prose now make me cringe. I look at it not so much for its ideas, which I've internalized and taught and repeated and come largely to reject, but for the enthusiasm behind them—the energy of thought, the sense of urgency. Even though it's not a book I would write today, I still find that I believe no one else has written it: a combination of Soloveitchik and Heschel, a *Halachic Man for Dummies*—a decoder of halachic spirituality.

The essential argument of the book was that *halacha* is a trans-subjective spirituality. Most forms of spiritual practice, Eastern and Western, have the individual as their zone of significance. I meditate, or I pray, or I dance, and I have an experience, in my mind, my subjectivity—even if the system in which I'm practicing denies that the individual ultimately exists at all. If I choose to evaluate the experience ('that was a really good davening" or "I didn't get much out of that service") it is necessarily in terms of my own subjective experience.

The distinction between trans-subjective *halacha* and subjective-Hasidic spirituality was less about relativism than about the place in which religion transpires. Although it's less familiar to us than the relativist subjectivist (you have your spiritual feeling, and I've got mine)—it's certainly possible to be a fundamentalist subjectivist too: to have an individual religious experience and still believe that it is universally the best, or absolutely true. This is happening all the time, in our community, in the evangelical Christian Right, and elsewhere. (See my article "Fetishizing the Trigger" for more on that.) So it's not about relativism and fundamentalism.

Rather, it's between subjective and trans-subjective. Much of traditional religion places individual experience beneath some other good: service to God, societal harmony, whatever. This is where most contemporary seekers get off the bus, because as soon as something else is placed above the individual experience, then all kinds of mischief—self-abnegation, repression, asceticism—is now permitted. Come to think of it, maybe many contemporary *baalei tshuva* get on the bus for the same reason: because now the individual's pleasure and pain is not the most important thing in the universe. What a relief—especially if you have a lot of pain.

What I found, though, as I wrote my book and went on my religious journey, was that there was a great liberation in not making the self the primary arbiter of value. I felt as if my religious life had gone through stages. At stage one, I did what I was told, lighting the candles when I was supposed to, eating only the right foods. I did this probably out of a desire to "do the right thing" and please authority figures—mainly I was just following orders. At stage two, I came to see that some of these practices really felt good; now I lit the candles when I was supposed to, but not to impress authority figures—to have an experience. Lighting candles felt good. But, of course, not always. Sometimes Shabbat coming in meant denying myself various pleasures or activities—what then? At stage three, I placed God ahead of me. Now I lit the candles not because I was told, and not because it felt good, but because it was part of a system in which the "right thing" was larger than "what felt good." And from that system, from the participation in a community and structure that was larger than myself, I derived a sense of value that was far more powerful than my individual pleasure. Even when lighting the candles gave me no subjective feeling at all, it had an objective reality that was outside my own preference—and that felt like the point.

Ten years later, it's hard to resist the urge to ask why I was so interested in that "sense of value," and to psychoanalyze this supposedly non-subjective religious experience. But at the time, it felt like a deeply healthy reordering of priorities, as well as an authentic reflection of what the Jewish tradition was actually saying. This was *avodat hashem*, the service of something greater than myself. This was what was meant by commandment. And this was revelation: that value exists, outside the mind, and out there in the material world. Not in some spiritual (read: non-existent) universe, but in the actual, tangible arrangement of reality itself. It matters that the food is this way and not that. It matters that at this time, this is done and this is not. Thus, as Soloveitchik wrote so eloquently (too eloquently, I thought at the time, since few people could understand him), the material world is both sanctified and signified.

But *halachic* spirituality was very subtle, I thought. It's hard to notice, this trans-subjective value—after all, its defining feature is that you might not necessarily feel it. Buberian and Heschelian Hasidism delivered the goods: do this practice, and you'll feel something. Soloveitchik's Misnagdism didn't promise any such reward. But in my practice, and my writing, I felt it was there, and appreciated it, and came, even, to love it.

2. Unraveling

Now, as I look at my life and my practice, it feels like I've lost it. Although my life is still almost orthopractic in its observance, at least in some areas, the theory is gone. And the "almost" undermines any pretension to the "ortho." What happened? And where am I now?

What's happened over the last five years or so has been a slow, gentle unraveling of the *halachic* tapestry I wove over the previous five. First, I came to see the supposedly trans-subjective values within *halacha* as, in fact, highly subjective—just someone else's subjectivity. For me, the most obvious example has been in the area of sexuality, in which ambiguous Biblical verses have been (subjectively) interpreted in excessively broad and oppressive ways, by (subjectively-minded) people with their own particular agendas. But it hasn't only been sexuality. It's clear that the dietary laws, the laws of Shabbat, and the laws of prayer all have undergone radical, extensive, and subjectively-oriented revision over the last several hundred years, often along paths that may once have been wise, but don't seem particularly so today. Does it make sense for the daily prayer obligation to swell from five pages in the morning and afternoon, to fifty pages in the morning, ten in the afternoon, and twenty in the evening? Does it make sense for the scientifically-minded *halachot* of *kashrut* to (d)evolve into something that resembles voodoo? I don't know the answers to these questions, but I know that the ways these laws have unfolded have been anything but objective.

Second, I've noticed that the predicted catastrophe of pick-and-choose just hasn't happened. Here again, sexuality led. I thought that when I came out, that that would be the end of my religious observance. After all, now the balloon had been punctured, and the whole system compromised. But in fact, the opposite was the case. Not lesser love, but greater. Not less spirituality, but more. Likewise when I began to allow myself small exceptions to the rules. Taking the subway on Shabbat, when there was nothing going on nearby but a good invitation somewhere else, made Shabbat better, and brought me closer to God. It still doesn't feel good swiping my MetroCard—but that moment is outweighed by hours of spirit.

Third, as my practice has slowly liberalized over the past five years, I've tried repeatedly to "check in" with why I'm doing it at all. As I wrote last fall, I think that guilt and fear play much larger roles than any of us would care to admit. I'm always interested, and bemused, when someone in the orthodox model refuses to answer the question of "why do it," insisting that it's not up to them, it's a commandment, and don't you see that's the whole point, that it's not up to us. I always want to ask (and sometimes do): well, why not disobey? Some, of course, will respond with an account of reward and punishment—but these are not the interesting ones. More subtle minds understand that, even if there is *s'char v'din*, it's got to be so different from any conventional understanding of reward and punishment as to be, essentially, not reward and punishment. One needn't even mention the Holocaust to point to it, and remember that the old worldview only makes sense with extensive redefinition.

So more intelligent folk rarely have recourse to such concepts. Rather, they'll point to the essence of covenant itself, either in the traditional mythic understanding of *Torah mi'Sinai*, or in some modified Kantian, or Maimonidean, or even Kaplanian sense. These accounts do hold water—and there are many more good ones as well—but I always want to ask why we need them to. Yes, the explanations make sense, but so do contrary ones. So do nihilistic ones. Why choose the righteous? Why choose the good?

Here's where it gets more interesting, because here, unlike within the mythic structures themselves, is the real juice of individual choice, and that, not communitarianism or covenant, is the defining feature of (post-) modern religious life. You can choose to subscribe to a system that says it isn't your choice, and that God has commanded you—but it's still your choice to buy into the system. And there are usually interesting reasons: a passion for justice, a yearning for God, a desire for order or for ethics... or in my case, love.

3. Post-weaving

Today, I regard my halachic observance not as the pursuit of a trans-subjective spiritual value, but as a dozen roses I buy for my lover. Why not eleven, instead of twelve? Why roses, instead of dandelions? There's no real reason, other than the fact that, in our shared cultural understanding, a dozen roses means "I love you" in a way that eleven dandelions does not. I find, when I break Shabbat or kashrut, that I can feel a little cut off from love—whether internal or external, I leave to theologians. It doesn't feel good. I concede that some of why it doesn't feel good is pure guilt—but alongside that guilt is, I think, a genuine desire for intimacy with the universe, which I conceptualize as God. As Buber said, I can't really say much about whether I believe in God in the third person, as an It with these or those properties. But when we are speaking of God in the second person, when I am speaking to You, then of course You exist and have been laughing the whole time at my all-too-clever brain's peregrinations in philosophy.

This perspective also helps me reconcile myself to other religions, and to my co-religionists who make different choices. Other cultures have different cultural understandings—lilies instead of roses. And so do other individuals. I have my practice, which brings me a sense of closeness and love of Heaven—and other people do their thing. No need for universality, even as I appreciate connecting with an ancient community in the forms of my own practice. It matters to me that tefillin have been worn for thousands of years, and that they have, I feel, old magic within them, far deeper than anything I could invent. There is still the urge to spread the gospel, to bring to other people these gifts which I feel I've been given—but thankfully, there's no real impulse to convert them.

This new view, though, stands in stark contrast to my earlier system of belief, and is as anarchic as it is seemingly inoffensive. It seems, on the surface, like an ordinary, unoriginal form of religious practice—to do what feels good. But it isn't quite that, because if one is attentive, a dozen complications arise. For example, "what feels good" in a deep sense often has little to do with what feels good at the moment. Maybe this week I'm not in the mood to keep Shabbos at all, but over time, I know from experience how that lack will come to feel. Which to choose? And how to know in advance—maybe davening every day will transform me in a way that I couldn't possibly imagine until I do it. And what about deliberately not making an idol out of my own preferences—as in relationships, sometimes it feels good to deny oneself what feels good. And, conversely, as in relationships, without boundaries that are clear ahead of time, all of life becomes a slippery slope.

I've come to make a home for myself on the slippery slope. It's precarious, but there's more open air than in the dense flatlands of *halacha*, a geography which never accommodated me as much as I wanted it to. So that's where I am now: honoring these ancient tools for connection, while not buying into their myths of origination; recognizing that sometimes the tools will work and sometimes they won't, but doing them even some of the times they won't; and, at the place which had at one time symbolized all that was wrong with subjective Jewish practice: the salad bar. There are practices I do, and practices I don't do. And there are those I do sometimes but not others. It's inconsistent, and it's not an ideology; indeed, I far prefer those who admit its heresy to those who try to rationalize it into some "evolving" conception of "Jewish law and tradition." That kind of theorizing has a place, since it gives thousands of Jews the sense that they are being good people and not heretics. But for myself, I embrace the apikorsus of the religious salad bar.

Lately the term 'flexidoxy' has begun to gain currency to describe this non-ideological (even anti-ideological) way of Jewish practice and belief. It still sounds a little too Orthodox for me—as if, well, "I'm Orthodox, but." Which I'm not. But of all the labels I've considered (neo-Karaite, Reconstructionist, Heterodox, postmodern-orthodox), it seems to fit the best. After all, the categories I'm working within are still those defined by the rabbis. And while flexidoxy is a break from the foundational belief that the rabbis are authorized to interpret law for me, it's not a break from the general categories of *halacha* as a mode of response to the Infinite.

Maybe thousands of other people make this break all the time, and think nothing of it. But as you, my readers, know, I don't like to think nothing of it. In my view, thinking nothing of it is disrespectful to truth, even to God. And it's imprudent, because if we think nothing of our heresy, we won't keep it under control. We (or our children) will slip down that slope, into a place devoid of value and connection, and wonder how we ever ended up there. The answer will be simple: like the Walmart and McDonald's consumers who bewail the loss of their small town's center, we will have created our reality through ignorance. So I want to conclude with a few principles of Thoughtful Flexidoxy, based on my last few years of working with them.

The first critical element, for me at least, is taking discernment seriously. At an actual salad bar, I don't think too much about exactly which ingredients to include. But if religious practices are chosen this cavalierly, the only god being served is the self—the same small ego that is responsible for all of my suffering and alienation. That, to me, is an exact inversion of the priorities of religion. To be sure, many of the so-called pious are practicing just that, making religious rhetoric and symbol the servants of their own egoic desires. But it's an even more obvious danger for those of us on the religious salad bar, picking and choosing. So it has to be not "picking and choosing," but carefully discerning, weighing, experimenting, testing the waters and the ice—processes which require both literacy with the sources (*Chicken Soup for the Soul* won't cut it) and spiritual attentiveness to the self. If subjectivism is to be the foundation, then it needs to be attended to, nurtured, and improved.

A second critical element of thoughtful flexidoxy is cultivating *ahavah* as seriously as the pious cultivate *yirah*. It's no use making love the ground of religious practice if love is left untilled. Just as the pious remind themselves of God's terrible judgment, and of the need to repent, so I need to remind myself—through meditation, walking in the woods, prayer, and study—of the abundance of love available in every moment, if I simply surrender my desire for it to be other than what it is. Then I remember, and then I can choose—not from a place of rationalization, or fear, or convenience, but from as close as I can get to authenticity. All this talk of love may be clichéd, intellectually speaking, but who wants to be an intellectual when it comes to love? Once again, the parallel to human relationship is apparent—since being an intellectual in bed isn't the best recipe for romance either.

Third, a subjective anti-system such as flexidoxy is authentic only insofar as it is recognized as being what it is: a heresy. This has two aspects: that of faith, and that of questioning. First, heretics are not unbelievers. After all, if I didn't believe, truly, that the *Avinu Sh'ba'shamayim* can be accessed by means of the ancient Jewish pathways of *halacha* and study, then I'd just junk the whole thing, do my Insight Buddhist meditation, and be done with it. That, however, is not my God. No, a heretic is a believer. And just as discernment and love require cultivation, so too does belief: in this case, an endless process of active remembering, with whatever practices work toward that end. Torah study (in its broadest sense), bodily exercise, enlarging the heart, acts of lovingkindness—these are a few very traditional, and very effective, ways to remember and remind. The alternative, again, is a religion of compromise and convenience that deserves to be rejected by the next generation.

At the same time, flexidoxy and the other salad bar heresies are not ideologies. I'm not claiming, as the Conservative movement does, that what I'm doing is God's will, or what *halacha* was always meant to be, or part and parcel of a centuries-old Jewish narrative. It is part of a very old Jewish practice, which is to be gentle and flexible in the adaptation of Jewish norms to life. But it won't do as an ideology, or as a practice that can be prescribed to others. I don't even trust it completely for myself, since I know how often even my best-intentioned discernment leads to disaster.

For those coming from a secularist or accommodationist perspective, all this may be much ado about nothing. So what, you eat fish in the *treif* restaurant—the rest of us are enjoying the shrimp. Certainly, I'm not making any claim that this "journey" is significant cosmologically, or objectively—that would be contrary to the pluralistic foundation of flexidoxy itself. But personally, since *halacha* is one of my core practices, and since it contains within itself a fundamentalist justification, the uprooting of that foundation is both catastrophic within the system's own categories, and of some moment to me beyond them. Frequently, it fills me with doubt and fear. But when I succeed in surrendering and remembering, I see again the laughing, patient face of God.

July 2006

Religion and Insanity

1.   Mother Eagle

A friend of mine has been communing with Mother Eagle, and I don't know what to do.

For the last several years, my spiritual path has been about cultivating more openness, more sensitivity, and more awareness to the subtle shifts of energy (whatever that means) that otherwise escape our notice. Beginning on my first meditation retreat, years ago, I learned that the reflexive doubt and cynicism which I had been so proud of, and which are such fixtures in contemporary literary culture, are often not the sophistication they pretend to be, but a defense mechanism, bespeaking not cultured sophistication but shame, fear, or even ignorance. I've learned this through my own subjective experience, and through conversations and interactions with other people: What seems to be analytical cleverness is often a kind of cowardice.

Cowardice—or culture. When someone tells me about UFOs, or the power of intercessionary prayer, or astrology, or 'energy,' the doubt kicks in immediately. It's how I've been raised. Am I really being more careful, critical, skeptical, and truth-seeking? Or am I just being committed to a worldview that Responsible People hold? Doubt is an instinct before it is a critique.

So a cultivated openness—not erasing doubt and judgment, but suspending them long enough for experience to unfold—feels important. And significant shifts do sometimes occur. Only a few years ago, for example, I felt sure that the notion of *energy* was nonsense. But then, in a non-chemically-altered spiritual practice, I experienced the phenomenon myself: How, with my hands inches above my partner's body and with his eyes closed, I could cause *energetic* changes in his body. I moved, and he moved; I concentrated energy, and he shook. Weird, yes—perhaps so weird that, as one of my editors once told me, I lose credibility by talking about it. But I'm not saying I know what happened; I'm just saying there was a phenomenon with no other explanation that I've been able to generate. I still don't know what energy is, but I know that there is more to heaven and earth than is dreamt of in scientific-materialist philosophy.

But openness still has its limits. As my excursions into the New Age progress, I've met weirder and weirder people. Usually, that's a good thing; the world would be a lot better off with more weird people than normal ones, and *weird* is often a reduction of *wise*. Other times, though, weird is just weird. I find myself having moments a bit like the scene in Augusten Burroughs' *Running with Scissors*, when Dr. Finch, the oddball psychiatric Svengali who acts as a surrogate father for Burroughs, says that the shapes of his bowel movements are messages from God. We've wondered about Finch's sanity throughout the book (and film), but in that moment, we realize that he has been nuts all along. In a narrative searching for a sane center, Finch reveals that he isn't going to be it.

So, when my friend tells me that he's in touch with Mother Eagle, I don't know what to do. On the one hand, I want to be open. On the other hand, I don't believe in the things he believes in, and don't see how a sane person could. To begin with, as Sam Harris has lately shown in his books, mythic religion isn't a harmless eccentricity. In the case of Mother Eagle, sure—but in the case of Jesus Christ and Muhammad, it's causing war all around the world.

Of course, few New Age practitioners are ethnocentric or violent. On the contrary, they tend to appreciate a potpourri of spiritual practices— darshan, diksha, davening, whatever—because these practices are understood functionally, in terms of what they do for the self, rather than mythically. Certainly, in my own life, I'm not fighting crusades or jihads. But I can see how my own religious beliefs cause me to be a little more violent in my own, limited domain. When Friday evening is approaching and I'm not ready, I get antsy, angry, and tense. I lash out at myself or other people. I get *really* pissed if my kosher meal gets lost by the airline.

And those peaceful New Age meditators? Watch what happens if you move their sacred yoga mat.

Still, it does seem to me that non-mythic religion successfully avoids the problems of violence and ethnocentrism that seem an inexorable part of mythic religion. Meditation provides the same sense of groundedness that religion provides, except that it is grounded in real, transitory, moment-to-moment experience rather than in myth, tribe, or code. Contemplation opens the heart, and makes one more, rather than less, appreciative of other religious paths. Indeed, that is a big part of the point.

But even if we set aside the dangers of myth, and recognize that, with the right pluralistic and contemplative training, many of them can indeed be avoided, there's still the issue of the beliefs themselves.

2. Don't worry, it's just an archetype

The most obvious way in which religious beliefs seem disconnected from rationality is when they make claims about reality that fly in the face of available evidence. For example, Rev. Ted Haggard, before he stepped down as president of the National Association of Evangelicals amid accusations that he paid a man for sex (repeatedly, over a period of three years—and did crystal meth to boot), told Barbara Walters that heaven was a real, physical place, beyond the known universe, where you could eat all you want and never get fat, and where there were mansions for all the faithful. Such ideas, like the belief in a physical Devil (held by 70% of Americans, according to Pew Institute surveys) or the notion that Christ will appear on Earth in the next 50 years (held by 50%), are so tied to supernatural myth, superstition, and unquestioned traditions received from authority, that modern and postmodern people can easily raise their eyebrows at anyone who holds them.

Intelligent spiritual practitioners today, and non-reductive scholars of religion, often take a different approach, which attempts to preserve the integrity of religious belief per se, even while dismissing the actual contents of those beliefs: to interpret mythic language in non-mythic terms that renders it scientifically OK. As Maimonides observed more than 850 years ago, the genius of religion is that it works on multiple levels. Yes, ordinary people really believe the myths—that there is a Mother Eagle out there, or a physical place called heaven, and a creation in seven earthly days—and that helps them order their lives, be more ethical, and have a sense of the sacred. Philosophers—that is, those of us with the privilege and aptitude for reflective thought—know that these myths aren't literally true, but that they still contain important truths, and truths which, when reduced to concept, are hard for most people to wrap their heads around, or care about. Thus all myth can be stripped of its dubious truth-value, and appreciated for its deep power to inspire.

So, following the Rambam, and modern Reconstructionist Judaism, and Unitarianism, and countless other thinkers and movements who have sought to demythologize religion while not dismissing it either, Mother Eagle isn't *really* a being, out there, with a consciousness and a self. She's an archetype, a representation of something deep in our unconscious—and more power to my friend for finding imagery to access it. Likewise, it's not that the Tarot cards are *really* magic; they just give his own deeply skilled intuition a structure in which to operate. It's just a matter of interpretation. Anyone can have a religious experience, but, as Ken Wilber develops at great length, that experience will be interpreted according to their stage of intellectual/emotional development. Similar experiences will be interpreted in different ways—and some interpretations are indeed better than others, ethically in particular.

Fair enough in theory, but put into practice, I'm not so sure.

First, the metaphorical/symbolic/archetypal understanding of Mother Eagle (or Jesus, or whatever) is so distant from the literal one, that I wonder if it really make senses to share a common vocabulary for such different phenomena as beings floating in the ether and archetypes in the mind. And do I really want to quiz my friend on where he is on a Wilberian spectrum of theological sophistication? Isn't that a bit arrogant—or at least alienating?

Second, functionally speaking, it's possible that myth only works when you *do* believe in it, when you make a commitment to it and say: Well, it's possible that the world operates according to wholly scientific-material principles, and it's possible that it operates according to mysterious spiritual ones—and I commit to the latter. And not spiritual in the way I usually refer to it—not in the sense of "waking up to the miraculous truth of ordinary experience." But spiritual in the juicy, mythic way— with Mother Eagle and the rest as actual energies both *out there* and *in here.* You have to really believe this stuff—even if, from my still-stuck-in-skepticism perspective, you seem totally nuts. That's when myth really gets going, and how evangelism gets out the vote.

Third, even the symbolic Mother Eagle can lead to trouble, because of the weight given to subjective, generally non-rational, experience, and the disconnect from reality that that seems to indicate. This is the point of Harris's observation (in *Letter to a Christian Nation*) that "If someone told us that God spoke to them through a toaster, we would conclude that this person is insane. I fail to see how the presence or absence of the toaster makes a difference." That is, even without ludicrous notions of a physical heaven where the saved eat cupcakes while the damned burn in hell, there is something about the religious experience itself that seems to bespeak a break from reality.

Which, given what most mystics say about the truthfulness of our concepts of reality, may be exactly what they want.

3. Are You Experienced?

What Western Buddhism, the New Age, evangelical Christianity, and Jewish Renewal all have in common is that, unlike much of traditional Western religion, they are tied to subjective experiences. Whether interpreted in terms of myth or not, whether mysticism is a mindstate or an encounter with God, these forms of religion are experiential in nature. The sense of unity, the holy spirit, conversations with angels—these phenomena differ in theology, but all weight the impulses of imagination and intuition over the hard data of the rational and perceptual faculties.

We may not like to acknowledge this similarity, but once one strips out the content of the myth, the experiential reality of the evangelical and the experiential reality of the Buddhist are more alike than not. Yes, one ascribes the experience to Christ, and the other purely to the mind—but both give weight to experience over apparent, conventional understandings of how the world works. For example, when I am on retreat, and observing how all the habits of the mind are thoroughly impersonal, I know, with a certainty, that the idea of a separate self is an illusion, and that this consciousness does not belong to me in any meaningful way. It occurs here, in this brain, but its contents are wholly borrowed from stuff outside. The sense of certainty—that's the kicker, because it's that sense that we're told to trust.

And more than that, if I admit it: I feel a closeness to some kind of larger consciousness; an access to an internal wisdom that feels as though it, too, comes from *beyond*; and above all an ease, and an overpowering love. It scares me, in my rational, normal state, how in love with God I can become. Because that love, that sense of closeness, all of it, no matter how I try to cleanse it of myth, is still a subjective experience that seems difficult to distinguish from madness.

So then, with whom do I have more in common—the Evangelicals who trust their inspiration, or the literate atheists with whom I like to go to dinner? Really, I and people like me are split down the middle: I am aligned with the atheists on matters of science and cosmology, but aligned with the religionists on questions of spirit and subjectivity.

Maybe that's why I feel myself increasingly distanced from my angel-channeling friend—because he's not split down the middle, but has instead gone over to the other side. Or rather, to *a* side, as opposed to my have-my-cake-and-eat-it-too perch, astride the fence of doubt. With my meditation practice, I can feel grounded anywhere—but perhaps that sense of groundedness prolongs my indecision. Whereas, if I trust my experience, then I, too, must admit that I am on the side of the Tarot cards, the evangelicals, and the New Agers—without all their myth, but necessarily open to the possibility that the myth contains deep and useful symbolism for the unconscious mind.

And why, exactly, do I not believe the myth? Because it is more accurate to interpret my *devekut* as a mindstate, and condescendingly look down on the 90% of the people in the world who mistake their mindstate for a real, live deity? Their inspiration for *divrei elohim chayim*, the words of the living God? Is that really wisdom?

From each side—the mythic-religious one, the non-mythic-contemplative one, and the materialist one—everybody else looks insane. Who's more nuts: the Orthodox Jew who believes that God, the creator of Alpha Centauri and the Virgo Supercluster, wrote a grammatically bizarre and narratively confusing text—or me, who thinks that Judaism is somehow important even though 90% of Jews think that I've got it deeply wrong?

Who's more nuts: the guy who gets off the treadmill and gives up on conventional success—or the businessman who spends most of his waking hours chasing money and possessions? Which is more nuts: the retreat center or Wal-Mart? The ashram or Le Cirque? The church or the television? I can make pro- and con- arguments for all of them, and all of them are internally consistent, and externally nuts. Is it all just a matter of taste? Which insanity you choose to embrace?

The trouble with non-mythic, it's-all-an-archetype contemplative practice is that, unlike mythic religion, it postpones forever the need to make a choice. You don't have to believe in the parting of the Red Sea, or the apocalypse of 2012; you just go on meditating. And yet, what religion most teaches, ironically, is the importance of choice. As Pascal formulated it, the question is not whether belief or unbelief are coherent—both are—but rather which world one chooses to inhabit. And in making that decision, criteria other than truthfulness are required: personal satisfaction, peace in the world, ethics, meaning, joy.

In the spiritual world, there's a cute saying that "Dancers look insane to people who can't hear the music." In the mythic religious world, that's a truth claim, really: that there is music, that it's not just our imaginations. There are angels, demons, forces beyond our ken. But even without those mythic claims, it's still a strong notion: that even if any interpretation of the mystical mindstate is imaginary—that is, even if God (or the gods, or goddesses) is just in my imagination—life is far richer for living a richly imaginal life. Yes, it's a bit like psychosis, but so is dancing, right? Shaking one's hips to some melody, rhythm, and tone? What's the point of *that*?

I hear those voices a lot, every time I get on the literal or figurative dance floor. But if I want to enjoy myself, I try to turn them off and hear the music instead. This is the call of the circle against the line, the spiritual against the secular, the sexual against the proper: it is the Presence, and She knows how to shake it.

The irony for me is that, in trying to avoid making the "insane" choice, I'm driving myself crazy. I don't know which part of myself to trust, and so I flit from side to side, occasionally admitting that I am a mystic, then backing up and making sure everything has a rational, scientific explanation. Going on retreats to have deep insights—and they are not really experiences, like drug states, as they are times when the mind is quiet enough to see clearly—but then coming back and doubting those experiences, or reducing them to phenomena of the mind. Back and forth.

There is, obviously, a time for both: a time to deconstruct, and a time to dance. But one thing I know that I'm tired of is this attempt to have it both ways, or make it just a matter of balance, or have some of each. I've grown tired of what looks like indecision, and it's a cop-out. Real spiritual growth, and real mainstream success, requires commitment and choice. Pascal was right, but he didn't say how hard it was to look behind at what is lost.

I find myself envying both my friends who've dived into the chaos of the spiritual imagination, angels and all, and those who have become householders, professors, and rich. Whereas I keep trying to have it both ways, still waiting for the thunderbolt to knock me to, or out of, my senses—once and for all.

December 2006

Stop Seeking:
Paradoxes of the Spiritual Path

1. Stopping Seeking Takes Seeking

The point of the spiritual search is to learn to stop seeking.

Unfortunately, doing so takes effort, because human beings are genetically and environmentally conditioned to seek all the time. Every moment, most of us are thinking about the future or the past, chasing something pleasant, or trying to avoid something unpleasant. It's what animals do. Thus contemplatives seek ways to learn to stop seeking.

There's nothing wrong with seeking, except suffering and God. First, see what happens if you seek distraction but can't find it. Or what happens when you can't sleep. For me, even when I do get what I want, there's the potential for suffering when it's taken away, or when it doesn't fully meet my desires. Or when, having enjoyed it once, I want to taste it again. Second, seeking necessarily privileges something which isn't here (i.e., that which is being sought) over that which is. From a religious perspective, if "that which is" happens to be What Is, that is, YHVH, the Divine, well, that's quite a shame. God may be everywhere—but how often can I say _hineini_, here am I? From a non-religious perspective, it's obvious that life is more worthwhile when you're there to enjoy it. How many times have we all eaten a meal and barely tasted the food? Let alone had sex while worrying about how it's all going. To "stop seeking" is thus to start living.

Once in a while, we are forced to stop seeking, as in peak experiences of amazement or delight or danger. And sometimes life is so pleasant— holding a baby, relaxing after sex, eating a gourmet meal—that seeking stops on its own. But most of the time, to learn to stop seeking requires some kind of work—in particular, a search for the ways in which seeking is still going on, and the ways it can be, if not stopped, at least relaxed a little bit. This "search for non-search" could be as simple as remembering to relax or as life-altering as having kids, or meditating, or religion. But what it really is about is the purification of the present moment from desires or fears of other ones. It's about showing up.

2. Seeking to Stop Seeking Can Stop Stopping-Seeking

Of course, there's always a catch: in this case, at least three of them. First, seeking ways to stop seeking can become, itself, a narcotically addictive search. Comparing this meditation technique against that one. Searching for ever-more-transcendent peak experiences—"well, I did really forget myself and stop seeking last time, but I'd like to do it even more." Falling into the trap of thinking that it's the particular way of walking that matters on the journey, instead of showing up for every step of it. Talking about meditation instead of doing it. And, despite oneself, turning the whole thing into a goal-oriented process with goals and accoutrements. It's said that spirituality can turn into a kind of narcissism, but narcissism doesn't quite capture the angst of unbridled self-reflection. After all, Narcissus just saw his beautiful reflection—in meditation, you see an ever-more-clarifying picture of the good, the bad, and the ugly. Thus endless self-reflection can end not in clarity and calm, but neurosis and paralysis.

Second, there is what Trungpa Rinpoche called "spiritual materialism," in which the path to non-self becomes instead a path of gratifying and pleasing the self. Yoga, meditation, prayer, entheogens, energy work—all of these can easily become about enriching, enlarging, and serving the self, when they are meant to do the opposite. Spirituality can become a consumer lifestyle, and a way of enhancing, relaxing, and generally pleasing Me—witness the success of the ego-empowering Kabbalah Centre, and the promises of eternal youth from some of today's most financially successful institutions. Even a sincere motivation for learning can becomes twisted: the search for occult, hidden realities can lead to both surprising truths about subtle energies that otherwise escape our notice—or a great cosmic treasure hunt, in which the goal is to know as much esoteric nonsense as possible.

Third, because spiritual practices bring about highly pleasant mind states, and among the most indescribably beautiful sensations I have ever experienced, they can spoil precisely what they are meant to enhance. Give me more of the mind-blowing contentment, bliss, and sensations of unity I feel on meditation retreat—the regular pleasures aren't enough. Like a connoisseur of wine no longer able to enjoy ordinary merlot, I only want the extraordinary stuff. Thus the practice of waking up to ordinary pleasure can undermine exactly that.

In all three of these cases, the search to stop seeking becomes, itself, a search with goals. It's tough, because, as goals go, bliss, contentment, and the deepest joy I've ever experienced are pretty good ones, and my experience is that meditation brings them about. But that is one of the paradoxes of the spiritual path: like love, you only truly experience it when you're willing to let it go.

3. Stop Seeking for a Reason to Stop Seeking

There's one final way that the search for not seeking itself becomes a search: searching for a justification of the search itself. Naturally, since spiritual practice takes a lot of time and effort, and since it gets sneered at by many smart people, those of us who do it spend a lot of time explaining why it's so important. Not just something we want to do, and not just something which helps life be a little juicier, a little more meaningful—but really Important. Thus one hears all the time that "the purpose of our being here is to awaken to who we are," or that people who aren't "awake" aren't truly happy. Nonsense. That's just the New Age version of Jews thinking they're the Chosen People, or Christians thinking that only Christ can save you. The fact is, we spiritual seekers want to be doing what we're doing. That's it. We notice that it brings us more happiness, more joy, more equanimity, and we want that. Maybe we're just more dissatisfied than other people. Maybe we just like new mind states. But the rhetoric that "what I want is the most important thing to want" is just odious, no matter how soothing the voice that says it.

I've come to a place in my meditation practice where I'm okay with saying that it's just my preference to do it. And I understand that, for many people, a less-reflective life is simply more enjoyable. My editor here at *Zeek* had occasion to say, as he reviewed my latest round of religious self-questioning, that "one reason why I am so much happier now that I was a few years ago was that I'm a) too busy to do much contemplation and b) 'settled.' I picked a city, a partner, and a level of religious observance and declared to myself 'Here I am.' It works most of the time."

There was a time when I would look down on this kind of "settling," either blaming it for all the unconscious evil we do in the world, or castigating it in the name of Socrates. But no longer. I do still think that some degree of "afflicting the comfortable" is necessary to keep us honest—without some way to disturb the calm of a peaceful, bourgeois life, it's quite easy to be ethically irresponsible and spiritually somnolent. But there are many ways to do that, and many comfortable, settled people who are, after all, quite responsible and awake.

Nor do I buy into the myth that meditation and spirituality are really for everyone. For many people, the resistance to meditation does indeed come from fear, but for many others, it's just not of interest. In fact, I sometimes wonder why it's even for me. Why am I not simply satisfied with the ordinary, un-enhanced, un-mindful pleasures that most people seem perfectly content to enjoy? Yes, at the extreme, such a lifestyle is a degraded form of human existence: draining away in front of the television, marching from mall to SUV and back again, being programmed by the vulgarities of pop culture. But that's just the extreme, and a bit of a cliché in any event. The reality is that there are many good ways to enjoy a good life. Contemplation is a minority interest.

Searching for the reason that spirituality is important is just the kind of "seeking" that the spiritual search is meant to arrest. Why do we contemplatives need to explain why everyone else is not a contemplative? Why can't we admit that we're on the spiritual path because it's what we like to do? Personally, I find meditative practice leads to more enjoyment of the simple pleasures of my home, my lover, my career. But I also find it interesting in and of itself. Exploring ideas, refining the mind, and learning the subtleties of attention and desire are not, for me, stages to go through until I "find myself." I find them interesting on their own. Isn't that enough?

Now, it's also true that I am just the kind of person who likes to explore, explain, and articulate. As Alan Watts once asked rhetorically,

> Why not sit back and let things take their course? Simply that it is part of 'things taking their course' that I write. As a human being it is just my nature to enjoy and share philosophy. I do this in the same way that some birds are eagles and some doves, some flowers lilies and some roses.

That effortlessness, that justificationlessness—that's the ticket. If I keep trying to justify my search for not seeking, the stories will never end. "Maybe I do dislike my ego more than some other people do. Maybe I was just raised neurotic, and so spiritual practice is more important for me than for other people. Or maybe I just can't figure life out, dammit, and am too weird to be successful like my more mainstream-writer and lawyer friends." Now, in the life that I have chosen—"integral" on good days, "fence-straddling" on bad ones—some of this "bad" seeking (comparing, striving, demanding, berating) is inevitable. It's hard to cultivate enough ambition to succeed but not so much that success becomes the only goal, and competition the only way to achieve it. It's also hard, having given up a lucrative mainstream career, not to look at my peers who stayed on the straight and narrow, and flourished. So... stay with me... I'm learning to stop seeking the reason why I'm seeking to stop seeking.

See, isn't spiritual life fun?

4.   The Kicker (God)

Much of the wisdom of "stop seeking" comes from the four noble truths of Buddhism, which boil down to the observation that suffering exists because of clinging/seeking/wanting/thirsting, and that it can be ended by learning to stop seeking so much. What's great about the Four Noble Truths is that, now that the Buddha said them, they seem intuitively correct, and, more importantly, can be tested in a relatively short period of time. But there is one final element, which might just be the kicker.

Stopping seeking is more than just good for you, in the way that flossing is good for you. It is the only way to turn down the incessant demands of the ego so that it's possible to identify not with the ultimately unreal "small self" created by the illusion of interior consciousness, but with the greater processes of which each being is only a part. This is the Buddhist teaching of *anatta* (non-self), the Vedanta teaching of *tat tvam asi* ("you are that"), the Chabad teaching of acosmism: that what seems to be "me" isn't really me at all. Sure, I seem like "Jay" most of the time, especially when "Jay" wants something. But when I look at this personality closely, I really do see how all of its myriad pieces come from somewhere else: my upbringing, or my education, or wherever. "Jay" is really just a bundle of these other things, a temporary one at that, and a bundle which, on its own, never actually does anything; it's always one of the other things. A tactic I learned as a child; a talent I was born with; a way of speaking I picked up along the way. Each act, each decision, and each preference is ultimately ascribable (and, on a quiet retreat, observably so) to one of these sticks in the bundle. So what is so important about this "me" that needs to get fed, and that thinks that if it doesn't get what it wants, the world is somehow in disarray?

The "me" is a phenomenon, but not an essential one, and it is possible to stop identifying with it so much... by stopping seeking. And then the "non-seeking, non-desiring mind" (in Zen teacher Genpo Roshi's words) appears sufficient, blissful, ever-present, enlightened. And not "me." If you've never actually experienced that mental space, this all probably sounds quite vague. But if you've been there, you know it transcends words.

Even in talking about the "non-seeking, non-desiring mind," however, there's a bit of seeking, of justifying, involved. Am I, at such moments, really in touch with Mind, Brahman, God, or whatever? Certainly, it makes sense on paper: if the self is an illusion, a phenomenon that only exists when seen from a certain perspective, who is doing all this knowing, if it's not "Jay"? And it also does feel that way, as if the quality of the universe's knowing is present in my own, miniature knowing as well. It feels quite certain indeed. But then, we feel certain about a lot of things that turn out not to be true. Which is it—cosmic consciousness, or a nice bit of relaxation?

What I've found, lately, is that the claim to cosmic consciousness is itself a form of seeking. As if it's not enough that meditation makes me happy and opens my eyes to pleasure and pain—it has to also take me to God, which is somehow more present when I'm relaxed than when I'm stressed out. As if "God," rather than simply experience or insight, is somehow necessary for the deal to be worth it—and that God has a certain flavor, which is exalted or great or wise. As if something has to be holy to be worthy.

Whereas, when I'm able to sit back and let be whatever will be, then real receiving (*kabbalah*) can take place. Then God, in the sense in which I can understand the term, really does show up—precisely because I'm not looking for God, labeling an experience as God, or in any way claiming something is or isn't God. This is not the God of special mind states, particular revelations, or spiritual "holiness" in the way that makes you want to wave your hands in the air, but the omnipresent God—the one who shows up not because God wasn't there before, but because I was looking somewhere else. And so, as one of my teachers once said, stopping the war has no limits. Again I relearn and relearn and relearn: Stop the war against what is, stop looking somewhere else for God.

February 2007

Jay Michaelson   153

Shifting from Myth to Function

What does religion do? Television entertains, travel inspires, law patrols the boundaries—but what about the practices of religion? What purpose do they serve?

Given the amount of effort put into preserving religion, and the amount of trouble religion causes in the world, I think these are important questions. But beneath them lies an even more important foundation: that religion is meant to do something in the first place.

Let me start with a story. Last Rosh Hashanah, I blew the shofar in the woods. Due to a variety of circumstances, I was away from my family and not near a synagogue. But I wanted to observe the holiday, albeit in a highly unorthodox way, and I wanted to do it in a setting that felt close to nature, perhaps even close to God. So, one cold day last September, I schlepped a shofar out into the forest, donned a *tallit* and sounded the blasts as prescribed by Jewish law.

It was a profound experience. Transcending theology and rationality, the ancient sound of a ram's horn instantly stripped away layers of ego, rationale, doubt and even the notion of time itself. I felt transported to some primordial moment of religious awe, at once pre-rational and trans-rational, nonsensical and deeply true.

I also felt a wave of gratitude for the weird, inexplicable technologies of the sacred, these keys to the soul that Judaism has preserved throughout the millennia. I felt so lucky to be the heir of this long, complicated and often deeply problematic tradition—not so much for its cultural or intellectual heritage, but as a repository of, for lack of a better word, magic.

This is what spirituality does: It transforms the self in ways that ideology, philosophy, nationalism and ethnicity do not. And it actually works. The recent findings by the S3K Synagogue Studies Institute that American Jews under 35 are more "spiritually inclined" than those of their parents' generation have surprised many people, but not those who have experienced the power of real spirituality firsthand. Because unlike tired clichés of persecution and tribe, this stuff actually works.

I do not claim to know why this is so. Maybe the shofar has *mana* or eros. Maybe its sound evokes angels, as the Kabbalah suggests. Or maybe it's just childhood memories, or something from a vast collective unconscious, or the knowledge that the same sound is resonating in Kathmandu, Tel Aviv, Mombasa and New York and has been heard for thousands of years. Who knows.

What matters more, in my view, is that the ritual objects of Judaism are tools—and tools are meant to be used. While perhaps this may seem obvious, I think many Jews have forgotten this fact, much to our detriment.

Now, to suggest that Jewish practices have a purpose (spiritual or otherwise) is heretical in some quarters—and dangerous, because if that same purpose (say, ethical refinement, or spiritual awakening, or communal bonding) might be accomplished some other way, then the commandments might seem superfluous. Thus, in many traditionalist circles, the only reason for any religious observance is that God commanded it or that it is part of *halacha*, Jewish law.

Within a holistic, usually Orthodox, framework, this view works well enough; everyone is doing the same thing, and the pieces fit together in a semi-coherent system—a whole that does very powerful communal and sacred work. Trouble is, at least 80% of American Jews do not live this way, and thus rightly regard much religious observance as empty of meaning, nonsensical or downright harmful. Thus, if we don't first admit that religious practice is supposed to do something and, second, address what that something is, we'll never make a case for those not already convinced of its merit.

The conventional answers one gets to why Jews perform certain actions are mythic; they are tied to belief and (pseudo-) history. For example, we eat matzo to remember the exile from Egypt, or because God commanded it. But most American Jews don't believe Jewish myths—or in a traditional God, for that matter—let alone notions of commandments, repentance, reward and punishment. Really, does anyone seriously believe in Rosh Hashanah's Book of Life, or Passover's miracles of the 10

Plagues? Maybe this stuff is okay for kids, but at some point, we grow up and leave childish things behind.

Spiritual practice, on the other hand, is functional, not mythic. It's pragmatic; we eat matzo because it calls us to reflection, or provokes some stirring of the soul, or brings us together as a family. See the difference?

In fact, as James Carse described in his 2008 book *The Religious Case Against Belief* (Penguin) dogmas and beliefs have nothing to do with spiritual life. Nothing. Not only is Judaism a religion of "deed, not creed." Not only do Jews hold every conceivable belief, from Divine determinism to materialist atheism. But if the point of religious practice is to shift consciousness—however that is understood—then it has nothing to do with what happened in 1446 BCE (a common dating of the Exodus) or 4004 BCE (a fundamentalist dating of Creation), and everything to do with what is happening now.

From this perspective, it doesn't matter whether God is a benevolent father looking down on us all, or a delusion of the mind. It doesn't matter whether the Exodus happened or not. What matters is that we possess technology that can transform the self, open the mind, unite a community, motivate ethical action and bring forth tears when your heart is broken. Before you light candles, you're thinking of your mortgage; afterward, you're thinking of your kids, or the meaning of life, or something else that actually matters. That's what counts. Of course, if the Passover story, or the Yom Kippur myth, helps you do those things, great. If not, drop them. It's the transformation, not the myth, that matters.

As I have already suggested, there is no one transformation that will hold true for everyone. For example, reciting a blessing before eating a meal may serve many functions: opening the heart, remembering our best selves, interrupting the demands of the ego or, for that matter, inculcating subservience to God's demands, community affiliation and maintenance of cultural traditions. Some of these answers I agree with, others I don't. That comes with the territory. United in action, we can diverge in interpretation. In an age of pluralism and multiculturalism, it is a very good thing.

But in all these cases, the doing is all. Objects and rituals exist to be used, and only in the using, in the experience, can they do their work. *Naaseh v'nishmah*, the Israelites said at Sinai: We will do, and we will understand. Religion and spirituality take practice, *avodah*, work. This is, unfortunately, why spirituality is difficult to communicate and why much spiritual writing reads like a cookbook. You have to walk the path in order to see the view; reading about it just isn't the same.

If we are to take recent poll findings seriously, we must shift away from a belief-centered, ethnicity-centered, and history-centered religious worldview and toward a pragmatic one. Spirituality need not mean the same thing to everyone, and it need not involve chanting with your inner child (not that there's anything wrong with that). But it does mean a shift from myth to function.

It also means a shift in how we understand excellence. American Jews have achieved intellectual excellence, financial and political power, and social organization. But there are no Harvards for spirituality, and no gold watches for enlightenment. This has always been the case; deep spiritual practice has always been an elite, rather than a mass, phenomenon, and one difficult to translate to the norms of householder life. But today, with spirituality often relegated to the mushy-headed New Age, it's especially easy to look down on the personal-growth crowd, with its parade of fads from Kabbalah to the Secret.

But let's not throw out the baby with the Kabbalah water. Spiritual excellence is every bit as real as physical or intellectual excellence, and to my mind, smart people who don't do any work on themselves are as out of balance as bookworms who never go to the gym. I submit that if Judaism is to thrive, we must take spiritual growth as seriously as we do academic achievement or financial success. Again, the specifics will vary; some people will favor intellectual contemplation, others work on the body or the heart; some will recoil at patriarchal language and primitive myth, while others will embrace them. But if you aren't doing something, you're the spiritual equivalent of a 98-pound weakling.

Admittedly, real spiritual practice isn't easy; it demands introspection and an unflinching look at the ways in which we live our lives. And it takes old-fashioned work. For example, I find, even after years of practice, that I almost never feel like meditating; I have to force myself to do it. But afterward, I marvel at how confused and off my game I had been without realizing it. Or, I may not feel like observing the Sabbath, but when it comes, I realize how exhausted, how obsessed with work, how out of balance I had been. Spiritual practice is transformative, but the nature of transformation is that you don't know you need to transform until you do it. It's most important precisely when it seems most pointless.

For all that, "spiritual practice" can be as simple as, say, pausing for five seconds before eating a meal: no blessing, no words, maybe a moment's reflection on where the food came from and how fortunate you are to consume it. Just the practice, the openness and the intention—that's all.

Although such advice may seem banal, even trite, it's a fundamental reordering of the way in which many Jews regard their religious observance. The notion that these spiritual technologies might actually do something is threatening to those who maintain (for reasons of conformity or rebellion) that religion is about following orders and believing in myths. Yet, waking up to the subtle delights of daily existence, relinquishing the ego's incessant demands and coming into the presence of the numinous—this is how Judaism creates a life well lived, not just for the walking wounded of the self-help world, but for all of us interested in living a full and rich life. Jewish religious practice is a technology for waking up to life. Use it.

April 2009

The Myth of Authenticity

American Jews of a certain age, class and culture have the scene engraved in their memories: Woody Allen's Alvy Singer in *Annie Hall* at Annie's goyish parents' house, suddenly seen through their eyes as a Hasid, in a long black coat and *peyos*.

It's a hilarious moment: Allen imagining how he is seen by non-Jews, giving us a great sight gag and, of course, capturing in just a few seconds of film the great anxiety of American Jews that we are 'too Jewish,' notwithstanding all our best efforts to assimilate.

I wonder, though, how many of us share the unstated assumption of the *Annie Hall* gag: that to be Hasidic is 'really Jewish,' to be secular is not really Jewish, and everything else lies somewhere in between. How often has our culture set up *Fiddler on the Roof* as an imagined Jewish ideal: real Jews in a real shtetl, practicing real Jewish traditions for the real Jewish God. Never mind that all these were creatures of fiction: what is most authentically Jewish, many of us believe, is the old-time religion (a non-Jewish term) of black hats and the Pale.

It's not, of course, that we want to be the shtetl Jews of Anatevka— only that we continue to see them as the real ones, and the rest of us, well, as a kind of hybridization, or adaptation. Thus there persists in the American Jewish imagination an anxiety of inauthenticity: that someone, somewhere, is the real Jew, but I'm not it.

The myth of authenticity, however, has got to go.

First, of course, it's not historically accurate. Traditional Jews didn't wear long black coats until the 18th century (notwithstanding some recent, and absurd, images of Moses crossing the Red Sea in a fur-lined *shtreimel*). Moreover, until the advent of modernity, the notion that if you were 'really' religious, you would dress anachronistically, simply did not arise in Jewish thought. Distinctive dress, modest dress, visible signs like the yarmulke, sure—but never the idea that to be 'real' was to be so radically other from one's own place and time. In fact, with only a few exceptions, everything that we think of as 'really Jewish' came along at a particular place and time, because of particular historical circumstances, and was never universally shared (by Sephardim, for example).

More importantly, however, the entire notion of authenticity is a false projection of particular historical quirks onto an imagined ideal of realness that artificially freezes culture, and thus spells its demise. The truth is that there is no single authentic Jewishness. Like any living culture, Jewish culture (and religion) evolves over time in order to remain vibrant. Of course, there are certain core values, myths and cultural traits that remain relatively constant. But bagels, bookishness and bar mitzvahs all evolved historically; none is more really Jewish than sushi, sports or a Sweet 16.

Orthodox fidelity to the law, anxieties of dislocation, reformist rationalization—all arose along the way. Even the ultra-Orthodox maxim that "innovation is forbidden by Torah" is, of course, a 19th-century innovation. To imagine that cultural forms must remain static to be authentic is to doom a culture to obsolescence.

It is also, of course, to privilege some cultural forms over others. Why bagels and not *jachnun*? Why Joseph Caro's legalistic *Shulchan Aruch* but not his radical, mystical *Maggid Meisharim*? And, of course, why a white male rabbi over an African-American female one. Any time we claim that one cultural form is more authentic than another, we are replicating privilege and marginalization.

And worst of all, by ossifying and reifying a fake authenticity as the real thing, we actually undermine the attempt to create true authenticity on the part of progressive Jews. Meaningful authenticity isn't about an old religious form or a Yiddish pun. It's when a religious, literary or cultural form—old, new or alt-neu—speaks to the depths of what it is to be human.

If a guitar-playing, meditating female rabbi resonates more with the souls of her followers than does a *nigun*-singing, Talmud-learning male one, she is the more authentic spiritual leader. If ecstatic prayer speaks to and from the spirit more than a supposedly consistent rationalism, then it, too, is more authentic, notwithstanding the howls of the secularist. Authenticity isn't about form, it's about getting to what matters.

For progressive, spiritual Judaism to succeed, it needs to jettison the myth of authenticity based on some real forms that some real Jews really believe in, and replace it with a personalized notion of authenticity measured by integrity and individual coherence. Is my Buddhist-Judaism less authentic than someone else's more carefully patrolled boundaries of permissibility? Quite the contrary: It is more authentic, because it is more faithful to the truth of my experience. Not preference, not whim—but carefully considered internal coherence.

Those who prefer traditional forms sometimes deride innovations as compromises. Yet which is the more objectionable compromise: bending the rules to eat hot food on non-kosher plates, or clinging to a ritual form that may no longer hold any meaning, is historical in its origin and may actively impede other ethical values (such as connecting with people of other faiths)?

Likewise, sometimes traditional forms are derided as intellectual compromises by those who insist on a more rigorous secularism. But which is the real compromise: admitting the irrational desire to pray, or maintaining some pseudo-intellectual purity that cuts off the heart despite the soul?

Progressive Jews don't do what they do to compromise the authenticity of Judaism; they do it to maintain it. For those who care about living an authentic life, values shift because of consideration, not spinelessness. To say "This works for me," based on discernment and introspection, is a mark not of irresponsibility but of integrity.

The myth of authenticity, in contrast, is an abdication of introspection and personal responsibility. It's a lot easier to say "This is real Judaism, and I do/don't practice it" than to look closely at what form might work to do the important stuff (afflict the comfortable, comfort the afflicted) for you.

Obviously, newer Jewish forms are not intrinsically superior to older ones; the books of the Bible have endured precisely because they continue to speak to so many people, despite the gulf in history and culture. And to be sure, the ancientness of these texts is part of their power: They bind us to history in a way that newer books cannot. But this power is not because of some imagined authenticity, or some unbroken connection between us and Biblical Israelites who, after all, imagined that the world was a small, flat place, had no concept of medicine or industrialization, had notions about nation, ethnicity and gender that hopefully would have no place in contemporary society.

No, Biblical Israelites are not the real Jews. Neither are Hasidim, 20th-century modernists, neurotic New York psychoanalysts, Moroccan saints, angst-ridden intellectuals, High Reformers or anyone else. Real Jews are all of the above, and the rest of us who take Jewishness seriously, in one form or another. Real Jews speak with Southern accents, keep one day of yom tov (the holiday), hike in the wilderness, eat shrimp, inter-marry, become *ba'alei teshuvah*, do karate, are bisexual, are neoconserva-tive. Real Jews are the ones who make Judaism real for themselves.

When I read about Jewish farmers, Jewish Sufis and Jewish pro wres-tlers, I think, good for the Jews. If there is one distinctive feature I love about Jewish culture, it's the exact opposite of the myth of authenticity: it's how, in our many diasporas, we have amalgamated so many con-tradictions, oblique angles and diverse perspectives on how it is to be human. Granted, that pattern also leads to Jewish mobsters, Jewish fi-nancial shysters and Jewish arms merchants. But the basic principles of change, growth and evolution are what has kept us going these thou-sands of years, as much as the basic bedrock values that remain more or less constant. For Jews, even more than for others, change is authenticity.

So let's get used to slippery slopes, murky swamps and the many oth-er geographies of blending and uncertainty. Whether or not Jews have traveled here before, they are where we live today. Finding authenticity without is ahistorical and self-defeating. Finding it within is holy.

December 2009

Theology is Rationalization

For progressive, Jewishly-educated twenty- and thirty-somethings, it's very fashionable to struggle. We encounter problematic texts, we wrestle with their meanings in the *beit midrash*, and we live in a state of tension with them. We interpret them freely, albeit bound to the traditions of our ancestors. We dynamically balance the call of our heritage on the one hand, and the moral imperatives of our day on the other. And to be Jewish, we know, is to be *yisrael*, a godwrestler, not content with fideism or despair, because the wrestling with meaning, the search, the uncertainty—that is the religious life.

I don't buy it anymore. Not that I doubt the sincerity of the conviction. What I don't buy is the intellectualizing, the theologizing, and the amateur philosophizing that disguises the more naked stirrings of the heart. Why can't we just admit that we're Jewish because we want to be? Could we recognize that wanting—and not theology—is the essence of religious life?

Somehow that's not good enough. Human beings can't just admit that we want a mother—or father—figure to hear our cry; we have to invent stories to justify what we want. So traditionalists unconsciously pretend to care about the age of the universe, or sin, or the afterlife. Progressives understand these doctrines to be meaningless, so we godwrestle, or redefine, or in some other way try to have both emotional comfort and intellectual coherence.

But all of these doctrines and ideas are there to answer emotional needs. Motive is always present, especially among the Orthodox who say "Motive? I have no motive! God commanded me!" That motive is the most obvious of all: the motivation to obey God's command; to feel alright; to feel like I'm doing the right thing, or that there is a right thing to do in the first place. Consider any sentence beginning: "I keep kosher because..." Or more generally: "I am Jewish because..." I'd be willing to wager that, unless the completion of the sentence has something to do with desire—that is, with the heart—almost any words will be deceiving. I am Jewish because it is my heritage? Not really—it's because I want to connect somehow with my heritage. I keep kosher because it is part of a halachic, precedential system that I subscribe to as part of the Jewish national experiment? Come on—you do it because some deep part of yourself actually wants to do so: to do something right, or please the parent, or experience a sense of purity. In a way, Orthodox Jews are the most New Age Jews of all, since, even if they deny it, their practice addresses deep emotional needs.

Faith, in its purest form, is inchoate. Unlike faith-in-something, which has a cognitive object, it is a disposition of trust toward the universe. It's an attitude, a way of being, that has no particular object and no theory to which it is beholden. ("Trusting your own deepest experience," Sharon Salzberg calls it in her book *Faith*; not letting it be undermined by a corrosive doubt). It's only when faith is combined with ideas, particularly about how the world should be, or about how it came to be the way it is now, that faith translates into self-deception, or distraction, or even dangerousness.

Oddly, some of the most traditionally religious people these days are the "new" atheists, who attack religion for its flawed intellectual foundations, as if its foundations were intellectual. A recent debate between atheist Sam Harris and Jewish conservative Dennis Prager, for example, touched on theodicy, on the necessity of God for morality, the argument from design. But everyone's mind is made up, and no one was talking about why it was really made up that way. Instead, each party marshaled all the arguments available to defend the position he (it's almost always *he*) wanted to defend. If we choose to believe—that is, if it is not simply a matter of replicating the ideologies of our childhoods—we do so for emotional, not intellectual, reasons. The intellectual part is just window-dressing.

What is the meaning of the yearning of the heart? Is it really as ridiculous as the intellectual 'answers' provided for that yearning? Is not the question, perhaps unlike the answer, as beautiful as the appreciation of painting, dance, or music? Some of the neo-atheists treat religion the way a bad junior high school teacher treats a poem: as really about its meaning, which is to say, the information it seeks to impart. Whereas, a student of art or of religion knows that the informational content of the myth is far less important than the way the myth functions in a self-examined life. I don't care about whether Abraham left Ur and came to Canaan; I care what his journey means to me, to my family, and to my people. I care about what it must have been like for Isaac to submit to the violence of his father, and about his soul, so strong, so willing, so bound. I care about these sacred texts not as pseudo-science or pseudo-history, but as myth. But what do we do with the yearning, the love, the connection, the stories, the traditions—is all of it really to be cast aside because some people take them too literally?

Of course, fundamentalists say that they believe their religious doctrines. But then they also say that if you don't believe them, you're deluded and damned. Is that really "belief"?

There are, of course, many ways to elegantly square the circle. For example, well aware of the fact that thoughtful religious people and thoughtless religious people believe different things, Maimonides set about creating a system whereby intelligent 'philosophers' could reconcile their faith-tradition with what they knew to be true about the universe. He did this for a number of reasons: so they could remain in their faith community, so that they could live with their families, so that they could be part of the historical continuum of the great Jewish experiment. And many neo-Maimonideans exist today.

Yet it seems obvious that whoever wrote the Bible really did think the Earth was flat, that the two lights God made revolve around it, and that the Creator of the world chose the Israelites to be the bearer of His message. Indeed, the more I allow these ancient texts to be weird and 'Other,' rather than try to adapt, interpret, or wrestle them into some 21st century psychological or spiritual frame, the more delightful they become.

Secretly, I feel as though Maimonides knew this. The jokes, subterfuges, and ironies of his project of doing so, *The Guide to the Perplexed*, leaves one with the strong impression that he knows he's playing a game. Of course, the Rambam says he is committed to an infallible Torah, so a wildly fanciful interpretation that leads to the right answer is necessarily more accurate than a seemingly plain one which leads to error. But come on. He knew full well, and wrote many times, that the teachings of religion mean different things to different people: a "common person" reads text one way, a philosopher another (more correct) way. It's how religion works.

I, like Maimonides, am more a contemplative than a mythologian. For me, no amount of immersion in the complexities of legend and myth really accomplishes the same cleansing of the mental faculties, spiritual intimacy, and clarity of vision as a meditation retreat. But that is a minority view. For many more people, the wisdom of narrative, myth, and archetype are irreplaceable. The stories and characters of the Bible are the results of centuries of folk wisdom, tale-telling, and insight into the human condition. These writers were ignorant of contemporary science, pluralism, ethics, but quite wise when it comes to the human condition, and easier to transmit than Shakespeare. And while it is obviously the case that we know much more about science than we did two thousand years ago, is it really true that we are so much wiser about religion and spirituality than our ancestors? Ethics, sure—but the stirrings of the heart? Hardly. If anything, our noisy, advertising-filled world makes it harder, not easier, for us to sense the splendor of a sunset. What was *de riguer* for our ancestors—an inky sky punctuated by stars, untamable forests, a sense of mystery—is now almost never experienced, save on carefully planned excursions into the remote wilderness.

And as for God, that irritating, misleading, non-indigenous word best gestures to something my heart feels, not a thing my head knows or believes. On meditation retreat, for example, I don't really get any information about God. But I do get the *sense* of God—the sense of holiness, sacredness, beauty, sufficiency, peace—all these purely from a mind that is quiet, relaxed, and concentrated. Now, is it wrong to move from the sense of God to "God"? Yes, if it includes dogma, or attributes imported from somewhere else, or intolerance. Yes, if it means saying something about how the world is, or how it ought to be, even if the 'sense' is quite certain—since you can be certain and wrong. But surely it's not wrong to speak the language of the heart, and give that mode of speech its due. Reciting the *Ashrei* is a way of buying a bouquet of roses for the universe. After all the tragedies of the world, I can't say what God hears and doesn't hear. I just know I want to express love.

And I want, more than before, to be free of justifying what I want, as long as I don't force anyone else to speak my heart's language. I don't want to construct a system that makes it okay to be religious in the way that I am, or wrestle with problem texts. I want to admit that I love and that's all. Definitely, one might create a non-theistic devotional practice that conveys the love without the problematic theistic trimmings. But for me, saying "God is What Is" just feels different, and juicier, than saying "This is What Is." Call me a failed Buddhist, but I'll take the path of love.

Even the projects of translating the text of Hebrew prayers to make them somehow less ethnocentric, sexist, homophobic, anthropocentric— these projects are important for contemporary ethical reasons. But not because doing so makes prayer coherent, or theologically kosher, or sensible. Prayer cannot be rescued, it can only be cried. Even the dualistic language—God, please help me; I need you; I want to be close to you—is philosophically problematic. When I read the old texts, it's obvious that God is a guy, who may or may not have a body but who definitely does have personhood and separateness from us. He tells us to follow his commandments in exchange for his making the rain fall, and He tells us to follow the rules. No gender-neutralizing of this language will make it make sense.

But would we demand that someone praying for her sick child 'make sense'? And if we wouldn't, why demand it of ourselves? Is it more honest to shoehorn those old texts into my theology, my ethics, and my understanding of how the world works, or to speak the language of a different world, united by love and history, not theory and meaning?

I am often asked why I practice two religious disciplines, Judaism and (Western) Buddhism. One response is that, really, I'm just practicing the dharma—only my *bhakti* (devotional) path is Jewish, rather than Buddhist. Western Buddhism is an anomaly: a contemplative path extracted from its religious, mythic, ritual, and cultural contexts. This extraction was first done by Asian reformers who sought to 'update' Buddhism for the modern era and fight colonial religious incursions. Then that already-reformed Buddhism was adapted again by Westerners for their own pragmatic purposes: they were interested in tools for liberation, not a religious system. But Buddhism as practiced by most Asian Buddhists is as steeped in myth, ritual, community, and supernaturalism as Western religions are: tales of the Buddha's past lives, of his miraculous powers, of the adventures of the Bodhisattvas; descriptions of pure-lands and hell-realms; libations and prayers galore.

Some Western Buddhists suggest that all that religious stuff is a sad corruption of an originally pure tradition. Like the Jewish Reform movement, they argue that such stories are later excrescences attached like parasites to a core of rationality. But come on. The tales are there because tales work; they teach us about ourselves and our ancestors; and they work especially for people who aren't lucky enough to devote weeks to meditation and reflection. They are part of the Buddhist *gestalt*, because they are part of the human *gestalt*. Last week, for example, my partner and I went to a huge Buddhist monastery near my home to celebrate the Buddha's birthday—occasioned by a "bathing the Buddha" ritual, chanting verses related to sin and atonement, and various pomp and circumstance. It was just like Yom Kippur, right down to the confused younger generation that didn't quite know what was going on, the well-meaning monks, and the misbehaving little kids. There were offerings of fruits and oil, and a nice Kiddush luncheon afterwards. It was religion, in all its essence and manifestation.

This is not just sociological accident; it reflects the nature of religious consciousness, which at times is reflective, at times reifies concepts into myth and story, and at times just wants to dance. There are many Zen tales of monks crying and laughing, and even in the staid Insight Meditation Society, which has carefully removed all the nonsense from the tradition, there are occasional chants, offerings, and references to deities and demons. It's just part of how we live as human beings. Just as proposition without enthusiasm, vocation without passion, and obligation without lovingkindness are all bereft of humanity, so too meditation without devotion is incomplete.

For me, the Jewish pieces provide the devotional elements. I sit, watching my breath—and when gratitude arises, I express it in terms of God and blessings and benevolence. I note phenomena arising and passing, and when my mind is quieted, I feel... something... which I identify with "holiness." And when I am lonely, and sad, and bereft, I continue with my religious ritual, lighting Shabbat candles and feeling the aching beautiful emptiness.

It's unpleasant, to be sure, sharing a vocabulary with bigots, zealots, racists, and ignoramuses. I sometimes feel as though I should just leave the God stuff behind. But it's not like religion has a monopoly on bigotry and ignorance. And if these touchstones of value work for people, if they really invite reflection and action, wisdom and compassion—does it really matter that they make no more sense than the Flying Spaghetti Monster? Can human beings really do without the myths and rituals, and all become Ivy-educated philosophers? Do we want to? And is it really the case that meditation provides all the spiritual goods, that a childless woman kneeling before a statue of the Virgin isn't feeling something important that exists irrespective of dogma and tradition, yet depends on it in a way we cannot easily replace, and that ought to move us to tears?

March 2007

How Not to Believe in God

According to today's crop of neo-atheists, our culture's ideas about God are remarkably adolescent: a 6,000-year-old Earth? A God who punishes the wicked? This sort of thing might have been convincing long ago—but not to anyone who uses the Internet.

Sophisticated religionists have long had more subtle conceptions of their religions, of course, without such fideism. For example, many progressive religionists understand God not as some old man in the sky, but as a name we give the reality of all of being, a God that does not "exist" but is, indeed, Existence itself. Others understand Scripture as myth—its literal truth is no more relevant than whether Hamlet really lived in Denmark. The point is its meaning and its purpose. And so on.

Of course, this is not the stuff you learn in Sunday School—but that's the point. Imagine if your education in literature ended with Tom Sawyer and the last math you learned was pre-algebra. You wouldn't take seriously the possibility that literature can be transformative or that math can put men on the moon. But that's the situation when it comes to religion: most people learn the simple stuff as children, and then, unsurprisingly, become either childish religionists or skeptics who regard religion as childish.

Both groups hold that religion is about beliefs and explanations of how things are: the age of the Earth, what happens after we die, et cetera. Yet this is not the case. A believer doesn't become convinced of the existence of the afterlife because of philosophical argument—she becomes convinced because of grief, or rage at injustice, or the inability to cope with loss. Eventually, more and more ideas accreted, and more and more solace, meaning, community, and perhaps even experiences of the sacred became attached to them. But it was never really about the ideas; it was about the pain of living and the healing one finds in religion. Religions do offer theological doctrine, but what they really offer is solace, love, sanctity, and value—all of them inchoate, all of them dear.

Fundamentalisms and orthodoxies may say they are about theological propositions, but the reason it's impossible to argue with fundamentalists is that they have so much at stake that they'll say or do anything to make it all work out. What's at stake? If the Torah isn't literally true, then something in my life is wrong. If Jesus didn't die for my sins, then I am not okay.

Beliefs and opinions are held because of the intense feelings beneath them. America's religious right has intense religious experiences and associates them with Biblical literalism. The Islamic world's religious right has intense religious experiences and associates them with keeping the *umma* pure of corruption and decay. Israel's religious right has intense religious experiences and associates them with notions of chosenness and holy land. In this way, fervent hope leads to fervent ideology.

Here in America, hundreds of millions of people believe in demonstrably false notions such as Intelligent Design, or life beginning at conception, or a just, retributive God. Why? Not because of science, truthseeking, or logical inquiry. They "believe in" these things (notice the locution) because they think religion is at the core of their lives. Our political debates are not about evolutionary biology, civil liberties, or pre-existing conditions; they are about a terrified minority, afraid that society is slipping away from all it holds dear.

And religion is dear. Just imagine the grief of a young boy whose father has died. And imagine the hope, the consolation, when that boy is taught that at the Rapture, he'll meet his dad again. (This was the 'conversion story' of Tim LaHaye, author of the bestselling *Left Behind* series.) All of a sudden, Biblical inerrancy is no longer a hermeneutical proposition; it is necessary for the dearest of dreams to be true. None of this is about science; it's about primal human needs. The mental stuff is just window dressing.

Personally, I am a religious person, in love with God, and a mystic. I think spiritual and contemplative practice makes us better people, and makes life worth living. But when those spiritual states become wedded to ideology, they become dangerous. Already, a third of our country believes itself to be at war not only with Islam but also domestically, in what used to be called the "Culture Wars." And our lunatic fringe has grown in size as the bulwarks of its hegemony have begun to crumble.

We are all implicated by their fury. If I make a political decision based on an irrational or subjective value I hold privately dear, because of the emotional connections I associate with it, I am committing the same sin as they are. Those of us who are religious bear a heightened burden to question our motivations.

Jews, in particular, would be better off without the phrase "belief in God." First, it is a Christian phrase, not a Jewish one, and it suggests that the essence of religion is faith—a Christian value. Second, the phrase implies a certain kind of God—a God in which one either does or does not believe, probably an anthropomorphic God, a cosmic puppet master who sorts the bad people from the good, and makes the rain fall.

This naive God-concept may be popular in the media, but it is not the God of reflective Judaism. Rabbi Moses Cordovero, a great theologian and Kabbalist, called anthropomorphic ideas of God "foolish," and insisted that we think of God not as some Big Man in the Sky but as filling every atom of creation itself. Rabbi Moses Maimonides, Judaism's foremost philosopher, saw traditional God-language as a mere entryway toward more sophisticated philosophical reflection on unity and morality.

For these and generations of other Jewish theologians, God does not exist—God is existence itself. "God" is the world personalized, addressed not as *It* but as *You*. It is how we humans relate to the inexpressible mystery of being alive, which reveals itself not just in religion but in art, love, and delight as well. "Belief in God" is a phrase we should consign to the lexicographic graveyard. "Experience of wonder" (Heschel) is better. So is Love.

A few years ago, I wrote a book called *Everything is God: The Radical Path of Nondual Judaism*, which conveyed some of these rarified philosophical and mystical notions in a contemporary idiom. Most readers I've met have expressed gratitude and appreciation for the book. Some, though, seemed to feel as though something had been taken away. One newspaper asked "Is Jay Michaelson's God too mushy?" Another wondered whether the *Ein Sof*, the Infinite, the All, was enough of a father-figure to inspire morality.

But the contrary is true. It's not mushy to think seriously about God and let go of cherished myths. Grown-up people need a grown-up God concept. Imagine if you stopped reading at the age of thirteen—would you have any appreciation for literature? Yet this is exactly what most American Jews experience in their religious education. Just when they're ready to start asking serious questions, the bar mitzvah is over and so is Jewish thought.

Worst of all, this has consequences. In my new book, *God vs. Gay? The Religious Case for Equality*, I talk about how my naïve God-concept kept me from coming out until late in my twenties. I thought God would hate me for being gay, and it was only after coming out that I realized that what brings me closer to the experience of "God" is honesty, openness, and intimacy. It took a while for me to let go of stories I'd been told since childhood, but doing so helped me open to authentic spirituality and meaningful religious life. And of course, I was one of the lucky ones; others suffer far worse abjection and violence because of bad ideas about God and religion.

Judaism without "belief in God" is stronger, healthier, and more open to the possibility of holiness than a Judaism which clings to it. So am I.

May 2011

Getting Over the Judging God

1. Is God a Good Idea?

The Jewish High Holidays are an ironic time. More Jews go to synagogue on these days than any other point in the year, yet their theology would seem least likely to appeal to most Jews, one highlighting sin and repentance, judgment and guilt. Is this a good thing?

This is not, strictly speaking, a theological question; it is a psychological one. Let us set aside the question of whether God actually exists. We know, most of us, that our images of God are metaphors, invented for our benefit. So the question really is whether this particular image—the judging God—is helpful or harmful.

To be sure, it's not an either/or decision. In Jewish tradition, God is both the *dayan emet*, the true judge, and *harachaman*, the compassionate/womb-like one. God is Mother, Father and Friend; Teacher, Consoler and Lover. For that matter, God is Everything and Nothing, Immanent and Transcendent, Earth and Sky. Surely, the Kabbalists were right that, experientially, we humans relate to the Infinite according to traits, genders, energies and perspectives that are different for different people and at different moments. So it is not that the judging God is the only God-image we have.

But on Yom Kippur, He (and He is a He) is the dominant one. So the question remains: Is it a good image to have, or a bad one?

Today, many object to the image of the judging God on the grounds of justice. How can we speak of a God who judges in the wake of the outrage of the Holocaust? Surely, this objection argues, whatever we may wish to say about God, we cannot say that God judges fairly.

Others object to the image on the basis of gender, politics and family psychology: This judging God is like an abusive father (or husband), they say, meting out punishment and doling out rewards from above. We would all be better off without such an exemplar of abuse, patriarchy and hierarchy.

Still others, and I may be among them, object to the image of the judging God on other psychological grounds. Much of what we ascribe to noble motives of repentance is really just guilt warmed over. I learned this the hard way, as I came to accept my sexuality, and slowly understood that so much of my own theological talk was just plain old guilt and self-hatred.

This is true for all of us. Is it really such a healthy thing to feel oneself to be inadequate, judged and deficient? Does it really make us better people, or does it just make us tougher, more defensive and more judgmental ourselves? Does it comport with mystical experience, which radiates acceptance and compassion? Does God judge us, or only love?

I do not have a neat answer to these questions, but I want to suggest that while the judging God is an image of God that is experientially accurate, it is ultimately something to be transcended.

2. Let's not try to make it fit anymore

There are, to be sure, ways to square the circle.

First, guilt is part of human nature, and not an entirely bad part; it keeps us honest, checks the ego, and reminds us that we all have the capacity to be selfish and cruel. The judging God, in this light, is simply the superego projected toward the heavens; it accords with our experience of remorse. And as a form of social control, it is an effective story that doubtless keeps many of us from acting on our baser instincts. It just needs periodic updating from time to time.

Moreover, the image of the judging God is not a static one. God judges in order to inspire us to change, in order that God can forgive. Again, let's stay with experience, not myth. The point is that we judge ourselves so that we can introspect, right our wrong behaviors, taste the sweetness of forgiveness—and then move on. The catharsis of Yom Kippur serves its function, and then ends. The shofar is sounded, the book is closed, the process is complete.

Second, one might craft a theology of Yom Kippur that omits the bad stuff. After all, all of us live within the delusions of the ego, the *yetzer hara*, which sees the world not as it is—as manifestations of a single Being, according to the Hasidic nondual reading of the Shema—but as divided into many different, separate objects. Most importantly, the ego sees itself as separate from the rest of the world, and evaluates the world according to how well what's outside is pleasing what's inside. It's as simple as "have a nice day"—"nice" being a term that means "pleasing to the self." This is our ordinary existence, conditioned by eons of evolution and natural selection, and without this ordinary frame of reference, we'd all be dead.

But it is, all the same, delusory. Yes, there are neurons at a certain location in the cosmos which behave in such a way as to create the cognitive phenomenon of consciousness. Yes, on a cognitive level, it seems as though that phenomenon is distinct from everything else in the universe. But *seems* is not *is*. Really, every thought you are having, at this moment as at every other one, is wholly conditioned by an uncountable number of causes, which are themselves wholly conditioned by other causes, ad infinitum—ad *ein sof.* "Yes! I get it now." "I don't agree." "What's next?" "That link looks interesting." All of these impulses, ideas, predilections— all that, together, comes to form our ideas of ourselves—are not "ours" at all.

Tshuva, translated as repentance but literally meaning "return," is, on the cognitive level, simply a return to the 'right view,' the view of how things really are, when the screen of the ego is lowered. It's the *shov* of *ratzo v'shov*, running and returning—coming back to the Source, the undifferentiated Awareness that somehow gives birth to the cosmos. Running out into differentiation, with (for all but the most awakened of us) all its traps and delusions—but then, at special times in the year, returning. And from that place of unity, reflecting on the actions of the small self, observing how they may have caused harm, and attempting to repair the harm by reconnecting with other people and with God. Hopefully, the day after this essay appears online, you'll consider spending some time doing that.

That's all well and good, but the reality is that, emotionally speaking, the predominant tenor of the Days of Awe is different, difficult, and not worth trying to save by redefinition.

3. You can't handle the guilt

The traditional Jewish path to Return is not through emptiness, but through *kapparah*: atonement, catharsis. It's messy and ridden with guilt: beating the chest, reviewing one's transgressions, fasting to break through the resistances of the ego—the mainstream Jewish path of Yom Kippur is one not of nondual Right View but of dualistic wrestling with the small self, involving a lot of judging and remorse and regret.

As I've written about before, this generally does not work for me and instead elicits anger and resistance. I feel like I'm back in Hebrew school again, being forced to sit still through lectures I don't agree with. And I get the sense that all this pietism is, itself, a tragic delusion: you're beating yourself up, but the sun is shining outside, and the delicious, sensual world is inviting you to play. Where does it end—with self-mortification? Denial? Repression? I've been there before, thanks.

And does catharsis actually ever show up? Actually, the tradition says, the Book of Life is really open for another couple of weeks. And God is always watching you and always judging. And it never ends. I remember, during my more observant days, debating whether to eat non-kosher-supervised cheese, a legal debate that goes on within the Conservative movement to this day. Believe it or not, I really racked my brain and searched my heart over this technical *halachic* issue. The rules seemed nonsensical—but was I just trying to rationalize doing what I wanted? Did God really care? Was the system out of whack, or was I being lazy and indulgent?

Today, the whole thing looks like neurosis. Yes, there's a certain nobility to suffusing every aspect of one's life with holiness and participating in a millennia-old tradition of law. But all this angst—about cheese! Couldn't the emotional energy be better spent on giving more money to the poor, rectifying the sins of racism and sexism, or, well, just about anything? Is the sense of God's judgment helping us do what's right, or making us neurotic about anything and everything?

The narrative arc of judging-introspection-forgiveness remains, for me, an important one, not because it is helpful, but the opposite: because it calls attention to my own tendency to judge myself and my attendant need to forgive.

It would be funny, if it weren't tragic. Because with judgment comes— if we judge ourselves worthy—arrogance, self-justification and the judging of others, or—if we do not—self-hatred, anxiety and defense mechanisms aplenty. We make ourselves tough, argumentative and always right because we fear that otherwise we will be found lacking.

The judging God is a stage along the psychological path, both individually and communally. It is important to hold ourselves to a high standard of ethical, and possibly ritual, behavior. But at a certain point, it becomes more important to forgive ourselves for not meeting that standard—and, as a culture, to learn to be more loving and understanding, less judgmental and strict. Of course, there are always personal and political instances where strictness is appropriate. But do we really think that what the world needs now is more judgment?

It's a shame that so many Jews go to shul only on the Days of Awe. I wish they would turn up for the Days of Love, Rest and Celebration (Sukkot and Shabbat are good starts). Those, it seems to me, are what we need more of: more love, more authenticity, more openness. And they yield experiences of something which deserves to be named as "God."

When love, rather than judgment, fills my heart, I see a natural world which we are lucky to inhabit, in bodies which are miraculous in construction, and I feel loved in return. I feel the imperative to pursue justice, not out of judgment or toughness, but out of compassion. Terrible things still happen. But I feel God's presence in the companionship and response to such adversity, in intimacy, in love, in the healing and the mending.

4. Try forgiveness instead

Fortunately, repentance is only half of the process of Yom Kippur. Forgiveness is the other half, and there, I can find more of a home.

I was inspired to consider these questions by an interview in *The Sun* magazine with Richard Smoley, author of *Inner Christianity*. For Christians, of course, forgiveness is even more central than it is for Jews: it's the essence of *imitatio dei* and one of the primary avenues toward opening the heart within the Christian tradition. Smoley, like me a nondualist, was interested in the same question I asked at the beginning: how the discourse of forgiveness fits into a nondualistic, panentheistic worldview.

His answer was that ordinarily, we think of forgiveness as something that really virtuous people do—people who are stronger than you and me, who are good at all those Oughts and Shoulds—when they accept that someone has wronged them, but somehow are able to get past it and move ahead. This, Smoley said, makes forgiveness an act of exceptional virtue—and he was having none of it.

What Smoley offered instead was forgiveness as an act of enlightenment. He invited us to ask just who we think is really "wronging" us. Why did that person make the choice, say the words, do the deed that s/he "chose" to do? Well, obviously, because of a thousand causes and conditions—and not a hair's breadth of soul more. Being angry at someone for an offense they have caused is like when we get angry at traffic for being there, or at a computer for not working right, or at a baby for crying. Sure, the offensive person is more intricate than the traffic patterns, microchips, and baby—but only different in degree, not in kind. Really, all of us are beautiful, glorious, wonderful machines, gathering together a thousand strands of God, and then sending them out in uniquely recombined ways.

Forgiveness, in this light, is actually seeing clearly. Everyone is doing the best they can—if they could do better, they would. If wisdom were stronger, they'd make better choices. If patience were stronger, they'd be less angry. But these dispositions which arise in the mind—is any of them "me"? Or "you"? When we feel ourselves to be wronged by another person, we are not seeing clearly. We are being wronged by the universe. And, take it from me, it's a bad idea to nurse a grudge against God.

The more I hold onto idea that the taxi driver who almost killed me in an accident this year is some separate guy out there—screwing me over, not paying me even for my medical expenses, lying about what happened—the angrier I get. But, once again, the truth will set you free. And the truth is that jerkiness arises. It's the result of many causes and conditions, which I don't know: his childhood, his cultural history, economics, class, or maybe the fact that he is in fact a jerk. It's a phenomenon that isn't 'owned' by the taxi driver. From the *mochin d'gadlut* (expanded mind) of God-consciousness, causes lead to effects—of which my sense of indignation is one.

The conventional ethical responsibility of interpersonal relationships does, of course, continue. But instead of being one of the actors on the stage, a nondual Yom Kippur focused on forgiveness rather than judgment invites me to watch the play unfold from the audience's point of view. It's still happening, and still quite moving—and I'll still hop right back onto the stage soon, playing one of the roles I've learned for decades. But there is also the great play of life itself, and the miraculousness of the actors that transcends their transitory (or even recurring) moments of chutzpah.

This is nonduality from personal, rather than theological, perspective: that the world of people who may harm or delight us is in fact a vast, self-less matrix of causes and effects, conditions and consequences. This is true *tshuva*, true return to the Source: seeing the self is an illusion—a blessed, vibrating, shining, dancing illusion, but an illusion still—and that there is only What Is, pretending to be wronged, pretending to be evil, pretending to be you. And where there is suffering—on the planetary scale, or in the political world, or in your own life—there the work begins.

October 2011

Spirituality as Satanism

> Without Contraries is no progression. Attraction and Repulsion,
> Reason and Energy, Love and Hate, are necessary to Human ex-
> istence. From these contraries spring what the religious call Good
> & Evil. Good is the passive that obeys Reason. Evil is the active
> springing from Energy. Good is Heaven. Evil is Hell.
> —William Blake, "The Marriage of Heaven & Hell"

When I was younger, the ideal Jew for me was a kid who would wear
a yarmulke but who also still smoked, or drank, or enjoyed secular pleasures. To this day, I'm not exactly sure what this figure signified, but I
think it has to do with having the best of both worlds, with not having to
make a choice. Yes, the symbol said, you can be both Jewish and in the
world; you can be Jewish and have a good time; you can be Jewish and
cool; even Jewish and bad.

As the kippa indicates, "Jewish" for me meant religiously Jewish. Obviously, I know, and knew, that there are plenty of Jewish identities which
are entirely compatible with, or even encourage, various forms of sensual celebration, hedonism, and/or dissoluteness. But when I was younger, the part that mattered was the religious part, which to most people
seemed antithetical to all of them. Was it possible, I wondered, to have
my challah and eat it too? To taste the sweetness of a devotional religious
life but not give up too much of the sensual world?

It's entirely possible that this early interest in *gam v'gam*—both-and—
was synecdoche for sexuality. That is, "Jewish and cool" really was about
"Jewish and gay." But the *gam v'gam* is so pervasive in my life, I think it's
more than that. Two decades on, the bad boy kippa wearer no longer
holds the same appeal, but as a queer, spiritual, progressive, meditating,
neo-Hasidic Jew, I am closer to the ideal I once sought than the ideal was
itself. I now am the heretic who preaches, the lawyer-poet, the Jew who
thinks that God loves him when he's at Burning Man.

This is not my personal idiosyncrasy. Contemporary spirituality is, in large measure, entirely about the great *gam v'gam*: the marriage of Heaven and Hell, as first articulated by William Blake. It's a refusal to surrender either the spiritual or the sensual, and more than that, to insist that religion and paganism, God and Satan, are at their core, one and the same. The rhetoric is rarely so extreme, but it is there nonetheless.

For example, in the Jewish world, we "Neo-Hasidic" Jews want it both ways: the authenticity and fiery love of the Hasidim, the "neo-" of feminism, progressive politics, and sex-positive values. One could argue, from a more right-wing perspective, that "Modern Orthodoxy" is a similar straddle. Or the Conservative notion of "Tradition and Change"—"Change" here being specified as accommodation of love, pleasure, and human potential. Or "Jewish Renewal"—Jewish, but also renewed, with altered mindstates, left-wing politics, sexual liberty, and the rest.

William Blake's great work of philosophical spirituality, "The Marriage of Heaven and Hell," is ostensibly a dialogue between heaven and hell but often feels like an advertisement for the latter. "Heaven" is the puritanical religious ideology that condemns desire and points skyward toward transcendent, and usually body-denying, values. It is what we now know as the mainstream of Western religion: the religion of sobriety, restraint, society, and objective values. Over two hundred years ago, Blake was already blaming it for repression, oppression, and war. But as we'll see, it has its role to play as well.

"Hell," for Blake, is that principle which holds that "Energy is Eternal Delight." "Those who restrain desire," says the Voice of the Devil in Blake's poem, "do so because theirs is weak enough to be restrained." The Satanic libertine is not weak; she is strong, and more in touch with her (and his) erotic being. Hell sees holiness everywhere, especially in eros. It is pagan, sensual, and vibrant. It is sex, freedom, self-actualization. If Heaven is the Hasidism of neo-Hasidism, Hell is the neo-. Blake's "Proverbs of Hell" include:

The road of excess leads to the palace of wisdom…
The pride of the peacock is the glory of God.
The lust of the goat is the bounty of God.
The wrath of the lion is the wisdom of God.
The nakedness of woman is the work of God.

To spiritual folks today, as well as readers of Philip Pullman's heretical *His Dark Materials* trilogy, this should sound familiar. Likewise to all of us who see God in the body, especially the naked one. As I've written before, there is, in my experience, a glorious holiness in the fire-dancers of Black Rock City, the misbehavior of rowdy schoolkids, the grandeur of nature. All this is God/dess as Manifest, as Shechinah, as presence, as Earth, as sex, blood, guts, and energy. It is the suppressed, shadowed half of Divinity, often aligned with the feminine, suppressed by centuries of patriarchy.

For Blake, as a poet, the tension between Heaven and Hell is not one which ought to be resolved. Hell without Heaven is total, sensual, Satanic anarchy. A less well-known Proverb of Hell, for example, is "Sooner murder an infant in its cradle than nurse unacted desires." Hell has no ethics, no restraint. It is a de Sadian libertinism, and is corrosive of all order. But of course, Heaven without Hell is all order, all stasis, all restraint. It is dead, devoid of true holiness, and governed by fear and Reason to the exclusion of love and human energy. This, too, should sound familiar to those of us who either grew up in such a world, or see its leaders on television. In our time as in Blake's, there are those who would extinguish all fire in the name of the occasional conflagration.

What Blake sought, and what I for years have sought, is not a "golden mean" or happy medium or vacuous "balance" between the two poles. It's trite to say that, yes, well, I'll have some of each, because where one draws the balancing line is entirely determinative of the substantive result. Rather, Blake sought a marriage, a union of the two, a messianic wedding of opposites.

Likewise and *l'havdil*, I've tried for years to square the Jewish circle with creative readings of Scripture which showed that Judaism, too, embraces both Heaven and Hell, spirit and sense, God and Body. But it's clear to me that, for many people, and probably most, Judaism is about Heaven. It restrains our desires so that civilization can flourish. It is monotheistic: there is only One God, and while He does take on many different images, most (like Goddess, Pan, Christ, Ganesh) are beyond the pale. It is indeed about traditional values; family and marriage are built upon the curtailment and constraint of human sexuality. From the perspective of Heaven religion, liberated sensuality, and arguably even humanism, are the workings of Hell.

And it is indeed a slippery slope down. Just four years ago, I wrote what I thought was an innocent essay called "Guilt and Groundedness," in which I noticed, *vipassana*-style, that the feeling of "deep down" is just a feeling; it has no particular claim upon truth. There, my context was sexuality, and noticing how self-hatred that has been reinforced for twenty years will seem more "deep down" than self-affirmation that has been taught for only five or six—not because it's truer, or what you really feel, but simply because of time. And so the slippage began, first moving away from Orthodoxy, then the notion of normative Judaism, then the pretensions of monotheism.

Yet I have not slipped into darkness. On the contrary, throughout the entire rake's progress, I have checked in with Light. And throughout, like Blake's hero, I have found Light accessible even where Heaven's angels say there is only darkness. From the perspective of Heaven, there is light and there is darkness. As one slides into Hell, there is only Light. But there is fear too. My ego won't let go of the notion that God wants some things, but not others. That God won't love me if I fail to do this or that mitzvah. That there is a force in the world other than Love. I see the heresy of this Manichean view, but it's the heresy of the Orthodox. Just try to follow the inversions: the voice of Hell, which is half the voice of God, sees everything as holy and the road to Hell as the spiritual path to enlightenment. Meanwhile, the choruses of Heaven who sing of dichotomies—the pious ones—are the true heretics, for they place divisions in

God and deny the omnipresence of love.

I see precedent for this Blakean "Satanic" spirituality in some strands of the Kabbalah, because uprooting the basic Manicheanism of normative Judaism is a central part of a certain Kabbalistic agenda. Theosophical Kabbalah insists on a radical re-understanding of evil, in which evil is merely that which is erroneously separated. Ultimately, it is not vanquished so much as reincorporated, reabsorbed. There is only Infinite Light (*ohr ein sof*) after all. For the Kabbalists, this only happens at redemption—but for Sabbateans, their Hasidic heirs, and today's neo-Hasids and neo-Kabbalists, it is an ontological fact at all times: God is *yotzer or u'voreh hoshech*, the source of light and dark. Division is apparent, unity is real. To see that everything is light: this is the realization of the *Ein Sof* that underlies nondual Judaism, neo-Hasidism, and, in very different language, Mahayana Buddhism as well ("To see the light in everyone and everything," Lama Surya Das told me when I asked him, à la Hillel, to summarize his entire Buddhist Torah in one sentence).

Experientially, I occasionally feel the truth of the nondual, of Infinite Light. There are still moments of alienation; and for now, I step back from them, retreating to Jewish practice with its boundaries and norms. But in general, as the cords loosen, there is more breath, not less. So both my experience and heretical neo-Kabbalah point to the same place, and that *Makom* is one of love, acceptance, compassion, truth, ease, awareness, being, consciousness, bliss. But my love quakes with an admixture of fear. What if it is true that what hides behind the greatest of taboos are indeed the greatest of truths? What if it is true that what is condemned is simply the light in a vessel too sacred for orthodoxy? When I can truly surrender, the notion makes all the sense in the world. When I cannot, I'm terrified. In either state, I feel that those of us, and we are many, who see spirituality as advancing eros rather than controlling it are a pole apart from our co-religionists who still worship in pews and believe the old tales. I'm not sure how many of them there are, outside fundamentalist communities. But they are not reactionary; they are decent people, and probably more numerous than the rest of us. So, fear asks: What if they are right?

Again, as with Blake, this must perforce be a marriage, not a regression. I am not suggesting that the worshipers of Baal lived in some Arcadian unity with the cosmos, and weren't possibly cruel, vengeful, and unethical. The values of Heaven are to be integrated, not rejected or reversed. Anyway, spirituality is not really the same as Satanism; it's only called that by the armies of Heaven, who burn witches and condemn shamans. Spirituality doesn't venerate the devil; it observes that he doesn't exist. If this is a marriage, it is one haunted by uncertainty and covetousness. As much as I have seen renewal and vitality in the unchaining of eros, I have also seen firsthand how it can overtake even sincerely meant intentions of ethical conduct. As much as I feel myself to be a kind of refugee from Heaven's suburban lawns, there are moments when I wonder about the lives of my peers who live there with their children. Maybe it is only a marriage of convenience. But there is a quality of love that I feel when nothing is surrendered, one I no longer seek to teach to others but nonetheless set my life beside. There is a kind of union between sense and soul, earthly and heavenly. It is fierce and gentle, sexual and spiritual, and it lights heart and body afire.

November 2008

Part Three

Unknowing

Monogamy and Monotheism

I so want to be in love
To believe monotheistically in you,
that you are my tender, most tender love
and give to you my sense of wonder —
worlds captured in words
—Abraham Joshua Heschel, "Youngest Desire"

Falling out of love is never easy, especially after a three-year relationship with someone I once hoped to marry and build a life with. For me, the last several months have been like a period of grief; some days are fine, some are filled with shadow, and most are a little hollow.

But as the winter has given way to spring, and spring begun to hint of summer, there has begun to be a bit more light. I fell in love, as Heschel wrote, monotheistically. I wanted my partner to be my primary source of love, affection, companionship, and support. I wanted to turn to him whenever I needed help, and to hold him when he did. Although I maintained many friendships, some of them quite dear, I loved that my partner was my best friend, my secret-keeper, the one who was dear to my heart. In the months since our separation, it's become clear to me that this monogamy of affection came at the price of my love for other people. Not just friends and lovers but others, too; people would come up to me after a workshop or retreat, for example, and tell me how inspired they were, how grateful, how I'd changed their lives. And often, I'd be unable to take it in. I'd try; I'm neither so famous nor so arrogant as to simply shrug it off. But sometimes, the words would almost bounce off of me, like so much small talk.

Or, I'd have lovely gatherings of friends, on special occasions like a birthday or book-launch party, and barely feel the love and affection they were offering me. Again, not always. But often, there would be an invisible disconnect between us.

No wonder that, when things were difficult with my partner, I felt so alone. I had offers of support, listening, and aid—but I felt unable to embrace them. I had been so emotionally monogamous for so long that I'd cut myself off from the love being offered to me by others.

Even more damaging than this alienation from the love of others, though, was my alienation from my own capacity to love. It's been observed before that perhaps the most joyous aspect of a loving relationship isn't being loved by someone else—it's being able to love them. To feel love, as well as beloved. Love feels delightful; warm, energized, buoyant; all the clichés turn true. And of course, it's possible to feel that love not just for one's partner, but for oneself, and for other people, even for God and trees and breath. But I became so dependent on the love I received from my partner that I stopped relying on myself (or anything else) to generate it.

It was a kind of self-impoverishment. I had seen, in contemplative and shamanic settings, how important it was for me simply to love—to love myself, others, God, the world. And yet it was almost impossible for me to do that, so accustomed I had become to receiving love from someone else. Indeed, trying felt like yet another betrayal: what if, by generating love for myself, I cut myself off from the love of my sweet partner? What if I had no need for him? Fate intervened, I suppose. Or, not fate, but the mutual choices of two people no longer fresh in their love, and at least one impelled to take the next steps on his journey alone.

Slowly, over the last several months, I have begun to open my heart a bit more to other people, other things, and myself—and new growth has emerged from the bare branches. I find my friends all the more beloved. I want to sing to my house, to the woods, and even to God in the sing-song love-talk once reserved for one person only. And I have learned—been forced to learn—some of the capacities of my own heart, to generate love like a furnace. No doubt much of this seems simplistic, or perhaps banal, New Age, or sentimental. But as the Kotsker Rebbe said, and as I've quoted more than once recently, "there is nothing so whole as a broken heart"—because in its brokenness is openness, in its fractured state a wholeness which transcends the individual. I have experienced that over these spring months, an awakening from a beautiful dream that was nonetheless a slumber. I am even, at times, grateful.

I have noticed a parallel between this process of de-monogamizing my affection and the, by now, years-long process of opening in my religious life. For some time now, I have been drifting away from orthodox, then traditional, then mainstream, then exclusive, and then even non-heretical Judaism. I don't fancy myself a heretic, exactly, but I do recognize that some of my beliefs and practices may be considered heretical by others: preparing to spend several months in silence at a Buddhist monastery, participating in (neo)pagan rituals like Beltane, having intimate visions of Christ, Ganesh, and the Goddess. For many, I'm sure (and I've been told by plenty of commenters), all this is so far beyond the pale of normative Judaism that for me to hold myself as a Jewish teacher, as I sometimes do, is utterly unacceptable. I understand that, and accept the judgment. But in my experience, none of it has undermined my love of God, and of the Jewish God in particular.

Quite the contrary. By gradually opening to these other forms and other manifestations, my capacity to love has increased. And so mysticism—by which I mean the direct, loving experience of ultimate reality—has flourished. The analogy to earthly love is, presumably, obvious. YHVH, we are told in the Torah, is a jealous god. He wants exclusive, monogamous, monotheistic fidelity—and elsewhere in the Bible, Israel is repeatedly referred to as a harlot, a slut. The traditional Jewish faithful today take this demand quite seriously, and comply with missionary zeal. They reject not just the idols of the nations, but their customs, their languages, their clothes. These latter-day Jewish pietists are, indeed, more faithful to their God than I am, and I know from my own past experience and their present testimonies that they experience love in return.

I see in my own past Judaism the same pattern as I see in my past relationship. For years, I feared that if I stepped outside the bounds of Jewish exclusivity, the intensity of my commitment to the Jewish God would wane. And I didn't want it to wane; I couldn't articulate it at the time, but it gave me a sense of connection and security and love. It was mother's breast and father's strong arms all wrapped up in one. And so I guarded those boundaries. Gradually, though, I succumbed to temptation. I danced at Burning Man. I sat (though didn't bow) before a statue of the Buddha. I stopped worrying about whether sacred sexuality was idolatry or not, because I felt the Divine presence within it. Throughout, I "checked in," committed to being faithful to the One I loved—and throughout, the One was still there. In the depths, I called to God, and God answered me. I raised my eyes to the mountains, and asked where my help would come from—and my help was there.

No longer "God" in any traditional sense, certainly no longer Yahweh, or male, or transcendent. Now nondual, now seemingly atheistic, now a motion and a spirit that impels all thinking things, now feminine, now queer. At times this "God" seemed to melt away entirely, into a mere mindstate, a pattern of the brain. But no matter; the knowing remained; and consciousness itself; and love. When I was younger, one of my greatest spiritual fears was that mystical experience was merely a delusion, a dance of neurons in the brain. Now, I barely care anymore. Either God is Everything, in which case the neuronal dance is simply a helpful way to see the truth, or there is no God and the universe simply is what it is, in which case the neuronal dance can only be judged by its fruits: whether it makes us kinder, wiser, and more in awe of existence. And that it clearly does.

I still maintain many of the ancient forms of faithfulness. I don't eat cultically forbidden foods, I rest on the seventh day. As I've written about before, though, I do so not out of fear of retribution but simply as acts of love. The other day, I sat around waiting for Shabbat to end, wanting to go out, and while I questioned why I was adhering to these Pharisaic restrictions, the answer of love remained. That is why I do it, I admit. I wish others would admit it as well.

So while I am not a polytheist exactly, I do no longer believe that there is but one avenue to the holy—not even one per person. I follow many paths, and like to see where they lead. I have come to trust in the same salvation being at the multiple ends of the roads, as long as when I get there I can still say *hinei*, here, and trust and not fear.

And of course, while this essay is about emotional, rather than physical, monogamy, I wonder about the nexus between monotheism and monogamy in all its forms. Following Christianity, traditional Judaism has demanded physical monogamy for the last thousand years, though it was never really practiced by men, and thus must be seen as part of patriarchal oppression. Today, too, America's fiercest religious battles are not about ethics and social justice (of paramount importance to the prophets) but sexuality, pleasure, and gender. Today, to question physical and relational monogamy is to question "traditional values," that is, religious values. Are traditionalists worried that if one form of faithfulness is abandoned, others will follow? That if we yield to, rather than repress, our hearts and bodies, that we will wander outside the bounds of propriety, safety, and tribe? That as we learn that love is available in many forms and faces, that we might think the same of spirit as well?

Perhaps the skeptics are right that when believers say, "I love you, God," they are really saying "I love." In my experience, there is no significant difference.

June 2008

Monotheism and the Spirits of Nature

Recently, on a trip to South Korea, I stood before at a rock formation venerated by Korean shamans. The place was so holy that the power of it, the energy of it, was immediately apparent and absolutely obvious. And it moved me to tell a story about irony, idolatry, and nature.

For many monotheists, nature-centered spirituality smacks of paganism, and thus idolatry. But for me, being cut off from nature is idolatry. When I'm surrounded by the noises of the city, and the incessant lures of consumer capitalism, I become diverted from my true self and my spiritual path.

I love urban life. Yet its pleasures evoke, sometimes within minutes, a consumption-based perspective of "What do I want and how can I get it?"—the *yetzer hara* becomes taken for granted. I define myself in terms of the pleasure or pain that is being provided, and confuse stillness with boredom. Surrounded by glass and concrete, I lose my connection to my Source, and have to work to get it back. So, to the extent I still subscribe to monotheism at all, I find it enriched, not compromised, by the spirits in nature my Israelite ancestors sought so hard to erase.

Theoretically, as a nondualist/pantheist/whateverist who thinks that "God is Everything" makes more sense than "God is in Heaven," nature versus the city shouldn't matter. My spiritual practice is oriented toward resting in the simple feeling of being, in naked awareness itself, regardless of what perceptions are occurring. So in theory, I should be as at home in a parking lot as in a meadow; awareness is in both. "Is"—the way I translate YHVH—is in both. And yet, I'm not.

Perhaps the pivot here is that while we often think of nature as a positive quality—as if it is something added to our experience—I want to suggest that nature is, well, our natural state. It is urban life that is something added to life as it is, something that covers up the natural state. Our ancestors lived in conditions more connected with the realities of natural life than all but the most rugged of our contemporary vacations.

Like other animals, humans are connected to the cycles of time and the seasons. Yet unlike other animals, we have created an artificial world that defies those cycles. That world, not nature, is the change. The artificial world is the idol we erect between ourselves and everything else.

So it's not that "going into nature" is adding ingredients to the soup of consciousness. "Going into nature" is subtracting noise. Maintaining contact with "the simple feeling of being" is easier sometimes than others, and when there is something interposed between the soul and its natural state, and that something is a giant titillation of the selfish inclination, it is more difficult to rest in the omnipresent truth. Nature does not condition God. But un-nature tends to block our awareness of Her.

There is, perhaps, even a third irony, which is that I am most able to be monotheistically devotional when I am polytheistically awake. When God is abstract, I am able to approach God-consciousness with wisdom. But when God is concrete, and manifest in form, then devotion becomes primary. When I'm in touch with the various spirits inherent in natural settings, my heart opens, and my religious soul awakens. The fact that the spirit in question resides in a sacred mountain venerated by shamans might trouble some monotheists, but at this point in my journey, the particular form in which God/dess manifests is much less important than the energy of the manifestation itself. I am a more ardent Jew—that is to say, a more heart-centered and devotional one—when I am in sacred spaces, regardless of the particular traditions which venerate them.

More ardent—and more firmly grounded in what matters. In my experience, religion denuded of religious experience is likely to have a very short lifespan. Of course, I know that many people are not interested in spiritual experiences, and do not want to have them. I didn't have them myself, until a few years ago. Ten years ago, if someone had told me they visited a shamanic rock and felt a surge of sacred energy, I would raise my eyebrows and confess that such experiences were not part of my spiritual path. But because I have trained, investigated, and explored, they are now. And as a result, I feel closer to, not farther from, the essence of religious life.

My intent is not to pronounce judgment on those who worship an abstract God, or an imaginary father figure derived solely from Scripture. I have also experienced God in traditional monotheistic ways—as a father figure, concerned with righteousness and integrity—and I appreciate that experience. But I appreciate it because it is an experience, not because it happens to conform with a text or tradition. It sits alongside my experiences of Goddess-in-the-form-of-nature-spirit, God-as-emptiness, Spirit-as-eros, and so on. Thus the last of my ironies is that precisely because I remain a monotheist, I am committed to the holiness of all of these encounters.

I confess, the spirit of the sacred mountain does not feel to me like the spirit in the ancient tree; they do indeed seem like separate, distinct things, and if I were differently inclined, I might well describe some as sacred, others as profane. But I am not so inclined. I want to know the sacred in all of its garbs, recognizing all our concepts and maps as so many attempts to interpret the uninterpretable. The counter-intuitive and revolutionary proposition of monotheism is that beneath all those forms, there is One Reality. And to me, the necessary consequence of that proposition is that all religious forms gesture at the truth. Of course, the interpretations we provide may well lead us astray from monotheism. But before and beneath those interpretations, there is the experience, and that is where truth resides.

I want to suggest that, today, monotheism needs the paganisms of nature in order to fight the new paganism of commercial capitalism, with its deification of desire and its technologies of satisfaction. Against the market, God doesn't stand a chance, unless religion offers a tangible alternative to Mammon—and that means experience. Indeed, we are seeing in our times a return to non-rational experience, to spirituality, and to personal mystical encounters with the Divine. This trend is both for better and for worse—all these moves are often couched in fundamentalist religious language, or still more crusader-like zeal. But if we open the doors to multiple forms and sources of inspiration, monotheistic religion can be radically pluralistic, rather than imperialistic, and, above all, deeply powerful. Dry religion cannot be felt—but nature religion can. Maybe it's possible to open our hearts to the spirits of the rocks and the trees. Hopefully they will forgive us our trespasses against them. We need them.

July 2009

The Nondual Goddess

The biblical religion which eventually became Judaism was but one of many authentic Israelite traditions. The priestly elite condemned those other traditions, banning their practices, outlawing their images, and insisting that God was only male, and only in the sky. But we today are not only their heirs, but also the heirs to those suppressed and marginalized voices who spoke of the earth, the goddess, and the sacred feminine. One of our generation's leading actualizers of that inheritance is my friend Rabbi Dr. Jill Hammer, co-founder of the Kohenet Hebrew Priestess program. We spoke on the occasion of the publication of her new prayer book, the Siddur HaKohanot: A Hebrew Priestess Prayerbook.

Jay: Let's start with a phrase from Raphael Patai's seminal book, *The Hebrew Goddess.* Who is the Hebrew Goddess? What do we mean, conceptually or experientially, by this term? In the Kohenet siddur, the goddess seems to stand for nonduality, but isn't the language of god/goddess dyadic? Another way of asking this is, why is the goddess female?

Jill: The Goddess as a feminine yet nondual force partly has to do with the mammalian experience of womb/child/mother as a unity/multiplicity experience. It also has to do with the cycles of birth and death, with which the Goddess is almost invariably associated (while God-stuff often has to do with the transcendent, the infinite, and/or the hero's journey through the cycles). I experience these characteristics deeply in my spiritual life, yet when I try to talk about them I feel I'm approaching gender essentialism. I struggle a lot with the nondual piece. My experience is that people (at least in American Goddess culture) see Goddess as nondual and this distinguishes their experience from the general Western experience of God. However, saying "the feminine side of the nondual" seems a bit absurd, since that by definition is dual.

Jay: Sometimes I hear people criticize any movement "back to the womb" as regressive, trying to fulfill some deep psychological stuff.

What's up with that?

Jill: One of my early Goddess experiences was studying with Layne Redmond, a percussionist who researches priestess/Goddess connections to drumming. While teaching about drumming as an echo of the maternal/fetal heartbeat, she noted the fact that ova—the actual eggs that will later produce children—are formed in a girl baby before she is born. This means that part of what became me was not only in my biological mother's womb, but in my *grandmother's* womb. This blew my mind. It completely transformed the way I thought about my body and the way I thought about time. It blows my mind even more now to think that if my daughter Raya has children, their earliest origin will have been in *me*. So for me, the idea of "back to the womb" is not regressive. It's more of an anchor in time and space, and a reflection of the truth that our bodies and spirits blend; we're literally not separate from others. This is true on all kinds of levels, but for humans, it's the womb where this unitive experience is deeply physicalized.

While my wife and I were visiting Newgrange and Knowth in Ireland, we saw how people five thousand years ago put immense time and resources into building womb-like dark tombs/shrines where the solstice light would fall once a year on the ashes of their dead loved ones. This seems so deeply related to the notion of the earth as the place of the seed, and the idea that the earth-womb (unlike the literal human womb) can bring life from what has died. That's also the "back to the womb" piece in a non-regressive way.

Psychologically, at least for me and for many other women whose writing I've read, returning to the womb is about experiencing our own creativity and our desire to fulfill our potential—and the potential of the world, which we sense through the unitive mystical uterine experience. The return to the womb is the journey to the underworld, which is a complex and integrative journey acknowledging one's separateness and one's merging at once. It's an engine for increasing emotional, spiritual, intellectual and physical fecundity (not necessarily biological fertility, though that's part of it for some of us). It's about entrainment, not about regression. Maybe for the male principle, returning to the womb feels like a regression or an escape, but for women, in my experience, it can be like taking a step into our own creative selves by entraining with the universe. The womb doesn't eliminate the individual; it re-awakens the fertile potential in the individual.

Jay: One irony here is that "paganism" is at once more multi-theistic and more uni-theistic than monotheism. On the one hand, paganism includes lots of energies, deities, etc.; it's very polymorphous, or even polytheist. On the other hand, in the pagan view, we're all part of one web and not separate. Whereas, traditional monotheism has only one big Energy, but yet maintains that I'm separate from it. Monotheism seems like more of "one," but it's actually more of "two."

Jill: I'm right with you on the irony of monotheism (where there is one god but many things) and paganism (where there's really only one thing). I want to talk about another subject, though. I've spent a lot of time the last few months thinking about the divine masculine and re-integrating that into my self-concept. For me, the divine masculine often corresponds with a sense of being supported, loved, or guided in my specificity (my sense of the divine feminine is much more about embodying and accepting the whole). I've also been thinking about the ways the male reproductive process (in which seed has to be given to another separate being) might relate to "masculine" kinds of spirituality that emphasize the letting go of attachment and/or the giving up of control to a higher power.

Jay: It's funny, when I think about it, I think masculine spirituality is connected with building, doing, standing on top of the mountain, as well as violence, war, domination, hierarchy, strength, linearity. To me, anything that is about letting go or giving up is about relinquishing control and thus a necessary counterweight to masculinity, rather than an expression of it. Personally, and I think this is true for many men, the reproductive process still seems to end with insemination. That is, of course, completely ridiculous. But I think that for many men, the subsequent nine months of work are rendered almost invisible. I mean, whole civilizations refer to children as a man's "seed"!

Jill: This is very powerful, what you're saying here. This may be related to the way women have a hard time not giving away the store—we're trained to nurture, so being told that we're focusing on ourselves too much is triggering. And yet—women have an internalized masculine that we need to deal with, not run away from. We have fathers, brothers, lovers, sons, and male-introjects, and these relationships are part of who we are.

I too experience the Divine masculine as being about building and achieving. I do think that the drive to achieve is connected to the frailty of human life. We build because we want to last, even though we can't. For me, this feels connected to the male process of emitting seed, which is ephemeral but has the potential to create life. This seems connected to the figure of Christ, who dies to create eternal life, or the ideas of the Buddha, who encourages non-attachment and yet deep engagement in the world.

September 2010

Ayahuasca and Kabbalah

In 1954, Aldous Huxley published *The Doors of Perception*, a famous essay observing that the effects of mescaline were remarkably similar to the unitive mysticism of the world's great religions, particularly Vedanta, the philosophical-mystical form of Hinduism which Huxley practiced. It caused an immediate sensation. Many in the public were outraged by its pro-pharmacological spirit, and many in the academy accused Huxley (like William James before him) of flattening different mystical traditions and disregarding distinctions between "sacred and profane" mystical practice.

But many more were inspired. Huxley's essay, and other works like it, set the agenda for 1960s spirituality, and what later came to be called the New Age movement. He provided a philosophical explanation of what was important about mescaline—that our perceptive faculties filter out more than they let in, and that mescaline, like meditation, opens those doors wider—and a personal account of what a "trip" was like. He showed how entheogens (as they later came to be called) could be a part of a sincere spiritual practice. And he perhaps unwittingly imported a certain Vedanta agenda of what the "ultimate" mystical experience was like: union.

As has been argued by some scholars over the last few decades, this claim of ultimacy—that *unio mystica* is the peak form of mystical experience, with others defined by how close they approach it—is actually a rather partisan one. Why is "union with the All" superior to, or more true than, deity mysticism, visions of Krishna/Christ/spirits, or the text-based mysticism of the Kabbalah? Sure, for Vedanta it is, but that's just Vedanta's view.

Two generations of spiritual seekers have been influenced, for better and for worse, by this hierarchy. From the naive hippie to the sophisticated yogi, Jewish Renewalniks to Ken Wilberites, hundreds of thousands of spiritual practitioners have implicitly or explicitly assumed the prioritization of the unitive over all else: the point is that All is One. Within the Jewish context, there have been at least two forms of this exercise. In the academy, scholars have debated whether true unitive mysticism is absent in Kabbalah (as Gershom Scholem maintained) or whether it is present (as Moshe Idel has countered), as if the presence or absence of this form of mystical experience is a prerequisite for admission to the Parliament of World Religions. And among Jewish seekers, mystical concepts which may or may not conform to unitive mysticism, like *devekut*, are redefined in terms of it, to the point that any spiritual state may be interpreted as a direct experience of the Divine.

Most of these latter constituencies are also, like Huxley, influenced by the psychedelic experience, primarily that of mushrooms and LSD. While most contemporary spiritual teachers have long since given these substances up, in favor of meditation and other mystical practices which afford the same experiences in a more reliable container (and one greatly enriched by self-examination and introspection), if you ask them, as I have, they'll admit that the psychedelic experience formed an important part of their spiritual initiation. Whether it's what got them on the road in the first place, or confirmed their earlier intuitions, psychedelics have set the agenda for a huge percentage of contemporary spiritual teachers, across religious and spiritual denominations, and many of their followers as well.

These two trends that "all is one" is the point, and that it accords with the psychedelic experience—have occasionally led to a distortion of religious and spiritual traditions. In the Kabbalah, for example, unitive mysticism is only a small part of a wide panoply of mystical experiences. Yes, there are texts which speak of annihilation of the self (*bittul hayesh*) and a unification with God (*achdut*). But these are, truthfully, in the minority. Many more are visionary texts, describing theophanies of all shapes and sizes; or records of prophecy or angelic communication; or less explicitly unitive accounts of proximity to the Divine. Yet there's a sense, among teachers of contemporary Kabbalah—and I'm not referring here to the Kabbalah Centre (where Madonna goes), which does not teach Kabbalah proper, but rather a unique and sometimes weird synthesis of Kabbalah, the Human Potential movement, and New Religious Movements like Scientology—that unitive mysticism is the *summum bonum*, the ultimate good.

Some Kabbalistic texts agree, but many others do not. For example, Rabbi Arthur Green, today one of progressive Judaism's leading teachers, in 1968 wrote an article (under a pseudonym) called "Psychedelics and Kabbalah," explicitly analogizing the psychedelic experiences to aspects of Kabbalistic teaching—but selecting those aspects of Kabbalah and Hasidism which fit the experience. Naturally, Green was also influenced by the many forms of non-Jewish mysticism popular at the time, most of whom asserted that all is One, but in that essay, he makes clear that the psychedelic experience affected how he understood Kabbalah. Green, like fellow practitioner-academic Daniel Matt, has been enormously influential: their anthologies of Hasidic and Kabbalistic texts are read far more widely than the texts themselves, and are widely assumed to represent the mainstream of their respective traditions.

I am not taking a position on whether this "distortion" is for good or ill; in my own practice, the nondual/unitive perspective plays a central role, and I am grateful for it, whatever its sources. But I have a hunch that it is about to change.

The reason it is changing is that more and more Jewish spiritual seekers are pursuing non-unitive paths. This includes earth-based ritual, shamanic ritual, and other disciplines which, while they may hold the view that "all is one," provide experiences of differentiation (energies, elements, visions, etc). But perhaps more importantly, it includes drinking ayahuasca, smoking DMT and related compounds, and visionary shamanic-entheogenic practices which offer different experiences from the unitive one. The ayahuasca trip, unlike the mescaline one, is not especially unitive: indeed, one of its hallmarks is the sense of communication with other life forms or consciousnesses. And while a sense of all is One is sometimes reported in the midst of the ayahuasca experience, it's more common to read reports of visions of phenomena—manifestation, not essence.

Some of these accounts are strikingly similar to texts from the Hechalot and Merkavah schools of Jewish mysticism, which flourished between the second and ninth centuries. In the texts from this period, we read detailed accounts of heavenly palaces, Divine chariots, and angels; of ascents to other realms which seem somehow to be in outer space or an extraterrestrial locale; of a sense of great danger, but also great awe, beauty and love; and of beings which travel on some kind of cosmic vehicle. The descriptions are visionary and auditory, much like the accounts of ayahuasca visions. They are "shamanic" journeys, both in the sense of being journeys of the soul to other realm and in the sense of a transformation of the self. They yield information, prophecy, revelation, theophany. And they are not really about "all is one."

Hechalot and Merkavah mysticism is studied in the academy, but it is little known in the contemporary spiritual world. It's complicated, arcane, and literally other-worldly. But just as the unitive moments of Hasidism appeal to those who have had a unitive experience on mushrooms, so too the visionary aspects of Hechalot and Merkavah mysticism appeal to those who have had a visionary experience on ayahuasca. The similarities are striking.

What's more, Hechalot and Merkavah mysticism, related as it is to gnosticism, provides one of world literature's richest libraries of other-worldly mystical experience. It's eerie how similar some of these millennia-old texts are to the records contemporary journeyers provide of the ayahuasca trip: the sense of being in "outer space," the tenuous links to consensual reality, the sense of danger, and above all the colorful descriptions of chambers, angels, songs, palaces, ascents, descents, fire, music, and so much more. It also provides a sense of history, context, and "belonging" to those who affiliate with Judaism, Christianity, or gnosticism; like unitive experiences, non-unitive visionary/ecstatic experiences have a lineage within these traditions. Perhaps, too, it might offer guidance for those seeking to integrate such experiences into their lives.

To reiterate, I am taking no position on whether unitive or non-unitive experiences are "better," and certainly not more true. I see nondual essence and dualistic manifestation as two sides of the same ineffable unity. My point, simply, is that much of contemporary Western spirituality derives from a particular psychedelic experience and a particular form of mysticism it approximates. With the increasing popularity of ayahuasca and similar medicines, the former element has changed—and I think the latter will too.

In the esoteric world, this kind of change and interchange has always been with us. Hechalot mystics learned from the gnostics, who learned from the Jews, who learned from the Babylonians. Medieval Kabbalists learned from the Sufis, who learned from the Hindus, who learned from the Buddhists, who learned from other Hindus. One need not make the claim that all mysticism is the same thing in order to recognize that mystics across space and time have understood themselves to be gesturing toward the same truths, albeit in very different ways. And those differences advance, not obstruct, the progress of realization. After all, when one can ultimately know nothing, it helps to learn from everything.

January 2008

Both Buddhism and Judaism

Many Jews meditate, and most meditate in ways developed in the Buddhist tradition. That this is so, is undeniable; why this is so, is a subject for sociologists. But what does it mean for the practitioner? What are the benefits of Buddhist-derived meditation for a Jewish spiritual path, and what are the benefits of a Jewish path for serious dharma practice?

I'd like to sketch a few answers here, based on my own experience and studies, which I'll describe briefly first. On the Buddhist side, I have done serious dharma practice for a decade, sitting two- and three- month silent retreats in the Theravadan tradition (familiar to Americans through institutions such as the Insight Meditation Society and the Spirit Rock center, as well as the teachings of S.N. Goenka). I have reached a level of "attainment" (so-called) that qualifies me to teach in that tradition. I do not have the type of Buddhist religious practice that would be familiar to, say, a Chinese Buddhist, but I do have a fairly typical Western Buddhist meditation practice, as that form has come to be understood in the last half-century .

On the Jewish side, I have studied and taught Kabbalah for fifteen years, am completing my Ph.D. in Jewish Thought at Hebrew University, and have written two books and about a hundred articles on Jewish theology, culture, and spirituality. My personal practice includes keeping Shabbat in a superficially Orthodox way, keeping kosher in a Conservative way, and celebrating all the major and minor holidays. I speak Hebrew fluently and lived in Israel for three years. I have sampled Jewish meditation traditions as well as Buddhist ones, and I am invested in Jewish cultural and religious life as a committed nondenominational American Jew. Finally, in both traditions, my teachers include traditionalists and innovators, spiritual teachers and academics; I am informed by all of these approaches.

There are, as many jokes attest, as many iterations of Judaism as there are Jews. Personally, I see my Judaism as a way of being in relationship with that which is beyond my personal concerns and self-centered nature. Jewish ritual brings me spiritual experiences, communal bonds, ritual forms, and a calendar that carries me through a variety of human experiences. And Judaism's orientation toward justice, as well as to familial and communal life more broadly, reminds me that what happens between my ears is not the true measure of religious significance.

Jewish sacred time makes visible an aspect of human life that is often invisible. At almost all waking moments, our minds are busy taking us somewhere else—into the future or the past, into evaluations about the thing rather than the thing itself, into a thousand different desires. The television may be playing and you may not even notice what show is on. You can be nervously twitching your leg without realizing it. You may be lost in thought and unaware even of your own emotions. So, rituals, prayers, shared moments of cultural connection are invitations to wake up out of the daze and into other, perhaps deeper, strands of our lives, including emotional connection and a sense of the sacred. The quiet leads to the sacred, and the sacred leads to the reminder of what matters.

Some this should sound familiar to Western Buddhists, and to spiritual seekers of all stripes. Buddhist and Buddhist-derived meditation is an excellent way of calming the mind ("concentration") and then, based on the foundation of that calm, seeing into the essential nature of experience itself ("insight"). In my Theravadan Buddhist frame, the former is primarily of value because it is a ground for the latter. The point isn't to relax because it feels good, or even because it leads to spiritual experiences, but because a quieted mind enables insight to arise.

There are many directions such insight takes. In Theravadan Buddhism, it is guided toward a direct experience of the Four Noble Truths: that suffering exists, but that it is caused by clinging (*tanha*) and thus may be ended as well. The intuitive knowledge of these truths is one iteration of liberation, enlightenment, the point of it all. Another conception of awakening is to understand the core characteristics of all phenomena: impermanence, unsatisfactoriness (i.e., nothing can make you happy forever), and emptiness or non-self.

In Western Buddhism, though, the realm of insight has tended to expand. Now it includes one's psychological "stuff" such as deep-seated traumas or habits of mind. It may also include realizations similar to mystical ones: seeing great beauty, or glimpsing the unitive aspect of existence, or seeing how greed, hatred, and delusion operate in our contemporary political and social lives. In these expanded forms, Buddhist insight and Jewish spiritual insights might converge.

One simile I've often used for how meditation works is that of the mind being like a radio, trying to tune into a station, but filled with the static of distracting thoughts and worldly concerns. To hear the music clearly, there are two choices. One is to turn up the volume, and the other to turn down the static. In life, turning up the volume means having intense experiences: peak spiritual moments, or other moments in life when things are suddenly crystal clear because you are really there. I hope you've had such experiences. Maybe you've felt this when you were really "on" in some artistic creation, or, if you have a religious practice, when your practice took you to heights of ecstasy you'd never experienced before. These peak experiences are really nourishing. They show us that there is far, far more to this miracle of life than what we ordinarily experience. They give us a glimpse of possibility, of Light.

Unfortunately, peak experiences tend not to last; you can't chase kicks forever. So, instead of blasting the volume, is it possible to fine-tune the perceptive apparatus so that we lose the static, the station gets tuned in really clearly, and we can be present? Yes—and meditation is a process for doing so. Through various techniques of slowing down the mind and letting go of thoughts and desires and the rest, we enable ourselves to see clearly. That's really the central point.

That's a Western-Buddhist way of saying it. In Jewish language, we might inquire into the mandate *v'ahavta et adonai elohecha, b'chol levavcha, b'chol nafshecha, u'v'chol meodecha.* You shall love YHVH your god, with all of your heart, with all of your soul, and with all of your might. Now, how do you do that? Once again, I come back to the image of the radio and the static: we can learn to turn down the distractions and focus on what really matters, on deeply-held values, or on the silence which gives birth to wonder. This is not about having weird or wacky experiences, but about showing up more fully for whatever life is offering. Rabbi Nachman of Bratzlav said: "The world is full of light and mysteries both wonderful and awesome, but our tiny little hand shades our eyes and prevents them from seeing."

Of course, meditation is not the only way to experience the sacred. Art, love, prayer, ecstatic experiences, sexual intimacy, being of service to others—these work as well. One advantage of meditation, though, is that it enables not just another peak experience, but the possibility to be with whatever experiences arise, including negative mind-states (sadness, anger, despair), and in so doing to gain tremendous insight into how the mind works, and how the forces of greed, hatred, and delusion operate in the world.

In addition, seeing directly, in your experience, how the "self" arises and passes can be a more stable ground for relating to nonduality than any delicious (and potentially delusory) experience. The self really isn't there, not because I had a groovy experience once, but because it disappears on close, careful inspection. Maybe we're waves on the cosmic ocean, or maybe we aren't; maybe God is an accurate description of the universe, or maybe it isn't. Either way, the existential fact is that we are suffering because of our desires and aversions, and there are some ways to work with them. Of course, we will always experience the arising of desire; enlightened people still get hungry. But that gnawing, thirsty, clinging desire—the kind that leads both to damaging fights with our friends and to racism and nationalism—that's what the Buddha taught how to lose.

Why Buddhism? Why not "indigenous" Jewish spiritual practices alone? There are several reasons. First, meditation has always been a marginal, non-systematic, and secondary practice within the Jewish spiritual (let alone legal and ritual) portfolio, whereas it has been a focus of Buddhist monastic life for 2,500 years. As a result, the technologies are better, the systems are better, the maps are better. Finally, I would be lying if I didn't admit the repulsive effects of those iterations of Judaism that have, of late, justified oppression, ethnocentrism, and ordinary meanness. The Buddha Dharma also has its racist and violent versions, but as a personal matter, I have more experience with the Jewish varieties.

Of course, there are important differences between Buddhism and Judaism, and I'm not one to efface them. Again, people have different approaches. Some teachers say that *satipatthana* (the cultivation of mindfulness) is actually found within the Jewish tradition, or that Jewish practice *is* mindfulness practice. I don't see how that is historically or textually true, but if it works to end people's suffering and make their lives more holy and just, *baruch hashem*. As for myself, I find my spiritual practice to be enriched by appreciating the differences as well as the convergences.

For example, I know that many Jews practice Buddhist or Buddhist-style meditation because of how it energizes and enlivens Jewish life. This was my motivation at first; when I first discovered meditation, it was like the answer key to my religion. Now I know what all those prayers and books are talking about! When I meditate, the sense of love and sacredness arises naturally; the mysterious quality of knowing itself... it is impossible to describe, and yet, it is accessible.

But that's changed. Over time, my dharma practice has been transformed and sometimes eroded by Jewish practice—mostly, I think, for the better. It has helped me see where there is too much *yirah* (fear, awe) in my Jewish practice and not enough *ahavah* (love). It has helped me purge doctrines I consider to be noxious, like that of a chosen people, or a particular culture/people/religion being better than others, or Divine reward and punishment, or the trans-historicity of sacred text.

The dharma also asks different questions than Jewish spirituality (and, again *a fortiori*, Judaism) does, and its questions align with what I find to be important and inspiring. The Buddha's teaching, at least in the traditions through which I access it, is focused on authentic happiness, the release from suffering, transforming the self to be more wise and more compassionate. Mainstream Judaism is much more interested in setting up a just society with laws, in something called "God," and in the Jewish people as a communal unit. Of course, from Ezekiel to the Sefer Yetzirah to the Zohar to the Tanya, Jewish spirituality is also frequently interested in contemplative wisdom, but even in those and other books, the wisdom tends to be more esoteric, textual, and mystical than experiential, psychological, or practical.

I've also found—and I think this was true even before I became more serious about the dharma—that compassion—not a belief in obligation, faith in an origination myth, or fear of punishment—is the best motivator ethical behavior. Jewish text is very good at articulating moral imperatives. "Do not oppress the stranger, for you were once strangers in Egypt"—if only American conservatives could internalize that norm, repeated a dozen times in the Torah. But it's often not as good at providing a roadmap for how such an ethical transformation is to be accomplished. Human beings, especially men, have inborn tendencies to dominate, oppress, and other-ize. How do we work with them? How do we strengthen the *yetzer tov* and weaken the *yetzer hara*? Of course there are Jewish answers to these questions, but in my experience the Buddhist ones are simply more effective, at least today.

Dharma practice has lowered the stakes of whether any particular experience is "really" a mystical experience, or a vision of God, or whatever. Experience is experience, but as I suggested above, the more lasting change comes about by the mind intuitively grasping the truths of suffering and learning, again intuitively, to profoundly settle back. Some of this "settling back" is profound, as in moments of enlightenment (sometimes described as "seeing the *dhamma*" or "taking *nirvana* as object"). And some of it is everyday, when I'm angry at not being able to find my keys.

Definitely, I'm no longer drawn to what Rabbi Zalman Schachter-Shalomi called "angel shit," the various baroque doo-dads of theosophical Kabbalah, esotericism, and secret doctrines of the soul. They are beautiful doo-dads, but as my own practice has evolved, I care a lot more about justice, ethics, and lasting, real happiness.

Some of the erosion does feel like a loss. Not long ago, I wrote this:

I cherish a personal relationship to a personal God... I love to read psalms, to speak to God in *hitbodedut*, to cultivate a love for the Divine—not just an awe or presence with it. I want to be with God when I'm ecstatic, davening, walking, on the toilet, bored, irritated, and, of course, having sex. I am not just being with what is. I am rapturously, deliriously in love of God. Some times more than others.

If I'm being honest, that's no longer true today. I love love, I love the experience of the sacred, I love small moments of extraordinary beauty. Maybe the word 'God' has just become too fraught and too contentious. Maybe it will come back into my heart. I don't know.

Certainly, the God which I can comprehend loving is not some deity which does or does not exist—God is Existence Itself. This is God as Ein Sof, as everything and nothing. Moses asks how he's supposed to describe God, and gets the reply "I Am That I Am," *Ehyeh Asher Ehyeh*. Take out the pronoun, and you get is, "It Is What It Is." And as heterodox as it may sound, I really see no difference between this nondual YHVH and the Buddhist Dharma with a capital 'D.' It is what it is—that's all there is to it. This is how God is always present, even with prophets in jail and saints in death camps. Because the present is always present. The biggest difference is pedagogical. In dharma practice, by closely observing experience, it's possible to see for oneself that there is nothing really here to call "me." In most Jewish traditions, however, the nondual truth is expressed "top-down." For example, the great Kabbalist Rabbi Moses-Cordovero wrote: "Realize that the Infinite exists in each thing. Do not say 'This is a stone and not God.' Rather, all existence is God, and the stone is a thing pervaded by divinity."

Personally, I find the bottom-up, Buddhist path to this realization to be easier to communicate than the Jewish one, because it takes nothing for granted. I find it to be a more relaxing perspective; there's less fear of being wrong, because if I'm wrong, I'll change my view. There's much less at stake.

Meanwhile, I keep practicing Jewish ritual because I love it, too. It's in my heart, even if no longer in my rational head. Putting on *tallis* and *tefillin* sometimes feels right, and loving, and beautiful. In this regard, I sometimes feel like I'm restoring a balance that Western Buddhist innovators may have lost. Asian Buddhists also have devotional ritual and mythic belief, of course—it's only the Western ones who don't. I love how Jewish ritual elevates concrete, embodied actions like eating and drinking; Theravadan monasticism can sometimes tend toward the ascetic.

I'm not worried about hybridization. First, if we're serious about spiritual practice, and not dilettantes, that will include close discernment as to when we're on a spiritual salad bar (some of this, more of that) and when we're being pragmatic and wise in choosing the practices that help us be the kinds of people we know we want to be. Second, we're all living in the salad bar anyway, or some vast cultural-spiritual bodega in which every option is available; any claim to singularity of path is already profoundly compromised. Certainly, Western Buddhism is already a hybrid, and so is every form of Judaism, especially Orthodox ones.

In fact, my real tensions aren't between Buddhism and Judaism so much as between spirituality and self-actualization. Still, after all these years, I really want success, I really want fame, I really want approval—I, I, I. This is a fundamental human (and animal) condition. Yet I have also experienced that when this loud, scared "I" relaxes that the deepest senses of meaning and contentment arise, and that from the settled mind comes compassionate, just action in the world that needs more of it.

August 2010

Rethinking Spirituality

What is spirituality?

To most people who think about it, I suspect that spirituality is about having certain feelings, and spiritual practices are those actions that bring the feelings about. Light candles, and feel "connected." Pray, and become inspired. One does spiritual practices in order to have certain feelings, or mindstates, to which one may attribute a range of mythic or psychological meaning, or not. When you go to services at a synagogue that cares about prayer or spirituality (or at least a good community feeling at services) you show up thinking about mortgages and to-do lists, in the middle you're feeling a holy presence and perhaps inspiration to ethical action, and afterward you feel refreshed and re-energized. This is what state-change is: moving your mind from one way of being to another. And all religious groups have developed a wonderful array of tools to enable it to happen.

Such spiritual states have the power to open the mind, nourish the heart, and change the world. They are, I think, the most important force for social and environmental sustainability on the planet. And they can be lots of fun, too.

But states can also become dead-ends, or misconstrued, or actually dangerous. For every one hippie becoming one with the universe, there are five fundamentalists ossifying their experience into dogmas of hate and ethnocentrism. So, do the costs outweigh the benefits? Is there a way to get the good stuff without the bad? And what lies beyond spiritual states for those of us experienced enough in the spiritual path to have grown weary of them? Let's take a look.

1.   The Benefits of (Temporary) Transformation

The first value of spiritual states is what might be called their 'negative' capacity: you get to see that you are not your 'box' of identity, predilections, and mind. You get a break from being you, and that is really important. This you can experience easily. Go to a drum circle. Let go totally; get into the rhythm. Forget yourself, like hopefully you do during sex. Lo and behold! Mind, ego, and all the rest of your personality finally shuts up—and look, you can experience life just fine without it! Maybe even better, and more alive! So, states are really useful, if only for that. Many people never do it, and I think that's part of why so many people seem locked into traditional values, conformity, and narrow thinking.

States also have a 'positive' capacity. There's something important about those experiences when the walls of self are lowered. Drum circle ecstasy isn't just Not-Usual-Me; there's a glimpse of an oceanic oneness beyond ego, a melting into the Goddess that is deeply profound and important. This is some of what Gilbert and I experienced on our first retreats: a dissolving into the One, a glimpse of the numinous. At least as an experience, holiness is real. All those spiritual weirdos—they're not nuts. I don't know what they're experiencing (more on that in a minute), but there is an experience, and that experience is really valuable. And if it gets mixed in with a notion of *Shechinah* or deities or spirits or whatever, these are useful concepts, even if they are only concepts.

Third, mystical states have a tendency to shift one's priorities in useful ways. You experience this joy and bliss and compassion, and you get a little less obsessed with competition, career, and materialism. At least for a while. These states, transient as they are, yield a deeper, wider perspective on life's 'stuff.' Would we really have as many angry people, hunters, sexual predators, stressed out neurotic nuts, or conservatives if everyone underwent a real state-change every Friday night? I don't think so. It wouldn't save the world, but it would help if we were all a little calmer, and more infused with a joy that doesn't depend on consumption.

More specifically, genuine spiritual states invariably lead to compassion. I don't know why that is; it's kind of a miracle. And that compassion leads to all kinds of good things: less selfishness, more justice, less greed, more generosity, less hate, more love. I can hear my social-justice-obsessed editor clucking her tongue at spiritual narcissism, so let me emphatically state that, in my view, nothing would be better for the global pursuit of social justice than for more and more people to meditate and cultivate compassion on a personal level first. As I suggested last month, there is just no convincing a conservative that it's worth caring about some unfortunate marginalized person. They have to feel it themselves, and that takes changing the heart—and that takes spiritual practice. I don't see any other way if what we're after is durable, systemic change rather than fighting about the cause of the moment.

Finally, states lead to lasting insight. Experiencing spiritual 'highs' can provide a little more perspective on, and a little less thirst for, highs of other kinds, like sex, spirituality, drugs, love, music, food, travel, and other experiences. Again, I've had a very rich and wonderful life filled with all of those, but as anyone can tell you, chasing kicks forever is both puerile, and a little addictive. Mystical states can provide some of that joy and ecstasy without the side-effects and without all the clinging. (I've described some of this in my other work in the context of the jhana states). They were so intense that afterward, I would sometimes feel like, *This is it, okay? I have gotten higher than I ever thought it was possible to get. Okay. Whew, that was great. I'll do it again. Okay. Now I'll do it fifty times over a two-month retreat. Okay. Now I'm even tired of it. So what's next?* What lies beyond 'kicks,' even the most sublime ones? This is very useful: good spiritual highs lead to a better relationship to highs in general.

In fact, states lead to insights of all kinds. Again drawing on my recent experience, coming out of *jhana*, insights into *dharma*, Torah, and Jay's messy life popped like popcorn. One time, the 'wisdom light' in the third and fourth *jhanas* healed me of grief over a broken relationship which I'd been carrying around for six months. Honest—it's much later now, and the anger and heartbreak are gone, replaced only by a reflective, wistful sadness that feels sweet and appropriate. Other times, I would exit *jhana* and instantly see the radical impermanence of all sensations: here one moment, gone the next. I could poke through any wall of loneliness, anger, or greed. These insights do last, even though the blissful or content or equanimous states which produced them do not. So, states heal us, they re-orient us, they motivate us, and they teach us. What could be bad?

2.   Narcissism? Meh.

First, secular critics of this type of spirituality (which often is derided as "New Age") complain that it is narcissistic. Essentially, they say, it's just another selfish thrill, and is overlaid with delusion. At best, these pleasant delusions are rather pathetic balms. But they may also be deeply counterproductive, as the happy spiritual practitioner blissfully ignores her own problems, and those of the world. At worst, if the spiritual practitioner actually believes Allah, or Jesus, or whoever, is speaking to him, the delusions of the New Age are little different from the fundamentalisms of our era.

Surprisingly similar criticisms are leveled in religious circles. Some religious critics argue that New Age spirituality puts the individual before God. The traditionalist complains that 'feel-good' spirituality doesn't obey authority and doesn't do all the dour, disciplining things that religion is supposed to do. Others argue that it improperly values experience over authority or over ethics—it is immodest, indulgent, and perhaps just too much fun.

I wonder if these critics, secular and religious alike, have ever spent much time with actual spiritual seekers, however. I have, to be sure, known some who are narcissistic and selfish, and who prioritize their own personal experiences over political engagement, ethical conduct, and obligations to other people. But I also know plenty of secular and religious people who do the same things. Meanwhile, most earnest spiritual seekers I know feel an immediate connection between the spiritual experience and the moral impulse. It is, mysteriously, as Heschel described: one is moved by a sunset, and moved to help those who are suffering.

So, I'm not especially moved by this critique. The worst it says is that spirituality is no better than golf: a basically harmless diversion (though golf has a much worse environmental impact), maybe with a little layering of delusion. Hardly the end of the world.

3.   Spirituality and Idolatry

A less common critique comes from within the world of spiritual practitioners itself. When it's serious, spiritual practice is not about getting high, but about waking up to both the miracle of ordinary reality and the counterintuitive realization that your conventional self only exists as an appearance, a mirage. Like the Big Dipper, it is "there" in some sense, but not in the deepest sense; it's merely a way reality appears when looked at from a certain way. Spiritual and contemplative practice, in this view, exist to wake us up from that "certain way," which also happens to bring about all kinds of suffering, selfishness, and violence.

To do so, spiritual practice must be all-pervasive. If you suppose that God is only present in the pleasant stuff—on a summer's day but not in a cancer ward, when you're feeling relaxed but not when you're tense— then you're still making the same dualist error: God is here, but not there. In fact, the best spiritual practice might be one that neither provides the allure of the present nor the expiation of the difficult—but one which is utterly transparent, colorless, and thus always available.

What really matters—God, the Unconditioned, Emptiness, Nirvana, call it what you will—is not the state, the bliss, the light, et cetera. It's natural to idolize certain states. Oh, that gorgeous warmth of lighting candles. Oh, we were so high during that drum circle/Kabbalat Shabbat /whatever, that was really it.

But that's not it. It is what's always here; *Ein Sof*, everything. If it wasn't always here, it isn't it. Real *devekut* has only one attachment: Is. Totally colorless, totally omnipresent, and in fact, if you look closely, the only thing that doesn't come and go. There is no state that is it. This is it; just this. Not feeling special about this, not feeling relaxed or wise or anything in particular—although sometimes those feelings may arise in the wake of letting go.

Yet even when they're not dangerous, states can lead to a whole huge pile of suffering when the conditioned state passes, and you're left wondering what the hell went wrong. Believe me, I've spent many months in just that sense of bewilderment. The answer is actually pretty simple: I mistook something conditioned for the unconditioned. You just can't relive those peak experiences after a while. I've tried. I've tried really hard. It just leads to suffering. The only thing you can do, over and over again, is let go. Let go of everything. Every desire, every identification, every place your ego is hiding out and saying "I'm this." Let go, let go, let go, and keep on falling—because there ain't no place to land. Yet this falling, I am here to tell you, is the same as flight. It is also bad, bad news to get addicted to bliss states, as many people do. It's a spiritual dead end, a kind of masturbatory spirituality that's basically not so different from being addicted to drugs. You get high, you get withdrawal, you get high, you get withdrawal.

It's kind of tragic, since as I just mentioned one of the many benefits of spiritual highs is that they tend to reduce clinging to getting high. But sometimes it doesn't work that way, and one addiction is simply substituted for another. I've met a lot of 'spiritual' people who really are just looking for their next fix, and it's sad. It is also irresponsible, imbalanced, and even in its less severe forms, can actually increase selfishness—as in, "Stop bothering me with your needs! I'm trying to have a bliss state!"

The worst case of spiritual idolatry is when it becomes a gateway to fundamentalism. The reason is "fetishizing the trigger," which I wrote about a few years ago. Fetishizing the trigger happens when we find a trigger to amazing mystical states, and then mistake the trigger for the state, the finger pointing at the moon for the moon itself. This is the root of fundamentalism: this ritual is holy, that one is not; this religion is right, that one is not. And it's the root of the "right-wing hippie" phenomenon in Israel, in which well-meaning neo-Hasidic types get really seriously high off of the holiness of the Land of Israel, and end up hating Arabs and being incredibly ethnocentric. States are powerful, and that means they can be dangerous.

4.   In Praise of Spiritual Retail

Now, again, some perspective. I was told on one of my first retreats that concentrated mindstates can become narcotic. I understood, but I wanted them anyway—and to be honest, I don't regret it. Those four or five years of awesome mindstates brought on all kinds of insight, compassion, and the other benefits from above. They were also freaking amazingly awesome and beautiful.

So, if you're just starting out: cultivate states! Just try not to get too attached to them, or think they're something they're not. Love, learn, and let go.

Really, where the work of spiritual teaching and the work of social justice actually intersect is not in the more esoteric or refined realms, but in what you could call the 'retail business' of spirituality: bringing spiritual change to more and more people, usually in somewhat gross ways. Ultimately, while I personally am interested in the further stages of the spiritual path, and try to write about them, as someone concerned about the fate of our planet, I am actually more interested in the initial stages. I believe that spirituality can bring more and more people over to the good side of the fence—the side with more concern about equality and justice, more respect for the environment, and more pluralism on global and local levels. And I think spirituality can make people less racist, violent, overly conservative, greedy, and materialistic. But to do that, spiritual teachers need to interact with the not-so-good side of the fence, and cheapen what they are doing in order to reach more people.

Eckhart Tolle, after the huge success of *The Power of Now*, took a year of silent retreat to discern what should be his next step—not as a matter of a career, but as one of mission. What he did next was not unveil the next stage of the path, what lies beyond "now," but rather adjust the way he was teaching, simplify it, and, in a way, translate it into more coarse terms. The result was *A New Earth*, worldwide success, and, through Oprah, the largest audience a spiritual teacher has received since perhaps Deepak Chopra. (Chopra himself is an educated, enlightened nondualist.

His teaching is often quite coarse in presentation—live forever, never age, etc.—but I think he's really trying to reach the most people with the most light.) So, to rethink Jewish spirituality does not mean to junk its reliance on spiritual states, because for most Jews, like most people, states are still what is necessary. We still need to promise that you'll feel good, and deliver the goods. And let's remember that the majority of synagogues in America can't do even that; they don't even know there are goods to deliver, or that there might be goods other than coming together as a community, celebrating our religion, and repeating half-believed notions about God or commandments. For most people, the first step is still yet to be taken.

5.   What's Beyond States?

But if you've read this far, I'm guessing you're not one of those people. I'm guessing that you've had powerful spiritual experiences, and that, like me, you've struggled with what to do next: how to integrate them, or have more of them, or perhaps move from "state to stage," in Ken Wilber's terms. This is the real goal, right? Not to go off on retreat and feel close to God but *shiviti adonai l'negdi tamid*—to set YHVH ("Is"/ Being) before you always. So for those of us who have eaten the apple, tasted the forbidden fruit, and been transformed by it—is there anything beyond? Are we just to go on loving and letting go? Or is there something beyond the holiest of spiritual states?

I'm still very much on this path myself, but here's what I've learned so far.

First, states must be refined and made increasingly subtle, so much so that they approach omnipresence. Interestingly, the sequence of states known as *jhanas*, cultivated by Buddhists for three thousand years and by me for the last five, provide a kind of parallel structure for this process. The first *jhana* is pretty over-the-top, filled with intense rapture. Then that gets too coarse, and the second *jhana* takes over, with pleasure and delight and amazing, shimmering light, but without some of the intense concentrated effort. Eventually even that gets coarse, and the mind moves to the third *jhana*, with pleasure and bliss, but not rapture and amazement. And eventually, even the love and bliss of the third *jhana* gets a bit coarse, and the mind moves into the fourth *jhana*, which is equanimous, transparent, and so subtle it's barely there. The first *jhana's* coarseness is its strength: without that brute force, it's very hard to get 'in.' As I write this now, transitioning out of retreat, the fourth *jhana* has become difficult to sustain—it's just very subtle. Likewise with all spiritual states. At first, we need to get our socks knocked off: some amazing, wild ecstatic prayer service, or an upwelling of love so beautiful it makes us cry. As we progress, however, what I've found is that the states become subtler—and thus approach ordinary life more and more. The title of Jack Kornfield's book *After the Ecstasy, the Laundry* is apt, and the book deals frankly with some of the painful hangover periods that inevitably come after ecstatic highs. But the ultimate point is for the laundry itself to be holy, to be good. That does not mean that the laundry provides ecstasy. Rather, it means that by refining spiritual states, you don't need ecstasy to feel connected anymore.

I remember after my first few retreats, I would try to re-experience the joy or *devekut* I felt on retreat. For a while, it would work, but eventually, I'd get too distracted, and eventually even bored with trying. Now, however, I'm looking less for a spiritual state than just to let go into 'what is.' It's tricky, because "let go into 'what is'" sounds like "relax, feel connected, be holy"—but I want to suggest that it is actually the opposite: that it's really just letting go into what is, and being deeply, profoundly okay with that. If you've not experienced any of these states and progressions, that must sound rather banal. But imagine having the sense of okay-ness that you have when you're snuggling with your lover—just now, snuggling in with the 'present moment.' Not the love, necessarily (though that too may arise), but just the... yes. This is it. This really is it. This is God, this is the point, this emptiness that underlies all of my transitory states of mind... yep, this is it.

The result need not be an aching sense of holiness, or the belief that you can fly. It is mostly a negative capacity rather than a positive one: it's mostly in the letting go, the relaxing, the un-distracting, the remembering. Poke your head up out of the huge flock of self-absorbed sheep that all of us collectively are—oh yeah, you're awake. Consciousness. Emptiness. Even "God," if you like, though that term is inevitably freighted with associations and expectations. My God is named "is."

So, for me, it's sometimes easiest to just say, "Is it is?" Which... it usually is. This is the process of making states so transparent that they slowly turn into stages. What we're looking for—"it", the goal, enlightenment, whatever grows increasingly thin. The 'trigger' is always available. What you're looking for is always available—indeed, it's just your ordinary awareness, if you can believe that. Remember: if it hasn't always been here, it isn't the unconditioned. And it is, in my experience, slow, gradual, and filled with fits and starts. But it does seem to be working. "To see the light in everyone and every thing," Surya Das told me. Yes—and not radiant, shining, first-jhana light—but just the ordinary light that is, all the time. Nothing special—and yet, with enough practice, just as special as that which is most special.

Sorry if that seems paradoxical. Walk the walk; you'll see what I mean. So, at first we have mundane consciousness, the space of I-me-mine and work and the rest. Then, we have spiritual states, where those boundaries and demands are relaxed. And then, we have some notion that the real goal is not any state, but what Wilber calls "the simple freedom of being." This is rather like negative theology in our own experience: not this, not that, not this thought, not that idea, not this ego, not that possession. Ayin is everywhere, but it has taken me, at least, a lot of work to be able to refine consciousness so much that I'm not mistaking it for a pleasant state of mind.

And then, finally, there is the re-embrace of the ordinary itself—but, please, don't do this too fast. First, have the states. Then, refine them away. And then see that in every ordinary moment, lonely ones and lovely ones, there is the unity of form and emptiness, nirvana and samsara, yesh and ayin. Don't rush, but do move forward.

6.   Here's Some Advice

In my experience, in order to cultivate this negative capacity of seeing God without "God," there are at least four factors that need to be present.

First is a regular spiritual practice: meditation, yoga, prayer, reflection, whatever works. You've just got to take out the garbage, every day. You have to interrupt the torrents of thought, to-do lists, plans, senses of self, and so on, because otherwise 'letting go' just won't take. A lot of times, when I ask, "Is it is?" I get a response of "Yes, but so what?" This is a good sign that I'm identifying with factors in my mind, such as restlessness or unhappiness. It's a good sign to take a nice, deep breath and try to remember that "I" am not restless; restlessness has just arisen. There is no "I." Okay, whew. Regular spiritual practice maintains the base level of presence of mind necessary to do that.

Second, you've got to extend the spiritual practice beyond the mat, beyond the mind, and into action. If it's all about you, you're going to get too wrapped up in your feelings, your journey, your states, your shit. Take some time out of your head and go work in a soup kitchen. Council somebody who needs help. Volunteer for a cause you believe in. Whatever it is, there has to be some measure of spiritual practice in the world— not just to heal the world, but to ensure that spirituality doesn't dead-end in you. Don't prove the secular critics right by becoming a spiritual narcissist. If acting compassionately doesn't emerge naturally for you, in some seamless, Heschelian way, then force yourself to do it.

Third, I think that in addition to awakening, there needs to be some kind of "purification of mind," to use the Buddhist term, because one can be an enlightened human being and still be a total schmuck. In fact, thanks to what's now known as 'spiritual bypass,' you might think doing so is actually just fine. How can that be? Because enlightenment does not have to do with being a nice person; it's about seeing through the veil of illusion, knowing all things to be totally conditioned and transitory and thus unclingable. What's left depends on how you see the world—it could be God, or Emptiness, or liberation; could be All Mind, or No

Mind; doesn't really matter—the point is what it isn't, which is any particular thing.

Now, if that's true, it doesn't much matter whether what's in the mind is peace and love, or sexual desire, or nationalism, or simple obnoxiousness. It's all God, right? In fact, didn't we just say that mistaking any particular mindstate for God is part of the problem? So maybe it's better to never pay any attention to mindstates at all! So what if I'm causing "harm" because of my "neurosis" or "deep-seated baggage due to unresolved issues from my childhood"? Those are all just ripples on the cosmic ocean.

Speaking for myself, I can still be a gigantic schmuck: selfish, angry, unkind. Sure, I can often "go upstream" to a place where those are all motes of dust on a sunbeam; but meanwhile, other people are getting those motes in their eyes. So for me, at least, the ongoing process of cultivating patience, equanimity, lovingkindness, and other illusory, transitory qualities remains part and parcel of the overall spiritual project.

Finally, I think you've got to take a good look at your life, and see if it is really conducive to taking the 'next step.' Maybe it just isn't. Maybe you're at a stage in your life where you're working really hard and building something, and so you need to stay with cultivating really juicy states once a week. No harm in that. Or maybe you're raising a family, and the stress is just too much for subtlety. This is why monks are monks, and not householders. In my own life, I've shed three entire careers in the last two years, and am working much less—for me, anyway. I've chosen to take large chunks of time out and focus on contemplative work. I've stopped fighting with Jews about how their religion should be, and I've cut back on my political writing and work. And I've stopped living in New York City. These steps have often been painful; I'm a greed type, and I want it all. But I want one thing more, and that thing requires quiet of mind and body.

So, that's what I've learned. It is possible and necessary to move beyond spiritual states, but it takes work, the right conditions, and ongoing maintenance. And to repeat, I am not claiming to have completed this work, or attained anything. As a final aside, if I were really beyond identifying with my 'ego,' I probably wouldn't be writing at all; the more awake I become, the less I am interested in teaching or writing, and even less in impressing anyone by doing so. Compassion still motivates me somewhat, but humility counters it: do I really think I am so wise, or that I am saying something that can't be found elsewhere? I can imagine many realized beings who see no possible purpose in doing anything or going anywhere except Being itself, except perhaps in direct, compassion-motivated helping of others. So, if you are reading any book or essay, including this one, you must be getting something less than the totally genuine article. Beware of anyone who writes or teaches.

At this point in an essay like this, I often try to conclude with a poetic image, or a recollection of a spiritual moment at which all the veils dropped away, and the nakedness of the Divine was so radiant and cleansing. Having just finished a *jhanas* retreat, I have a big satchel of such moments. But the point of Zen poetry and ritual, as I understand it, is to get beyond all that. Whatever it is you're looking at now—that's the scenery for your enlightenment. So I'd rather not write any conclusion at all. Get it? :-)

May 2009

What's Different about
Jewish Enlightenment?

Earth's crammed with Heaven
And every common bush afire with God
— Elizabeth Barrett Browning

"Enlightenment" is sometimes regarded as a purely "Eastern" concept, foreign to the Western monotheistic religions. Yet the most important book of Kabbalah takes its name (*Zohar*) from the prophet Daniel's (Daniel 12:3) prediction that "the enlightened (*maskilim*) will shine like the radiance (*zohar*) of the sky." Who are these *maskilim*? The Zohar says that the enlightened are those who ponder the deepest "secret of wisdom" (Zohar 2:2a). What is that secret? The answers vary from tradition to tradition. Sometimes the secret is the substructure of reality, the human, and God, organized in the *sefirot*. Other times it is that the Torah's literal meaning is not its true meaning. And sometimes, the deepest secret is nonduality: that, despite appearances, all things, and all of us, are like ripples on a single pond, motes of a single sunbeam, the letters of a single word. The true reality of our existence is One, *Ein Sof*, infinite. The appearances of separate phenomena—you, me, the book, the table—are just temporary arrangements of the letters of the alphabet, momentarily arrayed into words—and then, a moment later, gone.

One common Kabbalistic formulation of this principle is that God "fills and surrounds all worlds"—*memaleh kol almin u'sovev kol almin*. This formulation is found in the Zohar (for example, in Zohar III:225a, Raya Mehemna, Parshat Pinchas) and other medieval texts, such as the twelfth century "Hymn of Glory" which says that God "surrounds all, and fills all, and is the life of all; You are in All." For example, Rabbi Joseph Gikatilla, part of the circle of medieval mystics thought by scholars to have composed the Zohar, is recorded as saying "he fills everything and

He is everything." His colleague Moses de Leon wrote that his essence is "above and below, in heaven and on earth, and there is no existence beside him." *Leit atar panui mineha,* "There is no place devoid of God" (Tikkunei Zohar 57).

Similar utterances occur throughout Jewish mystical history, particularly in the writings of Lurianic Kabbalah and Hasidism. In the words of the sixteenth century systematizer, Rabbi Moses Cordovero, "Everything is in God, and God is in everything and beyond everything, and there is nothing else besides God." "Nothing exists in this world except the absolute Unity which is God," the Baal Shem Tov is reported to have said (*Sefer Baal Shem Tov,* translated by Aryeh Kaplan in *The Light Beyond*). A later Hasidic master, Rav Aaron of Staroselye, wrote that "Just as God was in Godself before the creation of the worlds, so the Blessed One is alone [*l'vado*] after the creation of the worlds, and all the worlds do not add to God (may he be blessed) anything that would divide God's essence (God forbid), and God does not change and does not multiply in them, and the worlds (God forbid) do not add anything additional to God" (*Shaarei haYichud v'HaEmunah,* 2b).

Such statements may be quite familiar to followers of other mystical traditions, and students of the "perennial philosophy." Yet there are some distinct, and related, features of the Jewish conception of enlightenment, both in content and presentation, that distinguish it from others. The one I want to focus on here is that "all is one" is not the end of the spiritual journey, but in fact, precisely at its middle.

Whereas some traditions regard the knowledge of nonduality as the ultimate wisdom—enlightenment is the last stop on the road, so to speak; the final teaching—in the Jewish mystical tradition, nonduality is, in a sense, the beginning rather than the end of wisdom. Jewish mystics begin with the shocking, and proceed to the ordinary. The Zohar, for example, spends much less time describing *Ein Sof* than it does with the details of the sefirot (emanations), not to mention angels, demons, and the mythical stories of Rabbi Shimon bar Yochai and his circle. Likewise Cordovero, who devotes many pages to parsing the details of emanation and cosmology. *Ein Sof* is the basis, rather than the conclusion, of Jewish mystical theosophy. Nonduality is also the ground of religious practice, rather than the culmination of it. Never antinomian except in its heretical movements, Jewish conceptions of enlightenment do not end by transcending the conventional.

Hasidim, in particular, understood the enlightened consciousness not as a 'steady state' but what they called *ratzo v'shov*, literally "running and returning." This phrase, from Ezekiel 1:14, has come to stand for any number of oscillations in spiritual life—for example, between expanded and contracted mind, being and nothingness. And it was understood that a mystic would have to experience such oscillation, as he (always he) contemplated the highest unity at some times, tended to the needs of his family and community at others. Often, the *tzaddik*, the leader of the Hasidic community, was expected both to enter the highest states of what we might call God-consciousness, and to provide for the community's material and spiritual needs.

For this reason, the experience of enlightenment is not a steady state, or even a permanent transformation of the mind (as in some dharmic conceptions), but a life of oscillation between what Rav Aharon called "God's point of view" and "our point of view." Both points of view are of the same reality—they are just different points of view. Ours sees objects, people, and things. God's sees only Godself. The object is to see both as two sides of the same coin. *Neti-neti*, the Vedantists say: not-this, not-that. Neither twoness nor oneness, neither *yesh* nor *ayin*, but both, and thus neither. It's not quite paradox—it's enlightenment.

For the Hasidim, unlike many Vedantists, even though everything is God, the manifest world still maintains some reality and value of its own. Responding both to general Jewish norms of ethical and ritual commandments (*mitzvot*) and to specific historical trends in the 18th century (mystical heresy), Hasidic texts insist that the apparent world does exist in some way (even if only as a matter of perspective), and that our actions within it still have significance. They almost never advocated antinomianism, quietism, or abrogation of ethical norms. Within a tradition whose centerpiece is a Torah of this-worldly commandments, it could hardly be otherwise.

This ambivalence was reframed and reaffirmed when twentieth-century Jewish spiritual innovators such as Rabbi Zalman Schachter-Shalomi encountered Vedanta and other spiritual traditions in the 1960s. These Jewish seekers were impressed by the comparative forthrightness of those traditions' nondual teachings, and the way they were placed front and center. One did not have to become a religious Jew, learn Hebrew and Aramaic, and one day encounter nondual texts; rather, one could chant and have the experience. Immediate spiritual experience was thus privileged over communal affiliation, ritual observance, and, one might add, belief. Indeed, twentieth century Vedanta, one of the primary sources of 1960s and New Age spirituality, was itself the product of multiple stages of reform and 'refinement' by generations of masters beginning with Ramakrishna and Vivekananda, and continuing through the major twentieth century teachers such as Satchitananda. By the time Vedanta encountered the 1960s, we may speak of a 'neo-Vedanta' that presented a popular, accessible form of mysticism. Rabbi Zalman Schachter-Shalomi called it "Vedanta for export."

And he sought to replicate its success. Where Kabbalah was obscure and text-centered, neo-Hasidism and Jewish Renewal became experience-centered—like neo-Vedanta. Where Kabbalah insisted both on outward performance and inward intention (shell and kernel), neo-Hasidism and Jewish Renewal emphasized the latter over the former—like neo-Vedanta. Where Kabbalah (and even Hasidism, for most of its history) was elitist; neo-Hasidism and Jewish Renewal were populist—like neo-Vedanta. And where Kabbalah was particularist and even ethnocentric, neo-Hasidism and Jewish Renewal were universalistic and ecumenical—like neo-Vedanta ("they filtered out all the ethnic stuff," Reb Zalman told me once). Yet the issue of engagement with the this-worldly—with justice, community, family, ritual observances—remained a differentiator. Judaism, it was said, is this-worldly, rather than other-worldly (notwithstanding Vivekananda's intense social and political activism);

Judaism is theistic and devotional, in contrast with a nontheistic, and contemplative Vedanta (notwithstanding Ramakrishna's intense devotional life). And Jewish spirituality generally rejects acosmism, again ascribing it to an imagined Hinduism.

These distinctions between Jewish and Dharmic conceptions of enlightenment are not a matter of "East versus West." A Christian monastic's conceptions of the good life may have more in common with those of a Hindu renunciate, while his or her theology may have more in common with Jewish ones. And certainly, Western religion can, at times, devalue the world. With eyes turned toward heaven, or the afterlife, it can ignore or denigrate the manifest world, criticizing those who love it too much as 'pagan' or, in our time, 'humanist.' This is true even in the worldly religion of Judaism, which, notwithstanding our legion of ethical and ritual requirements regarding the material world, can often lead to either valuing the legality of a thing more than the thing itself (as Rav Soloveitchik memorably proposed and as I discussed years ago [in "Fresh Baked Bread"]) or, quite simply, to spending too much time indoors.

This social and psychological orientation is reflected in theological and ontological principles as well. Nonduality, after all, stands not just for "all is one" but, rather, that it stands for "all is one," "all is two," and, for good measure, "all is zero" as well. To understand this "unity of union and duality" is, in such systems, the highest spiritual apprehension, even though it seems to be made of paradox.

It's not paradox. We can envision it this way. By the end of their first year, all functional human beings have understood the difference between inside and outside, between self and world. It is the first essential stage in human development—and most of us spend the great majority of our lives there. Our lives are comprised of dualities, binaries, and boundaries. Things to do, people we like and don't like, stuff we want more or less of. A further stage is possible: unitive consciousness which perhaps returns to the pre-differentiation of infancy. At first, this consciousness only occurs at certain peak moments—lovemaking, abject terror, encounters with the numinous. But gradually, it is possible to extend the light of the *Ein Sof* into everything; in the words of the Lubavitcher Rebbe, to be in unitary consciousness more and more of the time. As Rabbi David Cooper has written, in *God is a Verb*:

> As nothing can be separated from it [*Ein Sof*], everything is interconnected in a Oneness, a unity, that cannot be divided. Things that in relative reality appear to be polar opposites—light and dark, hot and cold, male and female, determinism and free will, heaven and earth, good and evil, and so forth—are in absolute terms inevitably contained in the Oneness of Boundlessness.

The knowledge of this oneness is conveyed, in Jewish contexts, in ecstatic unitive experiences, in prophecy, and occasionally in the mystical study of text. Obviously, rarely do any of us enjoy such experiences for more than a fraction of our lives, and ontologically, who knows whether they convey something true about the world or whether they are mere alterations in brain chemistry. Experientially, they are reservoirs of wisdom and compassion, comfort and joy. They impart a kind of knowingness that is more certain than everyday knowing. William James, for example, describes his mystical experience this way in his *Varieties of Religious Experience*:

> There came upon me a sense of exultation, of immense joyfulness accompanied or immediately followed by an intellectual illumination quite impossible to describe. Among other things, I did not merely come to believe, I saw that the universe is not composed of dead matter, but is, on the contrary, a living Presence ... that the foundation principle of the world, of all the worlds, is what we call love, and that the happiness of each and all is in the long run absolutely certain ... I knew that what the vision showed was true. I had attained to a point of view from which I saw that it must be true.

For many years, I was fascinated by these accounts, and determined to see if I could have such experiences myself. And so I did, many times, and in many different mystical contexts. And indeed, from my own experience, I can attest that if you follow the instructions of meditative, contemplative, and spiritual practices, the promised results do indeed occur: a dissolving of the sense of self; rapture in concentrated joy; transient feelings of immense bliss; and, for religious souls like me, a certainty that one is held and loved and engulfed by the Divine. It is worth the effort.

Yet even these exalted experiences represent but an intermediate phase. That "all is one" is exactly half of the picture. What about our experience of twoness? Is it merely illusion? Or is it not the case that, if the Infinite is really Infinite, it is present when we are experiencing unity, and when we are not? That is, isn't whatever is happening now, with whatever emotional valences or intellectual components, just as much an experience of God (if you like that term) as the highest spiritual ecstasy? If God is *Ein Sof*, infinite, isn't God in the toilet as well as the tabernacle?

In other words, at a certain point, the mystic moved beyond unitive experience to return to the experience of duality while maintaining the consciousness of unity. This is what David Loy calls the "nonduality of duality and nonduality." And it is what the Zen masters mean when they say "in the beginning, mountains are mountains. During zazen, mountains are not mountains. Afterward, mountains are once again mountains." That is to say: in the initial dualistic consciousness, mountains are experienced as mountains. In unitive consciousness, the mountains disappear as separate entities and are only motes on the sunbeam of consciousness. In nondual consciousness, the mountains are both: both everything and nothing, both existent and nonexistent.

I'd like to return to a symbol I refer to often: that of the two triangles of the Jewish star. The downward pointing triangle represents the 'first stage,' the world of ordinary experience, in which there is self and other, figure and ground. This is the view of *aretz*, of earth, of all of us, with our histories and loves and heartbreaks and joy. The upward-pointing triangle represents the 'second stage' of unitary consciousness, in which there is no self, no other, no figure, and only the one Ground of Being. This is the view of *shamayim*, of heaven, of ultimate reality, the way things actually are. The star together is the 'third stage' of nonduality: of both-and and neither-nor. It is the *Ein Sof* that is both Many and One, hidden God and manifest *Shechinah*, and in being both, is Naught, or *ayin*.

Nonduality is not only oneness. It is oneness-in-twoness, the extraordinary in the ordinary. Is it a mere coincidence that so many of the symbols of the world's religions are based upon this coincidence of opposites? The cross of heaven and earth, the six-pointed star, the yin and the yang. To what does their joining gesture? This is why so many nondual sages say that the only thing keeping you from enlightenment is searching for it. If only you'd stop trying to see yourself through your own eyes! You, with your neuroses and shadows and wounds—*tat tvam asi*, "you are that." This moment of your experience is God masquerading as you.

As a lived phenomenon, this is the experience of *ratzo v'shov*, running and returning, that we spoke about earlier. Sometimes we experience life as the ego tells us we must: as a separate self, with boundaries to be defended and needs to be met. Other times, we see this ego as being like a computer program, running according to causes and conditions, just like the trillion miraculous programs executing all around us at every moment. Or consider nonduality from the perspective of earth-based spirituality: sometimes, we feel at one with all, part of the great cosmic dance, the cycle of birth and death—and other times, we revel in our own uniqueness, our individuality, our humanity and sex and joys. Along such a path, we do not seek an Aristotelian midway point, somewhat godly and somewhat human, but rather a vibrant oscillation between the poles of everything and nothing, separation and union. As the nondual sage Nisargadatta said, "Love says 'I am everything.' Wisdom says, 'I am nothing.' Between the two, my life flows."

The Jewish spiritual tradition contains both trajectories. On the one hand, the abstruse speculations of the kabbalist and Hasid take him far from the mundane plane. Yet on the other, the Jewish mystic hero is required both to soar toward God and to provide for his family's and community's needs. Once more, *ratzo v'shov*: to hold both the divine and the human perspectives, absolute and relative, in a dialectical relationship is the goal of what some Hasidim call *hitkallelut*, the incorporation of all things into the infinite essence, and *hashva'ah*, total equality or equanimity of view. God in the abstract, God in the concrete: the utterly timeless and the exquisite fragility of our lives in time.

This view has several practical consequences. First, it changes what spiritual practice is supposed to do. The awakened life is not about reaching the highest high, but about being able to slide in and out of our point of view and God's point of view, with less and less effort. Changing one's state of mind is still useful—but the point is not that experiencing ecstasy is great and doing the laundry sucks. Rather, it's that ecstasy has certain uses, and mundane mindstates do too. Feeling low, alienated or distracted by minutiae? Try an ecstatic drum circle, Friday night service or meditation practice. Need to console a friend, fix a car or work to save the whales? The ordinary mind is probably more helpful. This may seem obvious, but it is the opposite of how many spiritual seekers see the point of their spiritual work.

Second, this view transforms how the ordinary is experienced. It brings back the everyday sensuality of surfaces, touches, smells; the feel of fabric, rough or smooth; the contact of finger with tabletop or with flesh. Of warmth and of cold. Of the dancing of light against fiberglass, of the surfaces of cars in the winter sun. And, too, of the play of manifestation in our own human conditions: the sorrows and joys of human experience, loving, losing, surrendering. The world as it appears is not a distraction, not an obstacle to be contemplated en route to immortality. It is, rather, God's erotic play (Kabbalah), Indra's web (Hinduism), Kali's dance (Hinduism, again), the amorous hide-and-seek game of Beloved and Beloved (Sufism). This world, in its particular phenomena, embodied, emotion-ed and ever new in its complexity, is the dance of God. Thus this form of spirituality, extrapolated from its traditional origin, is at home with sucking the marrow out of life, with drinking from the well of life's blessings, with the spell of the sensual. It is with Oscar Wilde, who reveled in surface and deplored piety and "substance." It is with Zen iconoclasts like haiku master Ikkyu and poet Leonard Cohen, who embrace both enlightenment and sensuality. It is with the Stage Manager in Thornton Wilder's "Our Town," who rejects both the ephemeral distractions of the living and the fatalism of the dead, insisting on a productive tension between the two perspectives. And it is with the sculptor, the painter, the artist and the poet, who find mystery not in the abstract, but in the concrete. This is nonduality: a re-embrace of the world as ripples on the pond—ripples only, perhaps, but ripples, beautiful, reflecting light.

Third, as with Eros, so, too, with ethics. Sometimes, the 'ordinary world' is awful; it denies, oppresses, despoils. If we take seriously the meaningfulness of this world, we must own its injustices and horrors, not only the delights of touch and taste. Unlike escapist spirituality, anti-humanist religion or the cold abstractions of neoliberal economics, the nondual embrace of the world is at home with Judaism's ancient and historic priorities: social justice, righteousness and this-worldly ritual. Yes, God is in the world, but, as Abraham Joshua Heschel articulated more poetically than anyone (especially in his early poetic work, translated as "The Ineffable Name of God: Man"), that means God suffers with those who are suffering, God's face shines and is hidden, God's revelation is contained in the interpersonal. Heschel's humanism is a nondual one: It begins with the intoxication of God in All and progresses to its consequences.

I can say with some confidence that these perhaps heady concepts have greatly influenced my own life. I still spend a majority of my time immersed in the world, as a professional LGBT activist and as a journalist. My avocation is spirituality; my vocation is activism. In an unexpected way, I am devoted to *tikkun olam*, which originated as a mystical term referring to theurgy but which gradually became the mission of Jewish social justice work. Ironically, I see myself reflected in that term's weird history.

In general, Judaism is a householder religion concerned with the proper ordering of society; it is nearly (though not entirely) univocal in its affirmation of this-worldly experience and the importance of sanctifying that experience for divine service (*avodah*). The Jewish revelation spends but a few words on theophany, yet offers chapters on tort law and hygiene. The Jewish paradise is a community that cares for its needy. And the Jewish altar is the dining table, the orchard, the bedchamber.

To be sure, silence and solitude remain indispensable steps along the spiritual path, and there are times at which renunciation and restraint are essential. Most of us spend the overwhelming majority of our lives at 'stage one,' experiencing ourselves as selves sandwiched between our ears—and we suffer as a result. So, for most of us, just getting to 'stage two,' in which the ego melts away for a blessed moment or two, remains the primary work. Besides, stage two is wonderful. If you're considering it, please let me urge you to spend time in the presence of enlightened masters, and see for yourself the palpable stillness of no-mind, the great compassion that emerges naturally from wisdom. Know that you can become such a person yourself. Please, do not rush to integrate too quickly.

Gradually, though, the mind states of spirituality, even the loftiest, will become less and less urgent, as God becomes more and more transparent. Slowly, not only may you see infinity in a flower, you may not even need to. The flower, having become infinite, may now be but a bloom—and wholly Divine in being so. Both-and, neither-nor, all of it, the emptiness and the form, yielding and wrestling. Duality and nonduality are the ultimate nonduality. In the language of the theosophical kabbalists, this is the site for the uniting of immanent and transcendent, goddess and god—and in that uniting, a transcendence even of the notion of transcendence. In their vocabulary, to call the entirety of existence the cosmic dance of *lila* is thus an invitation from the *Shechinah*: Come and dance with me.

October 2009

Is it All an Illusion?

God is true.

The universe is a dream.

—Vivekananda

Row, row, row your boat gently down the stream.

Merrily, merrily, merrily, merrily Life is but a dream.

—Anonymous

Two parallel questions: Is spirituality an illusion? Is the universe as it appears an illusion? (Or perhaps both or neither?)

For many spiritual seekers, the idea that there is only one thing happening in the universe, one vast unfolding play, causes a sense of resonance inside, a sense of rightness. The sense feels old to me, as if I knew it even before I had heard about it, twenty years ago now, sitting in an undergraduate religion class *Tat tvam asi*, you are that. Atman is Brahman: there is no ontological difference between the world outside and the world inside, the Self and God. It hit me then, it hits me now. And I've met people who are hit even harder than me, people who have become utterly, totally, without a doubt convinced that the mind-body process which, for most of us, dictates our wants, needs, joys, pains—that this is merely an illusory phenomenon. For them, reality is "perfect brilliant stillness" (David Carse) and what seems real is all but a dream.

But maybe that's all there is: a feeling, not a stirring of truth or consciousness What if this sense is just a feeling, just a neuron firing (or misfiring) in a mechanistic brain? Suppose, in fact, that consciousness is purely an emergent phenomenon that arises within the individual, wholly material brain. The 'oceanic feeling,' back to the womb, holiness—all these are mental events, entirely within the body-brain. (Of course, this would have to be true of love as well, but so what if it is.) Suppose it's all a sham! And not just unitive mysticism, but any spiritual feeling that pretends to be anything other than neurons jiggling in the brain?

Well, suppose it is. Look what happens: As soon as the sham is seen, and the pretension is relinquished—'progress' is made, because it's progress away from aggrandizement, away from being right or being enlightened or being anything at all. And toward: don't know, got no idea, have no business talking about it, writing about it, teaching, who would know anyway, just the knowing which isn't knowing.

The more beliefs and expectations are questioned, the better! As Chögyam Trungpa Rinpoche is reported to have said, "Disappointment will become your greatest ally." If you're still hoping for enlightenment to make your life radically different, you're still not quite there. Because 'there' is here, because this is it. So, in a way, better to be disappointed now and save yourself the time. Better for it all to be for naught. Surrender even the hope of progress, and progress will happen on its own, and your life in fact will be radically different, even though it may look the same from the outside, like you're carrying off a perfect drag performance that even you believe at times.

Except when, perhaps, you're a bit kinder and someone notices that something has shifted. Of course, shifts happen all the time as people (some people, anyway) get older and wiser. Maybe it's the therapy more than the spirituality that does it.

But then, what if the mystics are *right*? Is life but a dream? And doesn't the awareness that it is so necessitate a rupture, between pre- and post-? Won't it wreck my life? One consolation of *ratzo v'shov*, back and forth from one perspective to the other: you can have your cake and eat it too, your nonexistence and also your apartment.

Maybe this is a copout. For traditional Advaita, and especially its modern expositors such as Nisargadatta, his student Ramesh Balsekar, and Westerners such as Wei Wu Wei, Tony Parsons, Francis Lucille, David Carse, Jeff Foster, and others, that tentativeness is just the last gasp of the ego. Maybe the both-and view, the Tantric view, the nondual Jewish view, is too comforting. How convenient for me: I don't have to give anything up, don't have to make a choice. I can be enlightened and in the world. Maybe this is the ego making a desperate last stand to save itself. Maybe the real delusion isn't mysticism, but the resistance to mysticism.

Once during a shamanic ceremony, I had a death experience; moving toward the light, being drawn to it. I felt pulled back by my love for my partner, and my desire to create in the world. "Not yet," I thought. That was the beginning of a long, difficult few hours of resistance rather than surrender. At that time at least, I couldn't let go.

Most Advaitin sources suggest that once liberation happens, enlightened consciousness never again confuses itself with the apparent small self. (Most Jewish sources disagree.) And sure enough, that awakens fear within. I feel unready and even unwilling. From this side of the enlightenment divide, it seems impossible to distinguish between the enlightened and madness. Perhaps 'ego-death' is really a psychotic event.

I know people who experienced enlightenment in the stark, before-and-after-sense, and who live happy, full lives in the world. Most are in helping professions—doctors, teachers—suggesting that, indeed, compassion wins out over the ego's desire for more. Some are kind, others are not. They are not insane, and in fact, not as crazy as garden-variety 'spiritual' folk often are. And yet, my fear remains. Perhaps it is indeed the ego fighting for itself.

When there seems to be seeing from the other side, once-cherished and yearned-for objects on this side seem a little laughable. Beautiful boys, the charade of politics and power, status. What, then, of the worldly dreams I have cherished since youth? The ego must sense this danger to the status quo of appearance, which this mind-body loves, at times.

Or perhaps the pull toward *ayin* is just an ego wanting to be happy, and perhaps the fear of *ayin* is an ego wanting to be safe.

Actually, shamanic ceremony or no, I needn't have worried. The ego is quite good at forgetting the *ayin*, at perpetuating itself, distracting itself, finding other thought-forms to immerse itself in; entire discourses, really, which utterly take over the mind. Who has time for nonduality when discussing constructions of religion and sexuality in American political discourse (i.e., my latest book topic)? What is the relevance of the 'dream' when there are logistics to take care of, the 'real world,' and relatives and friends pursuing lives of relationship and community? Is the clinging to conventional reality fear, or sanity? Is it keeping me grounded or holding me back? Is it the nondual embrace of essence and manifestation, or is it indecision, the terror of letting go? I can't say.

Maybe all of it's a delusion. Could be, I don't know. But at least, if you doubt, doubt everything. Look into the eyes of the Dalai Lama, and doubt that he knows anything more than a pop star. Look into the eyes of generations of enlightened beings—sages, rabbis, bodhisattvas, crones—and find their gazes, and judge them all to be deluded. Keep doubting though. Doubt it all: atheism, religion, love, money, self, non-self, everything. Do not retain anything: not comparing oneself to others, not the hope that life itself is worthwhile, not the merest iota of value.

And in this doubting, in this rigorous, thoroughgoing rejection of every possible meaning, in this burning away of significance, lies the ultimate defeat of the self, the ultimate victory of what transcends it, the triumph of surrender. I don't know; I don't know; I don't know. I can't say, I can't tell you, I have absolutely no idea.

August 2011

Pro/Epilogue:
On Eighth Avenue in New York

Riding home in a taxi at four o'clock this morning, still a little bit stoned from the drugs and the music and the hormones all swirling inside the Roxy, I imagined Eighth Avenue, the lights cascading, as my country road, leading me home, John Denver style. The tall buildings on either side of me—not really skyscrapers, not in this town, though they would be in any other—rising up like trees, overarching the six lanes, our cars rolling to the distribution point at Columbus Circle, where we are filtered like products in the maze of a factory.

And then, the quiet Upper West Side. I remember when I moved here, the friend who lived in my apartment before me said, "It's a good place to come home to." My own suburb, really, with encroaching Starbucks and slightly tighter social codes than the neighborhoods I might really prefer. But still, a suburb with a symphony of lights still on, at 4:30am, visible from my rooftop. The hum of the city is faint at this hour, resembling the wind through desert mountains. The sky still grayish-orange, like Bayer Aspirin seen through heavy sunglasses. And everywhere, behind those windows, plants, books, furniture, and people living with other people, and facing them, every day, including today, now. The difference between country trees and the buildings that make up my 'suburb' is that within these buildings lie a dozen treehouses, with people sharing space, participating in culture, breathing the New York air.

I had been feeling very low earlier today, notwithstanding the outrageously beautiful weather—the third Saturday in a row that made me want to run outside and bathe in it all. I took a nice enough bike ride through Central Park, but I rode alone, while everyone else seemed to be thronging, mingling, chatting. I sat, dejected, still alone, in the Pinetum, wondering when I would ever find someone to share my life with, trying hard to resist the urge to wallow in the pity, and add "if ever." I am still young; I can be patient. And it's only been a short while that I've been healthy enough to look for love in a place that might actually yield it, instead of within the straight and narrow boundaries set by an extended childhood. So, I can wait—a while longer. But being able to endure the wait doesn't make the waiting easier.

New York does not always come to the rescue when you're feeling lonesome and sad, but sometimes it does, and when it does you know that, even if you could be living in a much larger house (or any house!) with much safer streets in some quiet backwater somewhere far from here, even when you wonder why, if you love the trees so much, you don't live where there are more of them—whatever your doubts, you know that this is the place for you, that this is where you live, in more senses of the word than you could make of it anywhere else. At least, this is so for me. I sometimes feel as though I'd be infinitely happier among the grasses in the country or the spirits in Jerusalem, and maybe I would; I wouldn't presume to know. But there are times in which the symphony of New York suddenly emerges out of the din, and I *remember New York in me*, in a way I cannot articulate or verbalize, like the memory of vanilla-frosted cake at a childhood birthday party.

The night, this night with the Eighth Avenue drive and the feeling of contentment in the *om* of the city—it was by no means unique, or even remarkable. I saw a great and underappreciated Peter Fonda film, *The Hired Man*, at the Tribeca Film Festival, thanks to my friend Ben's connections. Peter Fonda himself was there, as was Martin Scorsese; the red carpet, literally, had been rolled out. And the theater filled with film buffs—the sort of people who applaud the cinematographer's name in the credits—watched a beautifully restored print of an underrated, languidly-paced psychological Western, slowly spinning its Biblical-Homeric tragedy to the music and cinematography of the 1971 counterculture. Excellent art, fun celeb-spotting, and all surrounded by a hundred other cultural events of equal quality—where else?

And then a Yonah Schimmel knish, at a New York institution that wouldn't survive a week in chain store America, next door to a restored art house cinema, a few doors down from not one but four fantastic music venues, where I've seen everyone from The Moldy Peaches to Hasidic New Wave to Sonic Youth, surrounded by Indian restaurants, whiskey bars, lounges, lesbian bars, yoga centers—where else?

And a night clubbing. I checked out the scene in Dumbo, increasingly filled with annoying, visor-clad club kids, headed instead for the Roxy, filled as always with preening Chelsea boys and the rest of us. Moving from tribe to tribe, from blacklights to strobe lights, and later guided by the headlights of my car moving north on Eighth Avenue, listening to warm jazz tenor saxophone, a sound perfected not far from here, and not long ago.

Nothing remarkable, really. Thousands of bridge-and-tunnel Jersey kids did as well if not better. But even those kids and I are on the same team, the people who got out and chose to see what civilization had to offer tonight, rather than isolate ourselves. I don't blame anyone who opted to just relax with a nice video; this, too, is a joy. But to have the chance, in New York City, to *participate* in a weekly-regenerated organism of curiosity and desire—maybe this is what makes New York what it is, when it is what it ought to be.

And not only the activity, not only the kicks, but also the history. That this is Chelsea, not an imitation; that the knish resonates with generations of Jewish New Yorkers; the jazz, Brooklyn, the skyline, Scorsese—my night was filled with immediacy, presence, and history, even as it seemed to be all about whatever is happening now. The music came from *here*. The food, the culture, the sexual liberation, the film festival—all specific to this place, non-generic, genuine, not counterfeit. Other cities have comparable histories, but even the greatest cities struggle to compare with the level of specificity that attaches to the phenomena of New York. And in any case, this is the place I know.

Not to mention the sheer beauty of the city lights at night, driving northward at thirty-five miles per hour, dodging floating cars past 42nd and upward. At the Whitney Biennial this year, the art is dominated by works that involve the viewer in a whole environment. But New York is that every day. It takes a thousand cultural risks a day; it's filled with ambient music and absurdist video, loaded with the beauty and the poetry which helped me forget my loneliness as I forgot myself, as I joined in this mass movement of people wanting not to remain safe and fear the next attack, but, in some way, and in ways frivolous as well as sublime, to live—live, like I want to do, like I can't seem to help myself from doing, to look around and listen or enjoy or eat or dance or meet someone to love—all of this may be the reason too.

Did New York, in the end, cure me of my lonesomeness? Partly it did, mostly it didn't. But at least I remembered that, even in loneliness, I am not alone. That is partway there, I think.

June 2002

Enlightenment by Trial and Error

Acknowledgments

As I mentioned in the introduction, most of these essays first appeared in *Zeek*, a scrappy online magazine which I co-founded in 2001, and which lasted through 2015. We started *Zeek* because we wanted to publish work we weren't seeing elsewhere, work that reflected the "new Jewish culture" and that was intellectually serious and, often, spiritually audacious. Named after one of the Bible's most adventurous visionary poets, *Zeek* was the first to publish future rock stars such as Joshua Cohen, Adam Mansbach, Leah Koenig, and many others, and it was the only place I can imagine publishing essays like the ones in this book. So, deep thanks to my *Zeek* family, in particular (but not only) Dan Friedman, Michael Shurkin, Bara Sapir, Jo Ellen Green Kaiser, Joel Schalit, Sarah Chandler, Adam Rovner, Bob Goldfarb, Rob Mitchell, Leah Koenig, and Erica Brody. We really did change the world, in a tiny way, and I am proud of the work we did together. Most of *Zeek*'s content is still online at zeek.forward.com and www.zeek.net, and can be found by skillful googling.

Deep bows to the many spiritual traveling companions who helped this path unfold during the decade reflected in this book, including but definitely not limited to Ari Weller, Shir Yaakov Feit, Kenneth Folk, Daniel Ingram, Beth Resnick-Folk, Oren Jay Sofer, Eden Pearlstein, Adam Sher, Zivar Amrami, Jill Hammer, Shoshana Jedwab, Tamuz Shiran, Ezra Weinberg, Ohad Ezrachi, Eliezer Sobel, Jacob Staub, Yoseph Needleman, Rachel Barenblat, Amichai Lau-Lavie, Zvi Bellin, David Ingber, and a few folks who probably would prefer not to be named here (like my friend who was into Mother Eagle and who became a somewhat famous artist by the way).

Thanks also to my many teachers in three or four spiritual traditions. I've thanked them in previous books and am now thanking them again.

Finally, thanks to Larry Yudelson for building what is now the best publishing house for Jewish spirituality in the English-speaking world.

And of course to my life-partner and love Paul for taking care of Lila while I sat and typed.

I'd like to dedicate *Enlightenment by Trial and Error* to two of my teachers, Rabbi Zalman Schachter-Shalomi and Rabbi David Cooper. These profound mystics changed my life and the lives of millions of other seekers and finders. I owe them far more than this book—I owe them my capacity to love.

Works Cited

David Aaron, *The Secret Life of God: Discovering the Divine within You* (Shambhala, 2005).

Nissim Amon, *Eastern Wisdom: The Treasure Box* (Gatekeeper, 2017 ed.).[*]

Isaiah Berlin, *The Hedgehog and the Fox: An Essay on Tolstoy's Theory of History* (Ivan Dee, 1993 ed.).

William Blake, "The Marriage of Heaven and Hell," *Collected Poems* (Penguin, 1978 ed.).

Sylvia Boorstein, *That's Funny, You Don't Look Buddhist* (HarperOne, 1998).

Elizabeth Barrett Browning, *Aurora Leigh* (Oxford, 2008 ed.).

Fritjof Capra, *The Tao of Physics* (Shambhala, 2010 ed.).

David Carse, *Perfect Brilliant Stillness* (Paragate, 2005).

James Carse, *The Religious Case Against Belief* (Penguin, 2009 ed.).

Moshe Cordovero, *Elimah Rabbati* (Or Chadash ed.).

David Cooper, *God Is a Verb* (Riverhead, 1998).

Andre Gide, *The Counterfeiters* (Vintage, 1973 ed.).

Arthur Green, *Radical Judaism* (Yale, 2010).

Hafiz, *The Gift: Poems by the Great Sufi Master,* rendered by Daniel Ladinsky (Arkana, 1999).

Jill Hammer & Taya Shere, *The Hebrew Priestess* (Ben Yehuda, 2015).

Sam Harris, *The End of Faith* (Norton, 2005 ed.).

Abraham Joshua Heschel, *The Ineffable Name of God: Man: Poems* (Continuum, 2005).

Hermann Hesse, *Siddhartha*, trans. by Hilda Rosner (Bantam, 1982).

Aharon HaLevi Horowitz of Staroselye, *Shaarei HaYichud v'HaEmunah* (Ryzman, 1828).

Langston Hughes, *The Collected Poems of Langston Hughes* (Vintage, 1995).

---

[*] In a nice twist, the "Sufi tale" of the prisoner and the key that I cite in "Fetishizing the Trigger" appears to derive from a story by this Israeli Soto Zen master.

Ikkyu, *Crow with No Mouth*, trans. by Stephen Berg (Copper Canyon, 2000).

Louis Jacobs, *Seeker of Unity: The Life and Works of Aaron of Starosselje.* (Vallentine Mitchell, 2006).

William James, *The Varieties of Religious Experience* (Penguin, 1982 ed.).

Aryeh Kaplan, *The Light Beyond* (Moznaim, 1981).

Steven T. Katz, ed., *Mysticism and Philosophical Analysis* (Sheldon, 1978).

Jack Kerouac, *On the Road.* (Penguin, 2002).

Alan McGlashan, *The Savage and Beautiful Country* (Chatto & Windus, 1966).

Jay Michaelson, *Everything is God* (Shambhala/ Trumpeter, 2009).

Idem., *Evolving Dharma* (North Atlantic, 2013).

Idem., *The Gate of Tears* (Ben Yehuda, 2015).

Nisargadatta, *I Am That*, trans. by Maurice Frydman (Acorn, 1973).

Robert Pirsig, *Zen & the Art of Motorcycle Maintenance* (Harper, 2006).

Ram Dass, *Be Here Now* (Lama Foundation, 1971).

Rainer Maria Rilke, *Selected Poems of Rainer Maria Rilke*, trans. by Robert Bly (Harper & Row, 1981).

Sharon Salzberg, *Faith* (Riverhead, 2003).

Percy Bysshe Shelley, "Mont Blanc," *Selected Poems* (Penguin, 2017).

Friedrich Schleiermacher, *On Religion: Speeches to Its Cultured Despisers*, trans. by Richard Crouter (Kessinger, 2008).

Richard Smoley, *Inner Christianity* (Shambhala, 2002).

Joseph B. Soloveitchik, *Halakhic Man*, trans. by Lawrence Kaplan (JPS, 1983).

Frederick J. Streng, *Ways of Being Religious* (Pearson, 1973).

Vivekananda, *Living at the Source: Yoga Teachings of Vivekananda* (Shambhala, 2001).

Alan Watts, *The Book* (Vintage, 1989 ed.).

Ken Wilber, *One Taste* (Shambhala, 2000).

Thornton Wilder, *Our Town* (Harper, 2003 ed.).

Virginia Woolf, *Mrs. Dalloway* (Harcourt, Brace & Co., 1925).

Zohar, trans. by Daniel Matt (Stanford, 2003).

Glossary

Baruch Hashem: Praise the Lord!

Daven: To 'pray' in an ecstatic or contemplative way

Devekut: The mystical state of 'cleaving' to God in Kabbalah and Hasidism.

Halacha: The way of Jewish law and observance.

Hitbodedut: The Hasidic spiritual practice of conversation with God.

God: A term that usually denotes an anthropomorphic deity, but sometimes denotes the monistic One Being.

Jhanas: Highly concentrated mindstates cultivated in Buddhism and Hinduism.

Kabbalah: The Jewish mystical and esoteric tradition.

Katnut / gadlut: Contracted mind / Expanded mind.

Midrash: Legends based on the Bible.

Neti-neti: Not-this, not-that.

Samadhi: Concentrated, sometimes mystically-understood mindstate cultivated in Hinduism and Buddhism.

Sefirot: Kabbalistic term referring to the ten emanations of the Infinite, like stained glass refracting white light

Yin and Yang: Poles of shadow and light, yielding and penetrating, 'feminine' and 'masculine' in Taoist thought

Yetzer hara: Traditionally, the evil inclination, often associated with sex. In contemporary spirituality, the selfish inclination.

Index

dance, dancing, 9, 30, 44, 46-49, 130, 145-46, 165, 168, 183, 191, 244-45.

Darth Vader. *See Star War*s.

davening. *See* prayer.

Dead Poets Society, 47.

death, 54-56, 197, 240.

de Leon, Moses, 228.

delusion, 39-40, 84-88, 91, 115, 119, 156, 176, 177, 191, 208-09, 217-18, 238, 240-41.

diet, 2, 34, 96-102, 103, 104-05, 108, 133.

discipline, 41, 66, 74-83.

DNA, 23.

doubt, xiv, x-xi, 3, 4, 6, 14-16, 33, 35, 38-39, 42, 50, 67, 70, 76-77, 79-80, 86-91, 100, 139-41, 144-46, 164, 238-41.

Embodied Judaism, 12

enlightenment, meaning of, 24-27, 71-72, 227-237; stages of, 36-38, 211.

entheogens. *See* psychedelics.

ethics, 11, 20, 22, 25-26, 31-33, 46-48, 51-53, 65-66, 73, 91, 101, 134, 155-56, 166-67, 178-80, 214, 217, 236.

Everything is God, xiii.

evil, 3, 34, 52-53, 64-65, 100, 121, 123, 180.

"feminine and masculine", 126-28, 199-200.

flexidoxy. *See* Judaism.

Flying Spaghetti Monster, 169.

Fonda, Peter, 243.

Foucault, Michel, 82.

Forward, ix.

Foster, Jeff, 239.

Frank, Anne, 49, 52-53.

Freud, Sigmund, 78.

fundamentalism, 20, 32, 50, 53, 87, 100-1, 114-22, 131, 138, 156, 165, 171, 185, 195, 214, 217, 219.

Ganesh, 184, 190; see also Hinduism.

Genpo Roshi. *See* Merzel, Dennis.

Gide, Andre, 7, 11.

Gikatilla, Joseph, 227-28.

God: and realized beings, 71-73; as Being, xiv, 10-11, 17, 21, 23, 24-28, 47, 52-53, 65, 71-73, 90, 92-93, 170, 176, 221, 226, 233; as creator, 24, 145, 165; as Everything, 15, 19, 71, 191, 193; as "What is", 222-26; ethics and, 11, 20, 22, 46-48, 73, 91, 101, 134, 155-56, 166-67, 178-80, 214, 217, 236; experience of, 3, 34, 37, 47, 51-52, 84-93; fear of, 104, 137, 210; feminine/goddess. *See* Shechinah; immanence in multiplicity, 33, 39, 152-53; love of, 2, 16, 46-47, 93, 112, 188-92, 212; monotheism, 11, 20-21, 73, 99, 184, 188-92, 193-96, 199, 227; nondual conception of, xiii, 13-15, 18, 20-22, 23-24, 27, 28, 34, 37, 47, 91, 99, 147, 185, 191, 197-200, 209, 212, 227-37; polytheism and paganism, 73, 99, 126, 182, 190, 193-96, 199, 231; rejection of 'belief in', 21, 44, 69, 156-57, 170-73; skepticism and doubt regarding, xiv, 4, 15-16, 35 38-39, 70, 86-91, 100, 164, 238-41; theology regarding, 13-16, 21, 45-46, 69, 79, 90-93, 97-98, 104, 118-20, 134,

Kornfield, Jack, 46, 222.

kosher and treif, 62, 101, 105, 107-08, 112, 138, 140, 161, 163-64, 167, 177, 206.

Kotsker Rebbe, The, 189.

Krishna, 84, 201; see also Hinduism.

LaHaye, Tim, 171.

Lainer of Izbica, Mordechai, 110.

Last, Jonathan, 125.

Lennon, John, 63-64.

LGBTQ, ix, 2, 32, 46, 107, 114, 236, 173; and religion, 61, 68, 105-06, 114, 173, 181; homophobia toward, 32, 61, 107, 114, 128.

lila, 237

loneliness, 2-6, 169, 216, 223, 242-45.

love, 16, 210, 212, 222, 232-35, 238. *See also* meditation; God.

Loy, David, 233.

Lubavitcher Rebbe, 232.

Lucille, Francis, 239.

Lupolianski, Uri, 114.

Madonna, 202.

Maimonides, Moses, 101, 118, 134, 142, 165-66, 172.

masculinity, 5, 98, 127-29, 199-200. *See also* "feminine and masculine".

Matt, Daniel, 203.

Meditation: and doubt, x-xi, 6, 42, 50, 67, 76-77, 79-80, 86-90, 139-41, 144-46, 241; and "drug" experiences, 29-30; and ethics, 25-26, 49-52; and love, kindness, and compassion, 25-27, 31-34, 51-52, 66, 93, 137, 222; and sensuality, 28-34; and the sacred, 25, 28, 40, 166, 169, 208-09, 233; as seeing clearly, xi, 18, 25-26, 39, 51, 76, 87, 111, 146, 179-80; Buddhist, 52, 96, 111, 138, 206-13; concentration, 31-33, 85, 107, 111, 113, 166, 207, 220, 222, 233; *Hitbodedut*, 212; Jewish xi, 50, 52, 206, 209-10; pitfalls of, 26, 148, 153; retreat xi, 3-4, 15-18, 26, 29, 50, 66, 76-77, 80, 87, 96, 106, 112, 139, 144, 146, 149, 152, 166, 185, 188, 206, 215-16, 220-22, 226; secular xiii; subway practice, 18-19.

Merzel, Dennis, 152.

Milton, John, 11.

mindfulness, 32, 49-50, 55, 58, 82, 98, 117, 150, 210.

mindstates, 30, 47, 50-52, 72, 81, 89-91, 143-46, 182, 191, 214, 220, 225, 235.

mochin d'gadlut/mochin d'katnut, 31-11, 40-41, 180.

monogamy, 188-92.

monotheism. *See* God.

Moses, 159, 212.

mysticism 16-17, 37-38, 84-92, 111, 120, 143, 190, 201-05, 211, 230, 238-40; and acosmism, 152, 231; Hechalot/Merkavah, 204-05; unitive/*unio mystica*, xiii, 25, 38, 89, 198, 201-05, 231-33, 238. *See also* Kabbalah.

Mysticism and Philosophical Analysis, 85.

Nature, 19, 99, 126, 137, 154, 183, 193-96.

negative theology, 16, 91.

neo-Hasidism, 181-82, 185, 219, 230.

Neti-neti, 16, 229.

New Age, 36, 46, 60-61, 66, 87, 111, 140-44, 149, 157, 164, 189, 201, 217, 230.

New York, 8, 12, 27, 40-41, 48, 56-57, 155, 171, 178, 225, 241, 242-45.

Nietzsche, Friedrich, 75, 126.

nirvana, 99-100, 211, 218, 223.

Nisargadatta, 234, 239.

nonduality, 13-14, 24, 37, 40, 91, 97, 99, 172, 176-77, 179-80, 185, 191, 193, 197, 203-05, 209, 212, 227, 230-37, 239-41.

paganism, i, 73, 99, 126,182, 186, 190, 194, 195, 197-200, 231.

Palestine, ix, 71, 100, 114-18.

panentheism. *See*, God, nondual conceptions of.

Parsons, Tony, 239.

Pascal, Blaise, 39, 75, 145-46.

Patai, Raphael, 197.

peak experiences, xi-xii, 37-38, 79, 147-48, 201, 208-09, 219, 231.

phallus. *See* masculinity.

Prager, Dennis, 164.

prayer, 5, 21, 28, 32, 44, 49, 52, 62, 114, 118, 130, 133, 137, 139, 148, 160-61, 207, 214, 222, 224.

psychedelics, 29-30, 148, 201-05.

Ramakrishna, 230-31.

ratzo v'shov ("running and returning"), xiii, 176, 229-30, 234, 239.

Redmond, Layne, 198.

Reed, Lou, 4.

Reeves, Hope, 60-68.

relaxation response, 13

religion, meaning of, 35, 44-46, 50-53.

Rilke, Rainer Maria, 76-77.

Rinpoche, Chögyam Trungpa, 148, 239.

Sabbetai Zevi, 67, 110.

Salzberg, Sharon, 164.

samadhi, 3, 89-91, 120.

samsara, 99-100, 223.

Satan: in Blakean terms, 182-86; in Andre Gide's *The Counterfeiters*, 7, 11.

Schachter-Shalomi, Zalman, 44, 211, 230.

Schleirmacher, Friedrich, 44-46.

Scientology, 203.

Scorsese, Martin, 243-44.

service to others, 25-27, 209. *See also* ethics

sex, 31-32, 34, 40, 61, 78, 103-07, 112, 133, 146-47, 182-84, 186, 191, 209, 212, 215-16, 225, 234, 244.

Shakespeare, William, 8, 41, 75, 166.

shamanism, 46, 110, 186, 189, 193-96, 203-04, 240.

Shechinah, 128, 183, 197-200, 215, 234, 237.

Shimon bar Yochai, 119, 228.

Scholem, Gershom, 202.

Sith. *See Star Wars*.

skepticism, ix, 13, 40, 86-87. 139, 143, 170, 192. *See also* doubt.

Smoley, Richard, 179.

Socrates, 150.

Soloveitchik, Joseph, 5, 98-99, 130-32, 231.

spacetime, 23-24, 27.

Spinoza, Baruch, 91.

spirituality, 35, 46-48, 49-50, 72, 157, 214-26; and spiritual states,

49-50, 109, 171, 202, 222; and spiritual materialism, 148-49.

Star Wars, 123-25, 127-29.

Streng, Frederick, 45-46.

suffering, xii, 5, 14, 17, 19, 25-27, 41-43, 51-52, 55-57, 68, 71, 103, 109, 137, 147, 152, 180, 207-10, 217-19, 236.

Sufism, 114, 117, 120, 162, 205, 235.

surrender, 6, 53, 112, 137-38, 185, 240-41; and letting go, 11-12, 76, 112, 199, 208, 218, 221-24, 241.

Surya Das, 185, 223.

Talmud, 62, 96, 109, 111, 118, 127, 160.

Tantra, 31-33, 40-42, 239.

Tanya, 211.

Tao of Physics, The, x.

Thoreau, Henry David, 44.

time, 27, 98-99, 154, 184, 194, 198, 205, 207, 235.

Torah, 5, 37, 44, 61-62, 119-20, 134, 138, 160, 166, 171, 190, 211, 216, 230.

Truth: as feeling, 86-87, 91, 184, 191, 238; literal, 13-14, 35-39, 139, 145, 170-71; spiritual insight and , 13-16, 25-27, 65, 142, 152, 185, 195, 207, 211-12; and mystical experi-ence, 35-39, 84-93. *See also* delusion; doubt.

Twain, Mark, 105.

Van Sant, Gus, 68.

Vivekananda, 230, 238.

Vonnegut, Kurt, 96.

Watts, Alan, 151.

Wei Wu Wei, 239.

Whitney Museum, 244.

Wilber, Ken, 30, 35-41, 99, 142, 221.

Wilde, Oscar, 235.

Wilder, Thornton, 42-43, 236.

womb, 5, 45, 127, 174, 197-200, 238.

Woolf, Virginia, 8.

Wordsworth, William, x, 37.

UFOs, 139.

unio mystica. See mysticism.

Vedanta. *See* Hinduism.

yesh and *ayin*, 40, 223, 229, 234, 240.

yetzer hara, 16, 97, 176, 193, 211, 251.

yoga, 148, 224.

Yosef, Ovadia, 114.

Yom Kippur, 156, 168, 174-80.

Zalman, Reb, 230.

Zeek, ix, 12, 14-15, 38, 97, 120, 150.

Zen and the Art of Motorcycle Main-tenance, x.

Zevi, Sabbetai, 67, f110.

Zevon, Warren, 29.